AF710556

This book is a sophisticated comparative analysis of the doctrine of unjust enrichment in the North American and Jewish legal systems and in international law. By offering an explanatory theory which brings to light the normative underpinnings of the doctrine, it facilitates the prediction of legal outcomes and supplies the necessary tools for evaluating existing legal rules. Applying both theoretical analysis and comparative legal techniques, the study claims that the choice of compensation arising from a claim of unjust enrichment is not a matter of legal technicality. Instead it describes how the legal choice of a pecuniary remedy can be seen to embody a choice between competing values. This decision, writes Dagan, is implicated in the prevailing background ethos of the society at issue, and is deeply influenced by its own complex conceptions of self and of community.

Unjust enrichment

CAMBRIDGE STUDIES IN INTERNATIONAL AND COMPARATIVE LAW

This series (established in 1946 by Professors Gutteridge, Hersch Lauterpacht and McNair) is a forum for studies of high quality in the fields of public and private international and comparative law. Although these are distinct legal sub-disciplines, developments since 1946 confirm their interrelationship. Comparative law is increasingly used as a tool in the making of law at national, regional and international levels. Private international law is increasingly affected by international conventions, and the issues faced by classical conflicts rules are increasingly dealt with by substantive harmonisation of law under international auspices. Mixed international arbitrations, especially those involving state economic activity, raise mixed questions of public and private international law. In many fields (such as the protection of human rights and democratic standards, investment guarantees and international criminal law) international and national systems interact. National constitutional arrangements relating to 'foreign affairs' and to the implementation of international norms are a focus of attention.

Professor Sir Robert Jennings edited the series from 1981. Following his retirement as General Editor, an editorial board has been created and Cambridge University Press has recommitted itself to the series, affirming its broad scope.

The Board welcomes works of a theoretical or interdisciplinary character, and those focusing on new approaches to international or comparative law or conflicts of law. Studies of particular institutions or problems are equally welcome, as are translations of the best work published in other languages.

General Editors
James Crawford *Whewell Professor of International Law, University of Cambridge*
David Johnston *Regius Professor of Civil Law, University of Cambridge*

Editorial Board
Professor Hilary Charlesworth *University of Adelaide*
Mr John Collier *Trinity Hall, Cambridge*
Professor Lori Damrosch *Columbia University Law School*
Professor John Dugard *Director, Research Centre for International Law, University of Cambridge*
Professor Mary-Ann Glendon *Harvard Law School*
Professor Christopher Greenwood *London School of Economics*
Professor Hein Kötz *Max-Planck-Institut, Hamburg*
Dr Vaughan Lowe *Corpus Christi College, Cambridge*
Professor D. M. McRae *University of Ottawa*
Professor Onuma Yasuaki *University of Tokyo*

Advisory Committee
Professor D. W. Bowett QC
Judge Rosalyn Higgins QC
Professor Sir Robert Jennings QC
Professor J. A. Jolowicz QC
Professor Eli Lauterpacht QC
Professor Kurt Lipstein
Judge Stephen Schwebel

K
920
.D34
1997

Unjust enrichment

A study of private law and public values

Hanoch Dagan
Tel Aviv University Faculty of Law

CAMBRIDGE
UNIVERSITY PRESS

LAW LIBRARY
APR 23 1998
GOLDEN GATE UNIVERSITY

PUBLISHED BY THE PRESS SYNDICATE OF THE UNIVERSITY OF CAMBRIDGE
The Pitt Building, Trumpington Street, Cambridge CB2 1RP, United Kingdom

CAMBRIDGE UNIVERSITY PRESS
The Edinburgh Building, Cambridge, CB2 2RU, United Kingdom
40 West 20th Street, New York, NY 10011-4211, USA
10 Stamford Road, Oakleigh, Melbourne 3166, Australia

© Cambridge University Press 1997

This book is in copyright. Subject to statutory exception and to the provisions of relevant collective licensing agreements, no reproduction of any part may take place without the written permission of Cambridge University Press.

First published 1997

Printed in the United Kingdom at the University Press, Cambridge

Typeset in Swift 9.75/13 pt

A catalogue record for this book is available from the British Library

Library of Congress Cataloguing in Publication data

Dagan, Hanoch.
Unjust enrichment: a study of private law and public values/
Hanoch Dagan.
p. cm.
(Cambridge studies in international and comparative
law. New series)
Includes bibliographical references and index.
ISBN 0 521 58468 X (hb)
1. Unjust enrichment – United States.
2. Unjust enrichment (Jewish law).
3. Unjust enrichment (Islamic law).
I. Title. II. Series.
K920.D34 1997
346.7302'9 – dc21 96-49354 CIP

ISBN 0 521 58468 X hardback

VN

To the memory of my father
Moshe Dagan

Contents

Tables

Acknowledgments

This book is the culmination of six years' work, three as an LLM and JSD candidate at the Yale Law School, and three as a Lecturer in Law and Jurisprudence at the Buchmann Faculty of Law at Tel Aviv University. I feel privileged to have worked and studied within the unique scholastic environment of Yale Law School. I feel fortunate having joined the Buchmann Faculty of Law at a time of intellectual renewal and excitement, and grateful for the encouragement and support of the Faculty's late Dean, Ariel Rosen-Zvi.

Many people have read and commented on portions of this text. For comments, criticism, and encouragement, I would like to thank James Crawford, Ilana Dayan-Orbach, Zohar Goshen, Ron Katwan, Hagi Kenaan, Berahyahu Lifshitz, Avital Margalit, Ariel Porat, Peretz Segal, Omri Yadlin, and several anonymous readers. I am grateful to Anne Fernald who was my language editor, to Galia Feit for reference verification and indexing, and to Christopher Hart who has been a helpful and supportive editor at the Cambridge University Press. I am particularly grateful to Iris Schwartz who saw me through from start to finish and to Joseph Weiler who encouraged me in words and deeds to go through the completion of this project.

Special thanks are reserved to six special people. To Menny Mautner who introduced me to the world of law in the most fascinating and intriguing way. Through the years he has been a constant source of strength, guidance, and friendship. To Aharon Barak, Chief Justice of the Supreme Court of Israel, whose advice and support were crucial for both the initiation and the completion of this project. To former Dean Guido Calabresi, whose original ideas and enthusiasm for the law have been a source of inspiration. And to Alan Schwartz who extended his friendship and support and continually challenged me along the way. Our numerous conversations taught me the invaluable lesson of being rigorous in my reasoning and clear in my presuppositions.

I owe more than I can say to Tsilly Dagan, my wife and colleague, who is both my toughest professional critic and my most patient and helpful advisor. This work would not have been the same without her.

My greatest thanks goes to my JSD supervisor, Dean Anthony T. Kronman. I am very grateful for his faith in my ideas and fortunate for the helpful suggestions he has made regarding their elaboration and presentation and for his penetrating – but always constructive – criticism, which challenged me to be ever more precise in my thoughts. My interaction with him has affected my thinking about law and scholarship in ways which I may only fully understand in the years to come.

I acknowledge the Fulbright Foundation, the Cegla Institute for Comparative and Private International Law, the Buchmann Faculty of Law, and the Yale Law School for financial support which made the completion of this work possible.

1 Prologue

The task

This book is about the reflection of core social values in the technicalities of the law. At issue are those values which inform society's distributive scheme. This study analyzes the reflection of social values in the law through an account of the legal doctrine of unjust enrichment.

The law of unjust enrichment (or restitution) is a fundamental part of our law which has been neglected by legal scholars. To be sure, the basic maxim of the doctrine which prescribes that "a person who has been unjustly enriched at the expense of another is required to make restitution to the other"[1] is widely recognized. Moreover, private law scholars have devoted enormous energy to delineating the boundaries, skeleton, and anatomy of the doctrine.[2] This endeavor has contributed to the increasing recognition of the law of restitution as the third branch of civil liability (along with contracts and torts).[3] Nevertheless, courts and commentators alike continuously complain that applying the doctrine is difficult. This difficulty is not much ameliorated by separating the maxim into its (admittedly ambiguous) components: (i) a *benefit* (or *enrichment*); (ii) which has been received by the defendant *at the plaintiff's expense*; and (iii) the retention of which is *unjust*.

One of the main themes of this book is that this hardship can be remedied, or at least alleviated, only by studying the ways in which the law is connected to relevant aspects of the corresponding ethos. Only a

1 *Restatement of Restitution* § 1 (1937).

2 See, e.g., Peter Birks, *An Introduction to the Law of Restitution* (paperback edn. with revisions 1989).

3 See, e.g., I George E. Palmer, *The Law of Restitution* § 1.1 (1978 and Supplement 1995); Gareth Jones, "A Topography of the Law of Restitution," in *Essays on Restitution* 1, 2–3 (P. D. Finn ed. 1990).

particularistic cultural investigation can provide the doctrine with the coherence and integrity necessary to improve its predictability.[4]

Indeed, this book is not intended to study the abstract "principle against unjust enrichment" which is sometimes said to be the foundation of the law of restitution.[5] The principle against unjust enrichment is inadequate in resolving the doctrine's focal questions: identifying cases of unjust enrichment and delineating the appropriate legal response.[6] Hence, I believe that what is required is an explanatory theory which will bring to light the normative underpinnings of the doctrine, rather than a conceptual analysis of the principle against unjust enrichment.

Moreover, the law of unjust enrichment is rich, diversified, and often fairly puzzling. The doctrine encompasses a wide array of remedies, derived from many sources and origins.[7] More significantly, it covers a vast variety of social relations (herein termed "paradigms"), governed by an abundance of specific rules. Many of the paradigms give rise to overlapping claims, in restitution and contract, as well as in restitution and tort.[8] Such heterogeneity raises the suspicion that the applicable rules are not necessarily guided by the same considerations or enhance the same principles or policies.[9] It is thus advisable to direct the theoretical endeavor towards a relatively narrow category of cases within the field.[10]

Accordingly, this book is an inquiry into one important paradigm covered by the law of restitution: an instance where a defendant profits from a plaintiff's resource. It provides a positive account which can explain the law governing this paradigm and thereby improve its predictability. My goal is to focus on the considerations which guide the shape and development of

[4] For a strong support of the correspondence between law and social values see Ronald Dworkin, *Law's Empire* (1986); Lawrence Friedman, *The Republic of Choice* (1990).

[5] See, e.g., Andrew Kull, "Rationalizing Restitution," 83 *California Law Review* 1,196 (1995); Nicholas J. McBride and Paul McGrath, "The Nature of Restitution," 15 *Oxford Journal of Legal Studies* 33 (1995).

[6] *Cf.*, e.g., Steven Hedley, "Unjust Enrichment," 54 *Cambridge Law Journal* 578, 580–81, 592–93, 595 (1995); Stewart Macaulay, "Restitution in Context," 107 *University of Pennsylvania Law Review* 1,133, 1,139–40 (1959); Christopher T. Wonnell, "Replacing the Unitary Principle of Unjust Enrichment," 45 *Emory Law Journal* 153, 159–60 (1996).

[7] See, e.g., John P. Dawson, *Unjust Enrichment – A Comparative Analysis* 38–39 (1951).

[8] See generally Andrew S. Burrows, "Contract, Tort and Restitution – A Satisfactory Division or Not?" 99 *Law Quarterly Review* 217 (1983).

[9] See similarly Hedley, "Unjust Enrichment" at 589, 594, 599; Macaulay, "Restitution in Context" at 1,138, 1,145–46.

[10] The need for narrower categories in law was emphasized by the legal realists. See, e.g., Karl L. Llewellyn, "A Realistic Jurisprudence – The Next Step," in *Jurisprudence: Realism in Theory and in Practice* 3, 27–28, 32 (1962); Karl L. Llewellyn, "Some Realism about Realism," in *ibid.* at 42, 56–57, 62, 73.

the doctrine. Therefore, I fashioned the paradigm as simply as possible. Similarly, I do not delineate here the structure and subdivision of the law of restitution as a whole or define its outer limits. I believe that in order to be helpful, a taxonomy of the field must be informed by an analysis of the normative underpinnings of its various paradigms. Thus, I leave a more complete account of the law of restitution for future projects.

Still, my positive theory for our paradigmatic case is fairly ambitious. It attempts to account for the various manifestations of the doctrine in different legal systems. It strives for both transcultural and transhistorical applicability. It aims to be abstracted from the contextual contingencies of any specific set of restitutionary rules, and to extricate the essence – the common denominator – of the ways various societies implement the general principle against unjust enrichment.

Hence, this book is built upon three propositions. The first deals with the unchangeable aspects of the positive theory of restitutionary schemes; that is, each scheme gives weight to some perennial underlying values. The second proposition considers the changeable aspects of the theory. It contends that the support accorded to each underlying value is not constant but instead varies among both different legal systems and different protected interests. The third proposition is explanatory. It claims that the variability identified by the second proposition is explicated – and hence predicted – by reference to the prevailing background ethos of the society at issue, its own complex conceptions of self and of community.

The paradigm

Consider a case where A appropriates B's interest with respect to a resource without B's express or implied consent. B then files a complaint against A for his profit-making invasion. She asks for monetary recovery in restitution of A's resultant benefit, which she deems to be a wrongful gain.[11] A does not raise any affirmative defense.

Elaborating on this paradigm calls for underscoring its three distinctive attributes: the relationship between the parties, the object of the controversy, and the remedy sought.

The first characteristic worth noting is that A, the recipient of the gain, is an *invader*. He *appropriates*, i.e., takes or acquires in order to use or exploit B's interest without B's consent. The defendant, the only active party in the

[11] In the interest of simplicity, I have chosen to refer to all plaintiffs as "she" and all defendants as "he," unless the facts of the particular case dictate otherwise.

triggering event, infringes upon some part of the plaintiff's legally protected interest. The plaintiff, on the other hand, is entirely passive. The drama occurs without her having consented to the transaction, or even having given an appearance of consent.[12]

The relationship between the parties demarcates our paradigm from other types of restitutionary cases. One such type occurs where the defendant is passive, and the plaintiff herself confers the benefit upon him (due to altruistic motives, in order to serve her self-interest, or simply by mistake). In another set of restitutionary claims there is some pre-existing (contractual or fiduciary) relationship between the parties. Finally, a third type of case which should be distinguished from our paradigm concerns competition between the original owner of an appropriated resource and some third party to whom the resource has been transferred, or a trustee who represents the unsecured creditors of the invader who has become bankrupt. All these paradigms, as well as the more complicated cases which sit on the borderline between paradigms, are beyond the scope of the current study.

A second attribute of our paradigm is the object of the controversy, which I refer to as an interest in a *resource*. *Resource* denotes any means or capability of raising wealth, meeting needs, or supplying wants.[13] It can be an interest in what is defined in other areas of the law as tangible property (land or chattels) or intangible property (copyright, trademark, or patent); it can refer to one's interest in oneself or in a certain attribute of oneself; or, finally, it can be an interest in one's trade secrets, contractual relations, or even expectations and opportunities. *Resource* encompasses all these interests and is thus distinguished from two somewhat related concepts. On the one hand, a resource is not equated with wealth.[14] It is a *wealth-yielding interest* of a certain kind, with certain qualities that may distinguish it and the way it is treated by the law from other resources. But, on the other hand, a resource is not equated with property. Property is a concept which is overloaded with legal implications that may be of little, if any, significance

[12] Compare to the German law category of *Eingriffskondiktion*, i.e., a claim for the restitution of a benefit based on the interference with another person's rights, which is distinguished from *Leistugskondiktion*, a claim for the restitution of a benefit conferred by the plaintiff's own act. See Konard Zweigert and Hein Kotz, *An Introduction to Comparative Law: The Institutions of Private Law* 578–83 (2nd revised edn. Tony Weir trans. 1992); Reinhard Zimmermann, "Unjustified Enrichment: The Modern Civilian Approach," 15 *Oxford Journal of Legal Studies* 403, 404–07, 418–19 (1995).

[13] See *Black's Law Dictionary* 1,311 (6th edn. 1990).

[14] Contra Jack Beatson, "Benefit, Reliance, and the Structure of Unjust Enrichment," in *The Use and Abuse of Unjust Enrichment: Essays on the Law of Restitution* 21, 29–31 (1991).

for our paradigm. Thus it makes little sense to confine restitution *a priori* to proprietary interests.[15]

The last notable feature of the paradigm is the remedy asked by the plaintiff. She files her complaint *ex post* the invasion and asks for a pecuniary remedy. Hence, neither injunctions nor specific restitution of the resource appropriated will be a part of my agenda.[16] And, finally, she demands that the defendant give up the gains he reaped by[17] the invasion, rather than make good her losses. That is, her claim is in restitution, rather than in tort.

In Anglo-American law, our paradigm is rooted in the archaic concept of *waiver of tort* which views restitution as a parasitic claim, an alternative to tort damages. As such, the main advantages of restitution were perceived to be procedural, with respect to issues such as the survival of actions or the statute of limitations.[18] As these advantages were by and large extinguished, and as courts have come to grasp the significance of the main

[15] See similarly Jack Beatson, "The Nature of Waiver of Tort," in *The Use and Abuse of Unjust Enrichment: Essays on the Law of Restitution*, at 206, 208. A narrow property-based approach to restitution as a vindication of rights to property is vigorously espoused by Samuel J. Stoljar, *The Law of Quasi Contracts* 5–7, 93, 100 (2nd edn. 1989). See also Daniel Friedmann, "Restitution of Benefits Obtained through the Appropriation of Property or the Commission of a Wrong," 80 *Columbia Law Review* 504, 506, 509 (1980). Critical analyses of Stoljar's approach are collected in G. H. L. Fridman and James G. McLeod, *Restitution* 32–34 (1982).

[16] Specific restitution and injunctions are usefully discussed by Peter Birks, "Property in the Profits of Wrongdoing," 24 *Western Australian Law Review* 9 (1994); Douglas Laycock, "The Scope and Significance of Restitution," 67 *Texas Law Review* 1,277, 1,279–81, 1,283, 1,291–93 (1989); Dale A. Oesterle, "Deficiencies of the Restitutionary Right to Trace Misappropriated Property in Equity and in UCC § 9-306," 68 *Cornell Law Review* 172, 208–18 (1983).

[17] Some scholars complain that unjust enrichment law does not articulate its requirements of causation, and resorts to vague terms like "by" for "carrying the burden" of identifying cause (i.e., invasion) and effect (i.e., gain). Then, these scholars proceed to utilize a specific perception of causation to "better" identify the "true" gain in the scenario under consideration. See, e.g., E. Allan Farnsworth, "Your Loss or My Gain? The Dilemma of the Disgorgement Principle in Breach of Contract," 94 *Yale Law Journal* 1,339, 1,343–50 (1985). This strategy presupposes an abstract conception of causation, which is assumed to be "correct." Unfortunately, such a conception is neither elaborated nor defended. This book continues the tradition of avoiding any direct discussion of causation in the abstract. But it does so deliberately. Following Guido Calabresi's discussion of causation in torts, I refer to the "gain secured by an invasion" functionally, and attempt to identify the goals that are served by employing any given possible definition of the crucial term "gain." See Guido Calabresi, "Concerning Cause and the Law of Torts: An Essay for Harry Kalven, Jr.," 43 *University of Chicago Law Review* 69, 71 (1975). In fact, this functional analysis is the cornerstone of the first section of chapter 2.

[18] See, e.g., Palmer, *The Law of Restitution*, at § 2.3.

difference between restitution and tort – i.e., the former's focus on gains derived from the wrongful invasion rather than the mere harm it has inflicted – the two claims have diverged and restitution has gained an independent status. Thus, claims in restitution arise in many situations where no tort occurs. Furthermore, defenses from tort liability do not necessarily apply to their restitutionary counterpart.[19]

Thus far, I have restricted the variables that will be considered and discussed in this study. None the less, even within the realm of this simple paradigm there are important components that may vary from one case to another. Will the plaintiff succeed in recapturing the invader's enrichment, or will she have to be contented with damages for her harm? How exactly is "enrichment" calculated: that is, what is "the gain" the invader is forced to surrender? Is it the fair market value of the benefit or will the defendant have to give up all or part of his actual gain (and if so, can he deduct his expenses for obtaining such gain)? Does the answer to any of these questions depend upon the nature of the specific invaded resource? Does it depend upon the existence and proof of some improper means the invader utilized, or is the mere non-consensual appropriation sufficient to render the invader's gains wrongful and the restitution thereof appropriate?[20]

These critical questions are the primary focus of this book. However, before we turn to the development of some detailed answers, it is appropriate to begin with some methodological remarks and an overview of what lies ahead.

The method

A positive theory of law seeks to establish some correspondence between a legal doctrine and an underlying theory. A successful positive theory highlights the considerations – moral, political, economic, or otherwise – which shape the doctrine and guide its development. It thus enhances our ability to predict legal outcomes by conjecturing from the theory to the

[19] See, e.g., I *Restatement (Second) of Restitution* § 1 comment a (Tentative Draft, 1983–84); Beatson, "Waiver of Tort" at 210–24, 242–43; Friedmann, "Restitution" at 510, 538.

[20] The limited scope of my focus keeps this book manageable. It enables me to ignore all the other aspects of the relevant entitlement, notably its duration, the exact privileges it confers upon the resource holder, and the specific defenses, immunities, and privileges from liability in torts and/or restitution that are available to potential invaders. These components are important aspects of both property law and tort law. Considering these bodies of law from the theoretical perspective developed in this study may shed some new light on these well-explored doctrines and would be a fruitful realm for further inquiry. Such a discussion, however, is beyond the scope of this book.

probable results of a specific case. Moreover, a positive theory of law supplies the necessary tools for evaluating the existing legal rules by raising arguments for or against the underlying premises which are the proper target of one's critical (or justificatory) endeavor.

It seems advisable for a positive theory to resort to some comparative work. Comparative law is an important source for enriching legal theory by supplementing the often too narrow doctrinal discussion of a specific legal system, as well as the often too abstract normative argument, with some thick and contextual models. By studying the substantive law (as distinct from the legal techniques, categories, and concepts[21]) of different legal systems, comparative law reveals a variety of solutions for cases which are deemed easy from a narrow municipal perspective.[22] Furthermore, comparative law is instrumental in establishing a "liberating distance" from the dominant legal consciousness, thus uncovering the political and moral (often hidden) significance of legal doctrine.[23] However, in order to be able to enjoy this important advantage, the comparatist should refer to legal systems that are set in environments which are culturally remote from our contemporary Western circumstances.[24]

Positive theories are written in either an explanatory mode or a predictive mode. Under the explanatory mode, one starts by arranging the legal materials and then demonstrates their explicability by resorting to the theory. In contrast, when one writes in the predictive mode, the theory comes first, followed by a set of predictions it generates, and only at the last stage is the cogency of the theory examined by comparing the predictions with the actual legal rules. These alternative modes are two sides of the same coin, and choosing between them is merely a matter of preferring one

[21] Indeed, this study pays no attention to the doctrinal techniques or concepts (including that of unjust enrichment) which are utilized in order to prescribe one measure of recovery or another.

[22] See Mary Ann Glendon *et al.*, *Comparative Legal Traditions* 12–14 (1985); Jonathan Hill, "Comparative Law, Law Reform and Legal Theory," 9 *Oxford Journal of Legal Studies* 101, 105–06, 112 (1989).

[23] See Gunter Frankenberg, "Critical Comparisons: Re-Thinking Comparative Law," 26 *Harvard International Law Journal* 411, 447–48, 454–55 (1985); Hill, "Comparative Law" at 105–07, 114–15. *Cf.* Mary Ann Glendon, "Individualism and Communitarianism in Contemporary Legal Systems: Tensions and Accommodations," 1993 *Brigham Young University Law Review* 385, 387.

[24] *Contra* Alan Watson, *Legal Transplants: An Approach to Comparative Law* 7 (2nd edn. 1993) who argues that there is no worth in comparative law where there is no relationship between the legal systems; such claim, however, is apparently premised on the view that law is too often borrowed and hence not peculiarly devised for the society in which it operates: *ibid.* at 96, 107; needless to say that this book does not share such a view.

manner of exposition or another. Moreover, I believe that most positive theories are developed with both explanation and prediction in mind. Since theory and data are interdependent, we work from both ends, going back and forth, sometimes altering the theory, at other times suggesting an alternative interpretation of the doctrine.

Therefore it seems more accurate to discard the term "prediction" and use in its stead "retrodiction," i.e., the ability of a theory to predict *prior* events: here the details of the pertinent doctrines.[25] More importantly, it must be admitted that positive theories suggest new interpretations of the legal data, and are informed, like any interpretation, by the perspective of the reader and the purposes of the inquiry.[26] Thus, many positive theories – and the one offered herein is no exception – are disinterested in exploring the conscious motivations of the judges and legislators who have contributed to the molding of the doctrine. Instead, they attempt to provide new frameworks of thought that can capture the ethical intuitions of the myriad decision-makers involved. Indeed, my account does not purport to present the "original intention" behind the doctrinal rules which govern our paradigm. Rather, it is an attempt to look for patterns in the legal data that point to the presuppositions which shape the doctrine.[27] Exposing these presuppositions may provide a better understanding of the social significance of the doctrine, which may, in turn, enhance the predictability of future decisions and facilitate the normative legal discourse.

A roadmap

Much of this book is written in the predictive (or retrodictive) mode and it is structured accordingly. Chapter 2 elaborates my positive theory of unjust enrichment. I propose a model of how various communities employ this seemingly unified legal device, unjust enrichment, by loading it with their own core moral beliefs. The remaining chapters test this theory by examining the applicable rules of three different legal environments against their respective ethoses.

The first section of chapter 2, "From measures of recovery to rationales," develops the theoretical vocabulary to map the possible alternative rules. It

[25] The value of retrodiction is emphasized by Steven Weinberg in his *Dreams of a Final Theory* 96–97 (1992).

[26] See, e.g., J. M. Balkin, "Understanding Legal Understanding: The Legal Subject and the Problem of Legal Coherence," 103 *Yale Law Journal* 105, 110–12, 122–29, 131–36, 139–43, 150–51, 158 (1993); Frankenberg, "Critical Comparisons" at 442–45.

[27] *Cf.* William Ewald, "Comparative Jurisprudence (I): What Was it Like to Try a Rat?" 143 *University of Pennsylvania Law Review* 1,889, 1,947–51 (1995).

distinguishes the different *measures of recovery* which can apply in cases of our paradigm. These measures range (roughly) from compensation for the *harm* suffered by B, through payment of the *fair market value* of the resource involved, to the return of A's *profits*. The hierarchy of these remedies is quite apparent to lawyers since it differentiates among the actual contents of the possible doctrinal rules. But I believe that we can penetrate this first, exterior hierarchy and bring to light the values that can be promoted by the various measures of recovery. In this section I reconstruct this "invisible" hierarchy of *rationales*. As we will see, this inner hierarchy – ranging from the communitarian value of *sharing*, through the utilitarian value of *well-being*, to the libertarian value of *control* – corresponds to the hierarchy of measures of recovery. The hierarchy of rationales points to the ultimate justification of the doctrinal rules. Hence, an investigation of rationales may explain these specific legal rules. For this reason, positive analysis of the law should consider this inner hierarchy.

Thus, the "technical" choice of measures of recovery applicable to cases of the paradigm is in fact normative. In other words, prescribing the pecuniary remedies is instrumental in the vindication of certain goods (the rationales).[28] Hence, in order to appreciate the choice decision-makers face while shaping the doctrine, we need to explore the *intrinsic* moral, political, and social value of the underlying rationales.[29] The second section of chapter 2, "From rationales to distributive schemes," suggests that the three main possible rationales governing our paradigm – *sharing*, *well-being*, and *control* – represent particular, and to some extent competing, visions of the way people perceive themselves in relation to their social environment, their possible claims to other members in their legal community. I assume that most societies appreciate the value of these claims, but that the specific choice each society makes among them – its own *socio-economic ethos* – will

[28] The meaning of "vindication" here is two-fold: (i) a mischief – such as the diminution of one's well-being, or any disrespect to one's control – is remedied; and, at the same time, (ii) the available remedy generates such *ex ante* incentives that regulate a behavior which conforms with the aspired goal. Thus, for example, potential invaders will circumvent the market where the measure of recovery is *fair market value*, but resort to bargaining with the entitlement-holder where it is *profits*. See pp. 17–19 below.

[29] By contrast, legal economists, who are interested in the choice between some of the possible rationales identified herein, examine their instrumental consequences in terms of efficiency. See, e.g., Guido Calabresi and A. Douglas Melamed, "Property Rules, Liability Rules, and Inalienability: One View of the Cathedral," 85 *Harvard Law Review* 1,089, 1,106–10, 1,124–27 (1972); Peter K. Huber, "Mistaken Transfers and Profitable Infringements of Property Rights: An Economic Analysis," 49 *Louisiana Law Review* 71, 100–03 (1988).

none the less vary greatly. The latter point is crucial for our inquiry. Therefore, the third section of chapter 2, "Unjust enrichment and the socio-economic ethos," offers an explanation of the expected variability and some retrodictive guidelines this explanation prescribes.

A further refinement is still necessary. In addition to this inter-cultural diversity, some measure of intra-cultural variability should be expected. More precisely, I claim that the diversity of *resources* protected under our paradigm will generate a parallel diversity in the degree of protection accorded to such various resources. Accordingly, we should expect to find different measures of recovery applied to different resources.[30] The final section of chapter 2, "Unjust enrichment and the resource involved," provides an account of the reasons for such variability (this time in the intra-cultural dimension) and articulates the retrodictive strategy such an explanation recommends.

In short, the gist of my theory is that any analysis which aims at explaining, predicting, or formulating the rules of any given society must be particularistic. Respecting the law of unjust enrichment, such analysis should resort to two particular properties of the society in question: its socio-economic ethos and the particular social meanings it accords the various resources in question.[31]

As indicated above, vindicating such a theory of law requires some comparative work. This is the responsibility of the remainder of the book which implements the thesis, and, like most implementations, enriches the theory with nuances and subtleties. Chapter 3 collects the social data which is required in order to explain the legal rules governing contemporary American law and Talmudic civil law.[32] Then, based on that data, it actually produces a set of retrodictions as to the doctrine that is expected to be found in these two legal regimes. In chapters 4 and 5, I examine these retrodictions in some detail against the actual rules of these legal systems. Chapter 6, the final chapter, is added in order to further bolster the thesis. Chapter 6

[30] The existence of a spectrum of protected interests in unjust enrichment law was previously identified by Daniel Friedmann. See Friedmann, "Restitution" at 512–13, 556–57. But while his insight has inspired my approach, the theory of this book diverges from, without being necessarily incompatible with, Friedmann's theory: Friedmann demonstrates the existence of the spectrum by reference to a culpability component, while my analysis puts the emphasis on the measure of recovery; he explains the spectrum in terms of the difference between property and quasi-property, while at pp. 40–49 below I offer a different explanation.

[31] *Cf.* Margaret J. Radin, "Government Interests and Takings: Cultural Commitments of Property and the Role of Political Theory," in *Reinterpreting Property* 166, 168 (1993).

[32] I have deliberately focused my study on these two distinct legal traditions as a way of demonstrating the quite different results from quite different cultural contexts.

studies the pertinent rules of international law. Here, for methodological reasons, the representation switches to the explanatory mode. It is this book's positive theory that will serve as a source of explanation for the changing content of the doctrinal rules. With this then, we have the beginnings of a theory of unjust enrichment.

2 Theory

From measures of recovery to rationales

Measures of recovery

This section attempts to develop a "translation scheme" that will enable us to penetrate the possible measures of recovery and see their underlying rationales. It defines measures of recovery, clarifies the goods that can be achieved by law in cases of unjust enrichment, and studies the correspondence between the former and the latter. In short, it uses economic analysis in order to translate legal terminology into political philosophy.

The first stage of our task is to define and distinguish among the alternative measures of recovery – *harm* and four types of *gain*: *proceeds*, *profits*, *proportional profits*, and *fair market value*. The two most elementary terms in this lexicon are *harm* and *gain*. *Gain* refers to any value which is secured through the use of the appropriated interest. *Harm*, on the other hand, is any loss or detriment suffered by the plaintiff as a result of the appropriation. More precisely, in my terminology *harm* occurs only where the plaintiff has suffered a material loss, that is where the invasion has reduced the value of the plaintiff's resource or has diverted or prevented some expected gains she could have otherwise secured.[1] Hence, while the term *harm* includes lost profits, it does not include the "hypothetical loss" of not being paid for the use of the invaded interest where (but only where) the plaintiff was unable or unwilling, at the relevant times, to extract from the resource this "value of use." Put differently, *harm* does not cover the "mere" invasion, infringement, or breach of the plaintiff's protected interest.

The plaintiff's *harm* can be greater than, equal to, or less than the

[1] I do not mean to exclude emotional harms, such as pain and suffering, but assume, as is usually the case in the realm of this paradigm, that no such harm has been inflicted.

invader's *gain*. None the less, the law of unjust enrichment is most acutely concerned with the last category in which *gain* exceeds *harm*. This category includes cases where the invader is a more efficient producer (with regard to the appropriated resource) than the plaintiff or sells in a different market, as well as cases in which the plaintiff does not lose anything. This latter contingency occurs where the value of the plaintiff's resource was not diminished by the invasion *and* the plaintiff herself could not have made the gain or was unwilling to, or simply uninterested in, making it.

In cases of this type, where *gain* exceeds *harm*, a successful plaintiff obtains a substantive advantage in choosing the restitutionary claim rather than suing in its tort counterpart.[2] In these cases, a restitutionary claim has a distinctive bite. Accordingly, I assume throughout that *gain* is greater than *harm*.

But *gain* in itself is still an ambiguous concept, open to different possibilities for quantification and attribution. This book regards *gain* as a generic term that encompasses four quite different measures of recovery, all of which are important for our purposes. *Gain* can refer to the invader's gross *proceeds* from using the appropriated resource. It can also refer to the defendant's net gain from exploiting the invaded resource, i.e., to his *profits*. In this second instance, the defendant is allowed to deduct from his *proceeds* the costs he has in fact incurred in obtaining them.[3]

A third, and quite different, measure that courts employ when speaking of recovery of the defendant's gain is the *fair market value* of the plaintiff's interest or of its use in the period of appropriation. *Fair market value* is importantly dissimilar from *proceeds* or *profits*. This measure does not look to the actual events, but to the market. *Fair market value* is the price at which the resource or its prospective use would have brought through *bona fide* bargaining between a well-informed and willing anonymous buyer and a similar seller in the open market. It is the price at which *bona fide* sales have been consummated for similar interests.[4]

[2] See, e.g., Jack Beatson, "The Nature of Waiver of Tort," in *The Use and Abuse of Unjust Enrichment: Essays on the Law of Restitution* 206, 211 (1991); Douglas Laycock, "The Scope and Significance of Restitution," 67 *Texas Law Review* 1,277, 1,285, 1,287–88 (1989). But see Stephen Hedley, "The Myth of 'Waiver of Tort,'" 100 *Law Quarterly Review* 653 (1984).

[3] At times, the defendant invests not only out-of-pocket costs, but also some of his own time and labor to obtain the proceeds. Allowing him to deduct the fair market value of his services may raise some of the difficulties involved in the category of the intermeddler who officiously confers some benefit upon the defendant and claims reimbursement of the value thereof. To simplify the paradigm I assume that the component of defendant's unsolicited services is negligible.

[4] See *Black's Law Dictionary* 597 (6th edn. 1990).

A fourth possibility (and final at this stage) of quantifying the defendant's gain is represented by the *proportional profits* measure of recovery. When a court implements this measure it allows the defendant to deduct not only the reimbursement of his material contribution to the gain, but also a relative portion of any *profits* created by his expenditures in combination with the invaded interest. Thus, where *profits* are greater than *fair market value*, the *proportional profits* measure of recovery splits the difference according to the relative contribution of the parties' resources.[5]

Rationales

Thus far I have introduced five possible measures of recovery (*harm* and four types of *gain*). But how can we explicate the use of one measure over another? Or, more precisely, what does a legal system aspire to achieve by employing any one of these measures? This question is squarely addressed in the next subsection. Before exploring the underlying objectives of each of these measures, a short theoretical digression is needed, however. I take my theoretical premise from Guido Calabresi and Douglas Melamed's seminal article on property rules and liability rules. The following paragraphs discuss this celebrated essay as it informs my analysis.

For Calabresi and Melamed, resource allocation requires that the law decide "which of the conflicting parties will be entitled to prevail." Having made this initial choice of *entitlements*, the state must also make "second-order decisions" regarding the manner in which these entitlements are protected. The state has two rules to choose from:[6] a property rule or a liability rule. A *property rule* compels "someone who wishes to remove the entitlement from its holder [to] buy it from him in a voluntary transaction in which the value of the entitlement is agreed upon the seller." No one can appropriate the entitlement without first securing its holder's consent. In contrast, where a *liability rule* applies, "someone may destroy the initial entitlement if he is willing to pay an objectively determined value for it." Thus, liability rules are intended "to facilitate the [forced] transfer of the entitlement from [its] holder," and therefore employ "an external, objective standard of value."[7]

[5] If, for example, the proceeds which the defendant received from his use of the appropriated resource are 60, the market value of such use is 20, and the defendant's costs are 10, a measure of *profits* will enable the plaintiff a recovery of 50, *fair market value* of 20, and *proportional profits* of 40.

[6] Inalienability rules are not relevant for the purposes of this work and will not be discussed.

[7] Guido Calabresi and A. Douglas Melamed, "Property Rules, Liability Rules, and Inalienability: One View of the Cathedral," 85 *Harvard Law Review* 1,089, 1,090, 1,092, 1,105–06 (1972).

I believe that it is helpful to think of property rules and liability rules in terms of the good or goods they are aimed to promote (their "*rationale*").[8] As defined in the original Calabresi–Melamed framework, liability rules protect the economic value of the entitlement, which measures – since no better proxy is available – its (objective) level of well-being or utility to its holder.[9] However, a liability rule legitimizes the forced transfer of the relevant resource; where such a rule applies the *ex post* pecuniary recovery is intended as a surrogate for *ex ante* consent. On the other hand, an entitlement which is protected by a property rule requires any potential invader to seek and obtain the resource-holder's consent prior to the transfer. Thus, such an entitlement defines a domain of individual control over a resource. Where a property rule applies, the resource-holder's control cannot be reduced to a particular level of welfare; it cannot, in other words, be secured by a liability rule. Hence, property rules and liability rules should not be considered as merely different sorts of protection to entitlements; rather, the choice between these two rules requires a choice of the substantive content of the entitlement itself.[10]

The two goods – well-being and control – underlying the Calabresi–Melamed framework generate four, rather than merely two, different rationales which define people's entitlements in resources. One rationale aims at vindicating the resource-holder's *well-being*, but not her control over the resources at her disposal; another seeks to secure such *control*, but is disinterested in vindicating the plaintiff's well-being; a third rationale – I call it *well-being and control* – combines the two previous rationales; finally, the last rationale is aimed at vindicating either the resource-holder's well-being or her control according to the less demanding claim under the circumstances (*well-being or control*).

Choosing amongst these possibilities is not a purely theoretical enterprise; rather, it dictates and shapes the available remedies. To be sure, I do not claim that the underlying rationales are the only factors which dictate or shape the available remedies. Other considerations – institutional,

[8] This paragraph draws on Jules L. Coleman and Jody Kraus, "Rethinking the Theory of Legal Rights," in *Markets, Morals and the Law* 28 (1988); Robert Nozick, *Anarchy, State and Utopia* 57–73 (1974); John Christman, *The Myth of Property: Toward an Egalitarian Theory of Ownership* 21, 128 (1994).

[9] See, e.g., Robert C. Ellickson, *Order Without Law: How Neighbors Settle Disputes* 170–72 (1991). Aware as I am of the problems with the "objective" here, I use the term to emphasize that the protected utility does not include any psychological utility which an owner may produce by the mere fact of her control over the resource. Otherwise, the concepts of control and well-being would converge.

[10] *Cf.* Jeremy Bentham, *The Theory of Legislation* 111–13 (Richard Hildreth trans. C. K. Ogden ed. 1931).

procedural, and evidentiary – may well be at work when remedies are at issue. This, however, does not mean that the rationales and the available remedies are disconnected; it only implies that corresponding rationales with remedies is a more complicated task than it may first appear to be.

An obvious example for the connection between rationales and remedies is the preventive injunction. This remedy will surely not be available where the entitlement at issue seeks to secure only a resource-holder's *well-being*, and not her *control*.[11] Similarly, tying the discussion back to the possible measures of recovery in our paradigm, it seems plausible that these measures also stem from the underlying rationales. Thus, whereas vindication of the plaintiff's level of *well-being* may be effectuated by *compensating* her for any diminution of the value of her estate, only a measure of recovery which constitutes an effective *deterrence* from uninvited invasions can vindicate her *control*.[12]

In fact, I believe that one can hope to decipher the doctrinal rules governing our paradigm only by matching measures of recovery with underlying rationales. The remainder of this section provides the required translation scheme. The full scheme is summarized in table 1.[13]

A translation scheme

Consider first the *harm* measure of recovery which is, I claim, importantly different from the rest of our measures. At first glance, this claim of difference may seem obviously false. Is the *harm* inflicted on the plaintiff not the appropriate measure to vindicate her well-being and thus fully fit within the scope of rationales identified above? After all, once the plaintiff has been compensated for her harm, she is as well off as she was before. If the invader is even better off having paid the compensation for such harm, what possible objection remains where all we care for is the plaintiff's well-being?[14]

But this simplistic view of *harm* distorts the economic parameters. The economic value of any resource is the (discounted) sum of revenues from

[11] See Daniel Friedmann, "The Efficient Breach Fallacy," 18 *Journal of Legal Studies* 1, 15–17 (1989).

[12] See Jeremy Waldron, "Criticizing the Economic Analysis of Law," 99 *Yale Law Journal* 1,441, 1,444–49 (1990).

[13] See p. 22 below.

[14] See David Stevens, "Restitution, Property, and the Cause of Action in Unjust Enrichment: Getting by with Fewer Things," 39 *University of Toronto Law Journal* 258, 259 (1989); Henry Mather, "Restitution as a Remedy for Breach of Contract: The Case of the Partially Performing Seller," 92 *Yale Law Journal* 14, 32 (1982). *Cf.* I. M. Jackman, "Restitution for Wrongs," 48 *Cambridge Law Journal* 302, 303–04 (1989).

all future transactions.[15] Hence, in calculating the *well-being* "embodied" in a resource there is no justification – if we are indeed interested in the welfare of the *plaintiff* – to exclude any particular transaction, such as the potential agreement with the defendant. Accordingly, the resource-holder's *well-being* is restored only if she is compensated for the utility she would have captured had her consent been asked for.[16] Since the market at the time of appropriation set the price of such use at *fair market value*, the involuntary transfer has deprived her of the utility best evaluated by this figure. *Fair market value* is what the defendant would presumably have had to pay to the plaintiff had he not circumvented the bargaining process, even if we take the plaintiff's consent to the transfer for granted.[17]

Limiting recovery to *harm* evidences a unique rationale – I call it *sharing* – which focuses (at least also) on the interests of the defendant. Such a rationale vindicates the *defendant's* claim to share the plaintiff's entitlement. (It should, however, be noted that directing the measure of recovery to not less than *harm* implies a delicate distinction between *sharing*, i.e., foregoing the bargain with the defendant, and what may be termed *sacrifice*, i.e., actual diminution of the resource-holder's estate.) Hence, the underlying rationale of cases in which the law limits the plaintiff's recovery to her *harm* deviates from the kind of rationales underlying the rest of the available remedies, which all focus exclusively on the plaintiff's interests.

Since the accurate measure of the (objective) utility taken from the resource-holder is *fair market value*, this measure of recovery is the one which corresponds to the *well-being* rationale. Even where, as I assume to be the case in our paradigm, *fair market value* is greater than *harm*, an award of *fair market value* is justified from the point of view of *well-being* since it compensates the plaintiff for the lost opportunity of bargaining with the defendant for selling the use of her resource.

Three possible measures of recovery are still unexplored: *proceeds*, *profits*, and *proportional profits*. Which of these three alternatives vindicates the plaintiff's *control* over the appropriated resource? Or, more technically, which measure of recovery discourages potential invaders from circum-

15 See, e.g., Richard A. Brealey and Stewart C. Myers, *Principles of Corporate Finance* 73, 96 (4th edn. 1991).

16 See Nozick, *Anarchy* at 63–65; Waldron, "Criticizing" at 1,446.

17 See Robert J. Sharp and S. W. Waddams, "Damages for Lost Opportunities to Bargain," 2 *Oxford Journal of Legal Studies* 290 (1982). Sharp and Waddams apply the same explanation to an award of *profits*. This seems to me an overstatement of the power of this argument. See Andrew Burrows, *The Law of Restitution* 393 (1993).

venting the bargaining process and appropriating the protected interest without first securing its holder's consent?

The most suitable candidate among these three possibilities is *profits*. When the law supplies such a remedy, it returns to the resource-holder any net profit the invader may acquire from infringing the entitlement. Removing the possibility of profit takes the bite out of the forced transfer, and apparently deters (or at least aspires to deter) the invader from being engaged in what seems from the outset – given such a measure of recovery – a useless adventure from his own point of view.[18] Indeed, there is still a chance that the infringement will go undetected or that the resource-holder will fail to pursue her claim, which makes the defendant's expected gain greater than zero. Nevertheless, given the assumption that the plaintiff's *harm* is less than the defendant's *profits*, her opportunity to recover any excess gain creates the appropriate incentive to actually detect infringements and raise the restitution claim. Therefore, it still seems unlikely that a potential invader will prefer the non-contractual alternative.[19]

Hence, choosing *profits* as the measure of recovery appears to be directed at the point where it is no longer worthwhile for a potential invader to infringe upon the plaintiff's entitlement. It implies that transfers are legitimate only by obtaining the plaintiff's *ex ante* consent.[20] In other words, *profits* are the measure of recovery which vindicates the plaintiff's liberty to *control* the entitlement as part of her private sphere.[21]

Any pecuniary remedy which is less stringent than *profits* is inadequate in

[18] See John P. Dawson, "Restitution or Damages," 20 *Ohio State Law Journal* 175, 181 (1959); Peter K. Huber, "Mistaken Transfers and Profitable Infringements of Property Rights: An Economic Analysis," 49 *Louisiana Law Review* 71, 105 (1988); David D. Haddock *et al.*, "An Ordinary Economic Rationale for Extraordinary Legal Sanctions," 78 *California Law Review* 1, 13 (1990); Peter Birks, "Civil Wrongs: A New World," 1990–91 *Butterworth Lectures* 55, 86, 88. But see Peter Jaffey, "Restitutionary Damages and Disgorgement," 3 *Restitution Law Review* 30 (1995) who seems to conflate punishment and deterrence by treating *profits* to which the plaintiff is not "entitled" as premised on a rationale of punishment.

[19] See Huber, "Mistaken Transfers" at 105. *Cf.* Birks, "Civil Wrongs" at 87. In so far as the reason for plaintiffs' under-enforcement is related to inadequate awards of legal fees, this difficulty is external to the present discussion and requires a comprehensive solution.

[20] See, e.g., *Taylor* v. *Meirick*, 712 F 2d 1,112, 1,120 (7th Cir. 1983); Richard A. Epstein, "The Ubiquity of the Benefit Principle," 67 *Southern California Law Review* 1,369, 1,389 (1994).

[21] But *cf.* Christopher T. Wonnell, "Replacing the Unitary Principle of Unjust Enrichment," 45 *Emory Law Journal* 153, 180–84, 204–11 (1996): prescribing *profits* means embracing sentiments of envy and spite, unless the case is of a conscious taking of a well-delineated property right notwithstanding readily available alternatives to procure it consensually at a competitive price.

vindicating *control*. In particular, prescribing a remedy of *fair market value* cannot effectively deter the forced transfer (at times, it may even encourage it), since the profits the invader captures might exceed the value of the resource on the market.[22] Such a contingency occurs where the invader's efficiency exceeds (or even equals) the expected efficiency of buyers in the market.[23]

On the other hand, allowing the plaintiff to recover the defendant's *proceeds* would obviously deter him even further from circumventing the market, but it would do more than that. Whereas *profits* deters uninvited invasions while still keeping the defendant's capital intact, *proceeds* disallows the deduction of the defendant's contribution to the gain, thus confiscating a portion of his own estate.[24] Therefore, *proceeds* serves more than a means for vindicating the resource-holder's control; it also embodies society's condemnation of the invader's offensive behavior: the forfeiture of part of his own estate is the invader's punishment. Hence, a *proceeds* measure of recovery corresponds with a rationale – denoted here *control and condemnation* – which both vindicates the plaintiff's control and punishes the defendant for his anti-social conduct.[25]

The fifth, and most elusive, measure of recovery is the *proportional profits* which can be attributed to the appropriated protected interest. There are important similarities and differences between *proportional profits* and *profits* on the one hand, and *proportional profits* and *fair market value* on the other hand. Like *profits*, the *proportional profits* measure of recovery is calculated by reference to data particular to the specific circumstances (the *ex post*, rather than the *ex ante*, contractual surplus), and not by simply alluding to the price of the market. None the less, *proportional profits* shares with *fair market value* another quality, no less important, which distinguishes it from *profits*. Like *fair market value*, *proportional profits* requires a reconstruction of a "mutually benefiting transaction" the parties did not actually make. But whereas *fair market value* reconstructs the price, *proportional profits* reconstructs the way the parties would have divided

22 See George B. Klippert, *Unjust Enrichment* 88 (1983).

23 The expected profits of an average buyer is greater than the fair market value of the resource.

24 See Huber, "Mistaken Transfers" at 105–07; John P. Dawson, "Restitution Without Enrichment," 61 *Boston University Law Review* 563, 617 (1981).

25 Daniel Friedmann suggests that such a punishment would depend upon the reprehensibility of the defendant's conduct, the importance of the duty he breached, the extent of the defendant's contribution, and the justification for granting the plaintiff a windfall in the amount involved. See Daniel Friedmann, "Restitution of Benefits Obtained Through the Appropriation of Property or the Commission of a Wrong," 80 *Columbia Law Review* 504, 551 (1980).

the contractual surplus under circumstances of full information (hindsight)[26] and equal bargaining power. Indeed, an unarticulated assumption of judgments made according to *proportional profits* is that, if the plaintiff would have been offered the deal, and if she were equipped with the hindsight of knowing the profitability of the transfer, she *would have* consented to split its actual surplus in a *rational* fashion, i.e., according to the relative contribution of the parties' resources.[27]

But in cases of unjust enrichment no actual consent was obtained or expressed, and therefore a *proportional profits* measure cannot be said to *vindicate* the resource-holder's actual control. On the other hand, it cannot be denied that in comparison to *fair market value*, *proportional profits* is a remedy which *reflects some concern* for the plaintiff's control and not only her well-being. Although consent with regard to *proportional profits* is indeed hypothetical, it is not *contra*-factual as it is with respect to *fair market value*: the plaintiff could have gotten *fair market value* for her resource at the market, and the fact that she did not voluntarily sell it can only demonstrate that she did not want to; in contrast, it is somewhat more plausible, or at least not contrary to the factual circumstances, to say that, if she had been given the opportunity, she *would have* consented to a bargain which could have secured her a proportional share of a profitable enterprise.[28]

It should be noted that the preceding paragraph assumes that the defendant's *profits* are greater than *fair market value*, so that splitting the difference is a more favorable remedy from the plaintiff's standpoint than *fair market value*. This, however, is not always the case. Nevertheless, *proportional profits* is an intelligible measure of recovery only when *profits* exceeds *fair market value*. Awarding *proportional profits* where the measure of *profits* is smaller than *fair market value* fails to secure any one of the pertinent

[26] The expected profit of a transferee is obviously a valuable piece of information for any transferor in the market. If the latter knows or suspects that her bargaining partner can use the transferred resource more efficiently than the average buyer, she will no doubt try to capture at least some of this surplus. However, in many cases she will not be aware of this valuable datum. Moreover, even in cases where she actually knows it, she is obviously aware only of the *expected* gain, and no foresight is ever as good as hindsight.

[27] *Cf.* James G. Hodder, "Profiting from Tortious Use of Property: A Reply to the Lost Bargain Theory," 42 *University of Toronto Faculty Law Review* 105 (1984).

[28] The presuppositions of the reconstructed transaction represented by the *proportional profits* measure of recovery – i.e., full information, rationality, and equal bargaining power – may be contra-factual in a specific case. But the law needs to work at a certain level of generality and it is only reasonable for it to choose what may be perceived as the fairest contractual circumstances. See David Charney, "Hypothetical Bargains: The Normative Structure of Contract Interpretation," 89 *Michigan Law Review* 1,815, 1,823–24 (1991).

goals of availing the resource-holder with a remedy. On the one hand, it would not vindicate her well-being since the decrease in the value of her estate is *fair market value* which we assume to be greater than *proportional profits*. On the other hand, it does not vindicate her control: a *proportional profits* measure of recovery – unlike a measure of *profits* – does not deter uninvited invasions (knowing that he will be compelled to split any generated profit with a stubborn resource-holder will not deter a person who wants the resource from unilaterally appropriating it);[29] and, moreover, consent can certainly not be even hypothetically assumed where the terms of transfer (where price is less than *fair market value*) are inferior to what the market could have offered (where price is equal to *fair market value*). Finally, unlike *harm*, awarding *proportional profits* where it is smaller than *fair market value* cannot be explicated in any principled fashion in terms of the defendant's claim to share without unduly harming the plaintiff.

Hence, one can safely predict that *proportional profits* will be awarded only where this measure exceeds *fair market value*. In such cases, it corresponds to a rationale that vindicates both the plaintiff's *well-being* and her *hypothetical consent* to share in a profitable enterprise.

To complete the picture, two more rationales should be considered: *well-being and control*; and *well-being or control*. The first rationale aims at vindicating both the resource-holder's well-being and her control. Since *fair market value* secures the plaintiff's *well-being*, and *profits* vindicates her *control*, the measure of recovery corresponding to *well-being and control* is the greater of *fair market value* and *profits*.

Similarly, *well-being or control* – the rationale which is aimed at vindicating either the resource-holder's *well-being* or her *control* according to the *less* demanding claim – corresponds to the lesser of *fair market value* and *profits*. This, however, indicates that the *well-being or control* rationale reverses forced transfers only in so far as the remedy does not diminish the *defendant's ex ante* level of welfare. This creates an incentive effect of encouraging forced transfers, an incentive effect which is also generated by a *well-being* rationale (and its corresponding *fair market value* measure of recovery). However, unlike the latter, the former not only encourages efficient transfers, but encourages all transfers indiscriminately. This may be the reason why the *well-being or control* rationale is not evident in any case or statute covered by this book. It can thus be safely omitted from our translation scheme.

At this stage, we have matched six measures of recovery with six

[29] But see *Walker* v. *Forbes, Inc.*, 28 F 3d 409, 412 (4th Cir. 1994), suggesting a deterrence rationale for *proportional profits*.

Table 1 *Measures of recovery and rationales*

Measures of recovery	Rationale	Vindication of. . .
Harm	Sharing	the invader's claim to share the entitlement with its holder without unduly harming her
Fair market value	Well-being	the resource-holder's well-being
Proportional profits (when proportional profits exceeds fair market value)	Well-being and hypothetical consent	both the resource-holder's well-being and her hypothetical consent
Profits	Control	the resource-holder's control over the resources at her disposal
The greater of fair market value and profits	Well-being and control	both the resource-holder's well-being and her control
Proceeds	Control and condemnation	both the resource-holder's control and society's condemnation

rationales or combinations thereof. Table 1, which summarizes the conclusions of this section, will enable us to translate the legal terminology of the cases to the underlying values for which they stand.

From rationales to distributive schemes

Thus far I have suggested that the possible remedies in cases of our paradigm represent underlying rationales and have offered some tools for performing the conversion between measures of recovery and their corresponding rationales. Indispensable as it is, this stage is only the beginning of our investigation of the premises of unjust enrichment law. The third and fourth sections of this chapter[30] will complete my positive theory of unjust enrichment law by asking what is necessary in order to

[30] See pp. 34–49 below.

account for the rationales, and thus – utilizing the tools which connect rationales with legal rules – the doctrine of any specific legal system.

But before this question can be squarely addressed, some preparatory work is needed. In this section, I wish to support the claim – already implied by the introduction of the rationales governing our paradigm – that opting for any one of the available measures of recovery is not a matter of legal technicality, but rather involves a value-choice. I argue that the main underlying rationales – *control*, *well-being*, and *sharing*[31] – stand for important human values which represent competing social visions.[32] I further contend that the doctrinal rules of our paradigm rely on underlying distributive considerations.

The intrinsic value of the underlying rationales

Why would a legal regime be interested in conferring on its constituents the goods of *control*, *well-being*, and *sharing*? Or, in other words, what is it that human beings find attractive in each of these rationales?

Consider first the intermediate rationale – *well-being* – and recall that it requires the restoration of the *status quo ante* in so far as the plaintiff's (objective) level of utility is concerned. The case for protecting the *well-being* of agents seems obvious. A person's *well-being* is a means for the fulfillment of her desires, an instrument for seeking what she perceives as happiness.[33] Any derogation from one's *well-being* is an obstacle to the achievement of one's desires, an impediment to the pursuit of one's happiness. No one who cares for human happiness can disregard its curtailment or fail to understand the appeal of a rationale which guards against such a contingency.

If this is so, what then is the case for promoting an agent's *control*, and why is it not enough to restore the bilateral equilibrium of welfare? As we saw in the previous section, the *control* rationale is aimed at providing *ex ante* deterrence – and not only *ex post* compensation – against any non-consensual disturbance of the equilibrium of resources. It insists on the agent's consent being a prerequisite to any legitimate transfer of her resources. It thus seeks to guarantee the agent a private moral sphere free from forcible human interference; to disallow the use of the agent (*via* her

[31] The other rationales discussed in the first section of this chapter are combinations of *control*, *well-being*, and *sharing* and can hence, for the sake of simplicity, be omitted from the discussion in this section.

[32] *Cf.* Joseph W. Singer, "The Reliance Interest in Property," 40 *Stanford Law Review* 611, 627–28 (1988).

[33] *Cf.* James Griffin, *Well-Being: Its Meaning, Measurement and Moral Importance* 14, 22 (1986); Joseph Raz, *The Morality of Freedom* 289 (1986).

resources) as a means to serve someone else's objectives. In short, *control* promotes the agent's negative liberty;[34] and – all other things being equal – the greater the amount of resources one controls, the greater is the extent of one's negative liberty.[35]

Negative liberty is the second independent good which the rules governing our paradigm can promote. It emphasizes the importance of freedom (from) and independence as prerequisites to personal development.[36] Proponents of negative liberty put a great weight on the distinctiveness of individuals, on their voluntary choice of goals and their responsibility for such choices.[37] Therefore, a devotion to negative liberty entails an ideal libertarian legal system, the minimal state. As Robert Nozick characterizes such a regime, it attempts as much as possible to circumscribe a boundary around the individual moral space and to prohibit any "boundary crossing."[38] For libertarians, only a comprehensive scheme of legal rules which deter boundary crossing – i.e., rules guided by the *control* rationale – fully guarantees individual freedom.[39]

We see that *well-being* and *control* are quite straightforward rationales. *Sharing*, on the other hand, requires a more detailed discussion. So, my primary goal in the remainder of this subsection is to provide an account of this third rationale. This account characterizes *sharing* as an other-regarding rationale. It further studies its relation to the concepts of altruism, impartiality, community, needs, and equality.

Where the plaintiff was unable or unwilling to use or let the resource, *sharing* denies the resource-holder of the benefit she could have gained from a transaction with the defendant had the latter not circumvented the bargaining table. Thus, it derogates fragments of the entitlements of

[34] See, e.g., Steven Lukes, *Individualism* 66 (1973); Nozick, *Anarchy* at 71; F. A. Hayek, "Freedom and Coercion," in *Liberty* 80, 81–82, 89, 95–98 (David Miller ed. 1991). Gerald MacCallum argues that the distinction between negative liberty and positive liberty (freedom to do something or to become something) is unnecessary, and that both species of liberty can be analyzed within the same generic formula. See Gerald C. MacCallum Jr., "Negative and Positive Freedom," in Miller, *Liberty* at 100. None the less, the distinction between negative and positive liberty is still important for my purposes since *control* promotes only negative – and by no means positive – liberty.

[35] See Hillel Steiner, "Individual Liberty," in Miller, *Liberty* at 123, 137–38.

[36] See Isaiah Berlin, "Two Concepts of Liberty," in *Four Essays on Liberty* 118, 122, 124 (1969). But See Charles Taylor, "What's Wrong with Negative Liberty," in *Philosophy and the Human Sciences* (Philosophical Papers 2) 211 (1985).

[37] See, e.g., Charles Fried, "Is Liberty Possible?" in *Liberty, Equality, and Law: Selected Tanner Lectures on Moral Philosophy* 89, 94–95 (Sterling M. McMurrin ed. 1987).

[38] See Nozick, *Anarchy* at 57, 71–73.

[39] See F. A. Hayek, *The Fatal Conceit: The Errors of Socialism* 63 (1988); Milton Friedman, *Capitalism and Freedom* 8–16 (1962).

individuals in the resources they hold. It creates a common pool which others in the community – strangers to the resource-holder in our paradigmatic case – can utilize, as long as they do not actually harm the invaded resource, without incurring the costs they would have had to incur had they resorted to a market transaction with the resource-holder.[40] Therefore, *sharing* is concerned not only with the resource-holder's welfare, but also with that of other individuals in her legal community.

I suggest that proponents of *sharing* support this rationale as a form of institutionalized limited altruism: a legal device which calls for other-regarding action and seeks to inculcate other-regarding motives.[41] The concept of altruism is prominent in the writings of neo-Kantians and communitarians alike. I believe that the reason for such prominence lies in a certain feature of human nature to which both schools – different in so many other respects as they are – point. This feature is crucially important for our purposes.

In considering "the possibility of altruism," Thomas Nagel explains that altruism arises from the human capacity to view oneself simultaneously "from both the personal and the impersonal standpoints," that is, both as "I" and as "*someone* – an impersonally specifiable individual." This capacity, says Nagel, is premised on "a recognition of the reality of other persons, and on the equivalent capacity to regard oneself as merely one individual among many," all of which are included in a single world and are persons in as full a sense as oneself. Given such an ability to abstract oneself and to engage in reasoning to practical conclusions from both the personal and the impersonal standpoints, altruism is perceived as a rational requirement to which our reasons for action are subject.[42]

As I understand this neo-Kantian analysis, the driving force of Nagel's justification for altruism is the ability (and need?) he finds in us all not only

[40] *Cf.* Duncan Kennedy, "Form and Substance in Private Law Adjudication," 89 *Harvard Law Review* 1,685, 1,717 (1976).

[41] See Thomas Nagel, *The Possibility of Altruism* 79 (1978). I believe that the other-regarding commitment of the self cannot be reduced to the agent's own welfare or self-interest narrowly perceived. Any attempt to incorporate other-regarding motives into an enlarged notion of self-interest makes such notion of self-interest vacuous, since it still leaves us with the problem of distinguishing action that takes no account of the ultimate welfare of others from action that is at least partially concerned with the welfare of others. In contrast, in separating the notions of "self-interest" (narrowly perceived) and "altruism," we maintain, and are thus able to study, this important distinction. See, e.g., Amitai Etzioni, *The Moral Dimension: Toward a New Economics* 34–35 (1988); Christopher Jencks, "Varieties of Altruism," in *Beyond Self Interest* 53, 55 (Jane J. Mansbridge ed. 1990).

[42] Nagel, *The Possibility of Altruism* at 3, 19, 82, 88, 100, 144.

to dissociate ourselves from our personal perspective, but also to associate ourselves with our fellow community members (or, to be more loyal to Nagel's work, with the human species as a whole). This brings Nagel's explanation of the appeal of altruism closer than it seems at first glance to the community-oriented and sociological explications of the virtue we find in other-regarding ideas.[43]

The communitarian account emphasizes the human need for social solidarity, communal concern, and a sense of togetherness, all of which can only be satisfied in a moral community which is premised on a maxim of mutual responsibility. In so far as we understand ourselves as members of such a group with "a common identity," and not merely as a plurality of individuals, *sharing* need not be viewed as being used for others' ends, as libertarians undoubtedly regard it;[44] instead, it should be seen as a way of contributing to a community we regard as our own.[45]

It would be false to contend that the abstract neo-Kantian account and the contextualized communitarian account are identical. On the contrary, these accounts correctly perceive themselves as adversary theories of other-regarding phenomena.[46] None the less, these two theories converge in finding the source of the appeal of *sharing* in the other-regarding aspect of human nature. Both theories, more particularly, find the justification of responding to others' claims in the importance we attach to one another, whether as atomized human beings or as fellow members in one's constitutive community; whether due to rational deliberation or to innate emotions. In short, the appeal of other-regarding ideas lies in the other-regarding feature of the self.

Thus, I suggest we regard *sharing* as an institutional design which responds to, and supports this other-regarding perspective of human

[43] Sociologists explain altruism also in terms of empathy, or the identification with other people and the incorporation of their interests into our subjective welfare function. See, e.g., Jane J. Mansbridge, "The Rise and Fall of Self-Interest in the Explanation of Political Life," in Mansbridge, *Beyond Self Interest* at 3, 20. But surely the benevolent sentiments people actually have are confined to a much narrower circle than the range of beneficiaries of a *sharing* rationale, i.e., the whole legal community – typically the state. See generally Michael Ignatieff, *The Needs of Strangers* (1984). Hence, the empathy factor need not be considered here.

[44] See Nozick, *Anarchy* at 172.

[45] See Michael J. Sandel, *Liberalism and the Limits of Justice* 143 (1982); George P. Fletcher, *Loyalty: An Essay on the Morality of Relationships* 18 (1993); Robyn M. Dawes *et al.*, "Cooperation for the Benefit of Us – Not Me, or My Conscience," in Mansbridge, *Beyond Self Interest* at 97, 99; David Miller, "Distributive Justice: What the People Think," 102 *Ethics* 555, 560–62, 570–72 (1992).

[46] *Cf.* Brian M. Barry, *Theories of Justice* 238–39 (1989); Sandel, *Liberalism* at 52–53.

beings. It sees us as "divided selves," people who occupy both the personal perspective – which is preoccupied with our own self-interest, and the impersonal or communitarian perspective (according to one's theory of altruism) – which is the source of our other-regarding action.[47] *Sharing* appeals to the other-regarding standpoint of the agent. It seeks to sustain and inculcate her other-regarding side, or at least to create "an ecological niche" for altruistic behavior and altruistic motives.[48]

This vision of a self which is by nature divided between the personal and the impersonal (or communitarian) concerns, as well as the possibility (qualified as it may be) of a certain institutional influence on the equilibrium between the two standpoints of the self, are indeed two important presuppositions a protagonist of *sharing* must accept. These presuppositions provide preliminary hints as to the expected doctrinal implementation of altruism in the context of our paradigmatic case.

The metaphor of a divided self helps explain the limited altruism *sharing* prescribes: *sharing* does not entail actual sacrifice; it merely prescribes that in certain well-defined cases the defendant is required to pay only for the actual *harm* he had inflicted and not the full *fair market value* of the invaded resource.[49] This seems to be a sensible limitation on the level of altruism for a doctrine which acknowledges that we are of a "divided self"; that our primary attachment lies with our own personal interests, projects, and commitments; and that an altruistic institution can only insist that such attachment should be restrained by our occupation of the other-regarding standpoint.[50] Moreover, limited altruism prescribed by *sharing* may also mitigate the concern that institutionalizing altruism would create resent-

[47] See Thomas Nagel, *Equality and Partiality* chapters 2 and 3 (1991); Barry, *Theories of Justice* at 283–85, 357–66; Etzioni, *The Moral Dimension* at 63, 85, 253–54; Jane J. Mansbridge, "Preface" in Mansbridge, *Beyond Self Interest* at ix, xiii.

[48] See Nagel, *Equality* at 18, 20; Jane J. Mansbridge, "On the Relation of Altruism and Self-Interest," in Mansbridge, *Beyond Self Interest* at 133. My emphasis on the possibility of an institutional reinforcement for the other-regarding standpoint implies that the more rudimentary standpoint of the self is the self-regarding perspective. I do not think that this "hierarchical" picture is very controversial. At any rate, to the extent that it is, I might add that just as altruistic institutions like *sharing* reinforce the other-regarding aspect of the self, individualistic institutions like *control* reinforce the self-regarding standpoint. Therefore, my implicit presupposition regarding the hierarchy of the self's perspectives merely leads me to emphasize the first – rather than the second – way of institutional influence.

[49] *Harm* is lesser than *fair market value*, as may be recalled, where the plaintiff is unable or unwilling, at the relevant times, to use the resource in a way that extracts from it its *fair market value*.

[50] See Nagel, *Equality* at 37.

ment, and thus impede – rather than enhance – the possibility of inculcating altruistic motives.[51]

In other words, the altruism expected from such a divided self concedes its own intrinsic limitation, and the only (admittedly formidable) question is where to draw the line.[52] *Sharing* proposes one possible, albeit by no means inevitable, answer. The compromise it represents is local, and may not be well suited to other contexts. Nevertheless, in so far as the task of institutionalizing altruism in a private law arena and within a framework of privately held resources is concerned, *sharing* prescribes one sensible limitation on the "'call of duty.'[53]

Furthermore, if human nature is neither completely self-interested nor entirely altruistic, and if social institutions have some impact on the resulting mixture of opposing standpoints, then one can expect to find (somewhat) differently motivated selves in societies which resort to differing institutional designs. Such selves are, in turn, more likely to establish more institutions that respond to their ethical standards; hence there is a perpetuating process of cultural diversity.[54]

Some may try to refute this account of *sharing* by insisting that the question regarding the possibility of human nature having an altruistic component – which is one of the presuppositions underlying *sharing* – is more a matter of fact than of opinion.[55] But I have no interest in taking up

[51] For the dilemma of psychological reactance to which the text refers see, e.g., Viola C. Brady, "The Duty to Rescue in Tort Law: Implications of Research on Altruism," 55 *Indiana Law Journal* 551, 560 (1980). For a general discussion of the tension between normativity and coercion, which is mirrored in our conflicting attitudes towards authority see Meir Dan Cohen, "In Defense of Defiance," 23 *Philosophy and Public Affairs* 24 (1994). For the need of decision-makers to bargain against people's preferences see, e.g., Owen M. Fiss, "The Supreme Court, 1978 Term – Foreword: The Forms of Justice," 93 *Harvard Law Review* 1, 54–55 (1979).

[52] The difficulty of setting limits is aggravated when one considers altruism in the context of the large-scale nation-state (or even more obviously the world community), rather than of any smaller sub-unit thereof. When large numbers of potential beneficiaries are involved – as in the case of practically every legal community – small contributions add up to "heroic totals" which most of us would perceive to be "beyond the call of duty." See James Fishkin, *The Limits of Obligation* (1982).

[53] Regimes which do not admit the institution of private property may find the limitation of altruism to *sharing* far too biased in favor of the personal viewpoint, but such regimes cannot – indeed, need not – be considered here, since the paradigm with which this book is preoccupied is of the appropriation of private property.

[54] See Nagel, *Equality* at 177–78; Etzioni, *The Moral Dimension* at 63, 85; Jencks, "Varieties of Altruism" at 54–55; Mansbridge, "On the Relation of Altruism and Self-Interest" at 136.

[55] See, e.g., C. Daniel Batson, *The Altruism Question: Toward a Social–Psychological Answer* 11–13 (1991).

the empirical (or even philosophical) verification or refutation of this possibility, and the rest of this book accepts altruism as a given. Solving the immortal question of human nature is not required for my purposes. It is enough that *some* people (or, more precisely, *certain* societies) believe that human nature includes an altruistic side that can be reinforced by proper institutional design. Such a belief – even if it turns out to be mistaken – still explains both why protagonists of *sharing* find this rationale appealing, and why certain societies attempt institutionally to inculcate altruism. Moreover, the dispute surrounding the possibility of altruism can even be suggested as another reason for the expected doctrinal diversity among different socio-cultural environments.

A lot more has to be said on this emerging particularistic theme, which will be studied in some more detail in the next section of this chapter. Before moving on, however, I wish to conclude my discussion of *sharing* by exploring the relations between this rationale and the concepts of needs and equality.

At first glance, there seems to be little correspondence between the former and the latter: *sharing* is not sensitive to the specific socio-economic situation of the parties, while the focus of the social creed of needs is the recipient's shortage of basic needs and that of equality is the relative social status of the parties.[56] This difference notwithstanding, I claim that there is some resemblance between the *grounds* which support *sharing*, as studied above, and the *grounds* which support needs-based or equality-based social programs, to be sketched below. As we will see in the next section, this similarity is, in fact, the key to my positive theory. It will also help us to delineate with more precision the circumstances in which *sharing* can be expected to be operative.

Needs-based programs are premised on the moral priority of supplying individuals with certain basic needs – such as food, shelter, and minimal self-respect – over and above the satisfaction of the preferences of any other individual in society, including, according to some theorists, those of the needy themselves.[57] There is some divergence of opinion regarding the justification for such a priority.[58] On the one hand, there are those who

[56] *Cf.* Duncan Kennedy, "Distributive and Paternalist Motives in Contract and Tort Law, With Special Reference to Compulsory Terms and Unequal Bargaining Power," 41 *Maryland Law Review* 563, 584 (1982).

[57] See, e.g., David Braybrooke, *Meeting Needs* (1987); Fried, "Is Liberty Possible?" *Cf.* Garrett Thomson, *Needs* (1987) (a similar account respecting the intra-personal perspective). But see Griffin, *Well-Being* at chapter 3 (criticizing the indeterminacy of the concept of needs).

[58] Compare, e.g., Braybrooke, *Meeting Needs* at 131–32, 236–37 with Fried, "Is Liberty Possible?" at 107.

emphasize that meeting needs is premised on (and nurtures) a fundamental sense of sensitivity to other people's fate, caring for one another, or at least a willingness to give aid. Others, however, disagree, and contend that meeting needs can only be justified by a commitment to personal liberty, so only the prerequisites for free and fair choice for each individual are to be supplied. These differences in viewpoints – which I term "strong" and "weak" versions of the needs-based theory – lead to divergent views respecting the definition of "basic needs" and the appropriate standards for their provision.[59]

The concept of equality is importantly different from that of needs. Equality, as I use the term, encompasses social programs which favor those who are worse off, giving preferential treatment to improvements in their lives over adding to the advantages of the better off.[60] I cannot of course discuss in any detail the various egalitarian conceptions at the center of an ongoing philosophical and political debate. None the less, it remains useful to emphasize one common characteristic of at least two of the most prominent modern egalitarian theories. Both John Rawls' difference principle[61] and Ronald Dworkin's hypothetical insurance scheme[62] presuppose that our social circumstances and natural endowments are in some sense arbitrary.[63] To be sure, these features are by no means arbitrary from our personal viewpoint.[64] On the contrary, they are intrinsic to how we perceive our own identity.[65] Therefore, the appeal of the egalitarian creed can only be appreciated in so far as one accepts the appeal of resorting to the (neo-Kantian) impartial or impersonal perspective which urges each of us to

[59] Compare, e.g., Braybrooke, *Meeting Needs* at 50 with Fried, "Is Liberty Possible?" at 99–102, 107.

[60] See, e.g., Nagel, *Equality* at 12, 68–69; Raz, *The Morality of Freedom* at 225–27.

[61] The difference principle holds that social and economic inequalities are to be arranged so that they are to the greatest benefit of the least advantaged. For a full statement of the two principles of justice for institutions advanced by Rawls see John Rawls, *A Theory of Justice* 302–03 (1971).

[62] Dworkin's scheme urges us to imagine a world "in which, though the distribution of skills over the community were in the aggregate what it actually is, people for some reason all had the same antecedent chance of suffering the consequences of lacking any particular set of these skills." Dworkin further assumes that these people "were all in a position to buy insurance at the same premium structure," and suggests that the average insurance plan they would choose in such circumstances should guide us in fixing the lower bounds of a tax and redistribution program which is thus properly attentive to his conception of equality. See Ronald Dworkin, "What is Equality? Part 2: Equality of Resources," 10 *Philosophy and Public Affairs* 283, 315 (1981).

[63] See Rawls, *A Theory of Justice* at 15, 72–75; Dworkin, "What is Equality" at 311–14.

[64] See, e.g., David Gauthier, *Morals by Agreement* 221 (1986); Nozick, *Anarchy* at 192–93, 197, 201, 223, 228.

[65] See Sandel, *Liberalism* at 55, 79.

view himself as merely one among many, and thus his contingent endowments as morally arbitrary.[66]

If my analysis in the preceding paragraphs is correct, then both strong needs-based programs and those egalitarian programs which insist on the arbitrariness of our endowments, are closely related to *sharing*: the former programs are premised on the same solidarity which we found underlying the communitarian account of *sharing*;[67] the latter share the impersonal perspective rooted in our (rationally based) association towards other human beings.[68]

The distributive scheme

In this subsection, I formalize the claim I make in this section of the ideological premise underlying the law of unjust enrichment. I argue that the doctrine has an important distributive component. More precisely, I contend that it can usefully be described as constituting a distributive scheme.

Admittedly, analyzing our paradigm as a manifestation of the concept of *corrective* rather than distributive justice is more conventional. Nevertheless, I believe that such an analysis is inadequate. The concept of corrective justice on which such analyses are built is backwards-looking and conservative: it calls for the annulment of both wrongful gains and losses; it is indifferent to the justice of the pre-existing distribution of holdings.[69] Hence, the correctivist account of the law of unjust enrichment is apparently simple: once a wrongful gain has been demonstrated, restitution is to be granted.[70] Unfortunately, such a theory has a fairly limited

66 See Barry, *Theories of Justice* at 252; Nagel, *Equality* at 13, 63–64. Dworkin seems to deny the reliance of his scheme on impartiality, but in so far as he indeed denies it, it is not at all clear what the premise of his "abstract egalitarian thesis" is. See Ronald Dworkin, "Comment on Narveson: In Defense of Equality," 1(1) *Social Philosophy and Policy* 24, 31–35 (1983); Jan Narveson, "Reply to Dworkin," 1(1) *Social Philosophy and Policy* 41 (1983).

67 See Robert Nozick, *The Examined Life: Philosophical Mediations* 288–92 (1989).

68 There is no sanctity in the dichotomy suggested by the text. Thus, David Miller advocates an egalitarian program which is based on a communitarian justification. See David Miller, "In What Sense Must Socialism Be Communitarian?" 6(2) *Social Philosophy and Policy* 51, 59–60, 68 (1989).

69 See, e.g., Jules L. Coleman, "The Structure of Tort Law," 97 *Yale Law Journal* 1,233, 1,248–53 (1988). But see Jules L. Coleman, *Risks and Wrongs* 369–371 (1992) (corrective justice has nothing to do with wrongful gains; claims for wrongful gains are grounded in "restitutionary justice").

70 See, e.g., Kit Barker, "Unjust Enrichment: Containing the Beast," 15 *Oxford Journal of Legal Studies* 457, 468–74 (1995); Gregory Bordan, "The Law of Construction Privileges: Corrective Justice or Distributive Justice," 2 *Canadian Journal of Law and Jurisprudence*

explanatory (or normative) value, since – like the principle against unjust enrichment – it does not specify what renders a gain wrongful nor is it informative as to the specific measure of recovery applicable where such wrongfulness is indeed established. These questions, which are the focal ones the doctrinal rules should settle, must be resolved by distributive criteria.

In order to understand what is distributed and what exactly the distributive underpinnings of the doctrine are, consider the following Aristotelian account of the notion of distributive justice. Justice in distribution, according to this account, is perceived in a broad sense as any ratio between persons and things, any proportionate division of benefits or burdens among a group of potential recipients. Thus perceived, the notion of distributive justice – which I prefer to denote "a distributive scheme," a value-neutral term which seems more appropriate to this formal conception of justice – only requires that each recipient receives a measure according to *some* criterion.[71] The specific criterion according to which the proportion is calculated is what distinguishes distributive schemes from one another. In any case, it should be noted that the distributive criteria are not aimed at prescribing results for particular disputes (taking into account the charateristics of the specific parties involved). Rather, they operate in designing (shaping and reshaping) the general norms that govern any one of these disputes.[72]

The doctrinal rules of our paradigm respond to this formal description of distributive schemes. The doctrine prescribes which non-consensual appropriations of resources from their holders are wrongful and thus justify monetary recovery. Conversely, it also determines which appropriations are permitted, so that repair is not an inescapable result of the invasion. In cases of impermissible appropriations, the doctrine further establishes the appropriate measure of recovery. In all these respects, the rules of our paradigm affect the ability of each individual to make claims regarding various scarce resources.[73] Therefore, these rules constitute a society-wide

57, 67 (1989); Andrew S. Burrows, "Contract, Tort and Restitution – A Satisfactory Division or Not?" 99 *Law Quarterly Review* 217, 256 (1983).

[71] See Aristotle, *Nicomachean Ethics* 122–25 (Terence Irwin trans. 1985). The account of the text draws on Ernest J. Weinrib, "Aristotle's Forms of Justice," in *Justice, Law and Method in Plato and Aristotle* 133, 135, 137, 139 (Spiro Panagiotou ed. 1987).

[72] See Anthony T. Kronman, "Contract Law and Distributive Justice," 89 *Yale Law Journal* 472, 501 (1980).

[73] Scarcity inheres in our paradigm by the mere fact of non-consensual appropriation which implies conflicting claims over the resource at issue. Where resources are not scarce there is no need to set entitlements, and therefore no need to resort to distributive schemes. See, e.g., Barry, *Theories of Justice* at 154.

distribution of burdens and benefits, or – to use the term just coined – a distributive scheme.

The justification of one distribution or another is rooted in the applicable rationale – *control*, *well-being*, or *sharing* – which serves as the criterion according to which entitlements in resources are distributed to their holders.[74] But once these rationales are reintroduced, one can readily see that the distributive scheme constituted by our doctrine is far more subtle than the one sketched in the previous paragraph. It assigns not only claims regarding the use of some specific resources, but also certain primary social goods[75] with respect to these same resources: individual (negative) liberty, individual security in one's wealth, and social responsibility (i.e., responsibility of other members of one's society) for one's fate.

At least in so far as our paradigmatic case is concerned, these second-order goods conflict, so that opting for the one necessitates the neglect of the others.[76] For example, *sharing* infringes upon the individual's security and judgment with regard to the resource she possesses, and thus undermines negative liberty. Moreover, as an altruistic *institution* – as distinguished from freely initiated altruistic conduct – *sharing* may be said to coerce cooperation and hence to threaten, in an even deeper way, the individual's efforts to live her life according to her own choices.[77] In contrast, granting the resource-holder *control* over any specific resource necessitates the curtailment of other people's claims to share. Furthermore, the self-regarding attitude *control* inculcates may be perceived as frustrating the aspirations of those who applaud *sharing* to live in a society which nurtures the other-regarding standpoint of its constituents.[78] Indeed, each equilibrium along the *control-sharing* spectrum is a choice, an inevitable sacrifice of some ultimate values to others.

Hence, the doctrine governing our paradigm constitutes a distributive scheme which allocates claims to the primary goods of *control*, *well-being*, and *sharing* corresponding to the distribution of entitlements in resources and with regard to the very same resources. This distributive scheme is informed by the virtues of the underlying rationales as studied above. Therefore, it is this distributive scheme of primary social goods which should be the direct target of our explanatory effort.

[74] The rationales, as discussed here, have no bearing to the question of which resources are to be allocated to whom.

[75] The term follows Rawls, *A Theory of Justice* at 62, 92.

[76] *Cf.* Berlin, "Two Concepts of Liberty" at 125.

[77] See, e.g., Fried, "Is Liberty Possible?" at 95.

[78] See Nozick, *Anarchy* at 286–92.

Unjust enrichment and the socio-economic ethos

With the groundwork behind us, we can now address the second stage of my positive theory of unjust enrichment law: a retrodictive strategy for the rationales underlying our paradigm's doctrinal rules. Here I confront this task as effected by the social context; the final section of this chapter refines this still-too-abstract picture to include the specific relationships between individuals and their various resources.

My present claim is that one can expect to find some diversity across cultures regarding the rationales for judging our paradigmatic case. Furthermore, I claim that the socio-economic ethos of a society can be expected to effect its restitutionary doctrine.

Cultural diversity

I begin by considering a general contention: that one can expect to find a wide range of cross-cultural variability in the distributive schemes constituted by our doctrine. This claim is premised on a recognition of the existence of plurality of values across cultures.

Many writers have commented on the plurality of human values, but perhaps the best spokesman for this idea is Isaiah Berlin. Berlin insists that where the claims of two (or more than two) ultimate values prove incompatible in a particular case, and where the conflicting values are absolute and incommensurable, clear-cut solutions cannot, in principle, be found. He argues against the vision of philosophical monism which seeks to discover an ideal world in which all competing values are reconciled, all legitimate wishes capable of being truly satisfied, and nothing of value ever lost or sacrificed. For Berlin, such a vision is not merely utopian, but incoherent. Instead, he recommends that we face the intellectually uncomfortable fact that since some values may conflict intrinsically – since ends collide and since we cannot have everything – we must make choices. "The need to choose, to sacrifice some ultimate values to others, turns out to be a permanent characteristic of the human predicament."[79]

As we have seen, the primary goods distributed by unjust enrichment law are – at least in the context of our paradigmatic case – the very kind of ultimate, competing, and incompatible values Berlin discusses. Accordingly, one can expect to find various choices emphasizing different primary goods while discouraging or repressing others in both the personal and the

[79] See Isaiah Berlin, "Introduction" to *Four Essays on Liberty* at l–li.

social arenas.[80] In particular, every society can be expected to pick out its own preferred equilibrium along the continuum from individual *control* to societal *sharing*. Hence, we can expect different societies to adopt different distributive schemes for our paradigm.[81]

This conclusion is quite general and should be further refined. Is the expected variability a matter of pure coincidence? Or is the choice among rationales – and hence, the doctrinal rules and the distributive schemes – more predictable?

The underlying rationales and society's ethos

I claim that the choice of an equilibrium along the *control–sharing* continuum is predictable. More particularly, I wish to suggest as my working hypothesis that we can base such predictions on a correlation between the distributive scheme underlying the doctrine and the larger normative ethos of the society at issue.

This hypothesis is already implicit in my discussion of the intrinsic value of the various rationales.[82] Recall the libertarian thrust I attributed to the rationale of *control* as well as my insistence on the similarity between the grounds for supporting *sharing* and the reasons proposed for needs-based and egalitarian programs. These were not merely theoretical reflections. Rather, they have already done some work, linking *control* with libertarian ideals and *sharing* with more egalitarian systems and strong needs-based societies. The latter link also prompts another important conclusion: *sharing* is likely to be supplemented by a doctrinal assurance that the defendant is needy or worse off than the plaintiff.

Indeed, I suggest that the distributive scheme underlying the law of unjust enrichment corresponds with the level of *control*, *well-being*, and *sharing* the relevant legal community seeks to accord its members. Hence, given value pluralism, there will be no "best" doctrinal rules for our paradigm around which all legal regimes can be expected to converge.[83] Instead, a positive theory which aims to account for the rules of unjust enrichment must be specific to the particular society.[84] It should consider that society's ethos: its general ideas and pattern of ethics; the "distinctive

[80] See, e.g., William A. Galston, *Liberal Purposes: Goods, Virtues, and Diversity in the Liberal State* 30–31, 172 (1991); Raz, *The Morality of Freedom* at 395–96.

[81] *Cf.* Coleman and Kraus, "Rethinking the Theory" at 37.

[82] See pp. 23–31 above.

[83] *Cf.* Jonathan Hill, "Comparative Law, Law Reform and Legal Theory," 9 *Oxford Journal of Legal Studies* 101 (1989) (criticizing "better-solution comparative law").

[84] *Cf.* Clifford Geertz, "Local Knowledge: Fact and Law in Comparative Perspective," in *Local Knowledge: Further Essays in Interpretive Anthropology* 167, 215–16, 218 (1983).

human types" it nurtures; and the antecedent common understandings its members share.[85] An ethos is not easy to identify and isolate, and any account thereof is open to challenges.[86] None the less, it is possible to identify in every society – at least on the level of generality in which the law operates – some "'distinctive core," some "central tendencies; strong and enduring aggregations of belief that substantially define a political culture," which are expressed in the society's public rhetoric, foundational texts, ceremonies, and rituals.[87] I believe that this kind of data is required to explain the choices societies make from among the possible doctrinal rules of our paradigm.

But must there be such correspondence between our private law doctrine and society's ethos? Are rules of distribution from within our paradigm necessarily connected to society's general distributive scheme of primary goods?

Certain theorists – I call them "private law libertarians" – think it need not. Typically, they advocate a "division of labor" between public law and private law. Thus, in discussing tort law – the sister doctrine of our paradigm – Ronald Dworkin maintains that the concern for the well-being of other people is the responsibility of (only) the government, through its tax and redistribution mechanisms. In contrast, individuals are not required to treat others with care or concern in utilizing their private property. On the contrary, they are entitled (maybe even expected) to employ a self-interested attitude. The reason, according to Dworkin, for such a division of labor – pervasive public responsibility guided by his egalitarian program on the one hand, and (very) qualified private responsibility on the other hand – is to preserve personal liberty (leaving the agent enough moral private space free of the claims of others) while still being loyal to the strong egalitarianism of Dworkin's political theory.[88]

[85] *Cf.* Michael Walzer, *Spheres of Justice: A Defense of Pluralism and Equality* 5–6, 27, 313 (1983); Martin Diamond, "Ethics and Politics: The American Way," in *The Moral Foundations of the American Republic* 75, 77–78 (Robert H. Horwitz ed. 3rd edn. 1986).

[86] See, e.g., Martha C. Nussbaum and Amartya Sen, "Internal Criticism and Indian Rationalist Tradition," in *Relativism: Interpretation and Confrontation* 299, 301 (Michael Krausz ed. 1989).

[87] See Galston, *Liberal Purposes* at 16–17; Walzer, *Spheres of Justice* at 29.

[88] See Ronald Dworkin, *Law's Empire* 292–94, 296, 299–304, 309–12 (1986). In a different vein, Ernest Weinrib vehemently resists the injection of either distributive or communitarian considerations into the realm of private law. His arguments, however, are radically different from Dworkin's. For Weinrib, the immanent nature of private law justifies the private–public division of labor. See Ernest J. Weinrib, "Liberty, Community, and Corrective Justice," 1 *Canadian Journal of Law and Jurisprudence* 3 (1988); Ernest J. Weinrib, "Legal Formalism: On the Immanent Rationality of Law," 97 *Yale Law Journal* 949, 976–85 (1988). A full consideration of

Anthony Kronman has criticized the desirability of such a division of labor. In particular, he has demonstrated that taxation – as distinguished from private law regulation – is not inevitably the method of redistribution which is less intrusive, and hence less restrictive of individual liberty.[89] Kronman's conclusions are strengthened in our context. *Sharing* does not entail pervasive private responsibility (as Dworkin seems to believe it must), but rather constitutes a certain compromise that requires resource-holders to give the interests of others *some* weight. This may further ease Dworkin's concerns about the "liberty costs" that private law altruism entails.

Moreover, I would like to offer an argument that challenges the intelligibility of the dichotomous scheme promoted by private law libertarians such as Dworkin. I contend that the distributive scheme of a society's private law doctrines, such as the one governing our paradigm, cannot conflict with the desirable distributive values that society wishes to promote. Put differently, I believe that public law egalitarianism and private law libertarianism cannot be accommodated within one coherent legal regime.[90]

A full-blown defense of this thesis would require a rich account of the nexus or interdependence of political (in particular, distributive) programs and the conception of human agency. It is not my purpose to attempt such an ambitious enterprise. None the less, I think that identifying two premises on which such an account may be established can render my claim against private law libertarianism plausible.

My first premise regards the relation between the choice of a distributive scheme and the disposition of the persons who make such choice. The desirable distributive scheme of each social order can only be justified (and hence explained or predicted) by reference to a conception of the self. Any social arrangement inevitably depends on the prevailing societal equilibrium between each individual's self-regarding and other-regarding standpoints.[91] Hence, normative ethoses correspond to the different dispositions

Weinrib's formalistic theory would take us too far afield. Suffice it to say that this book – like most contemporary legal works – does not share his presuppositions of law's autonomy and inner intelligibility.

89 See Kronman, "Contract Law and Distributive Justice" at 503–07. For a recent suggestion of the inadequacy of distributing wealth through public law mechanisms see "Note, Distributive Liberty: A Relational Model of Freedom, Coercion, and Property Law," 107 *Harvard Law Review* 859, 867 (1994).

90 *Cf.* Guido Calabresi, *Ideals, Beliefs, Attitudes and the Law: Private Law Perspectives on a Public Law Problem* chapter 3 (1985).

91 See Nagel, *Equality* at 4, 16; Taylor, "The Nature and Scope of Distributive Justice," in *Philosophy and the Human Sciences* at 289, 291, 299; Nussbaum and Sen, "Internal Criticism" at 312.

of the differing selves typical to the pertinent communities: for example, if the other-regarding standpoint of such "typical self" is dominant, that is, if most people in a society perceive themselves more as members of a group and less as isolated and self-sufficient agents, they can be expected to opt for other-regarding institutions and regard the libertarian ones as less attractive (and *vice versa*).[92]

The second premise of my argument against private law libertarianism relates to the impact of social practices and institutional design on the constitution of personal identity. Communitarians, as well as other authors, often remind us that the values endorsed by the constituent selves of a community are themselves partly defined by the communities they inhabit, that our world is divided into constitutive communities, each composed of (somewhat) different selves, which are typical to their own particular socio-cultural environment.[93] According to this "social construction" thesis, the institutions of every society – modern or traditional, egalitarian or libertarian – also (at least partly) determine the identity of its members, and create in each of them a particular equilibrium between their self-regarding and other-regarding innate perspectives.[94] The law appears to be one of those important social institutions which shape the constituents' perceptions of their selves.[95] Hence, distributive schemes which underlie legal doctrines also serve – intentionally or inadvertently – to preserve, sustain, and reinforce a specific equilibrium between the self-

[92] In other words, our ideas of justice are powerfully affected by – and, to be sure, powerfully constitute – our perception of the relationship generally prevailing in the set of people within which the distribution is going to occur. See Miller, "In What Sense" at 58; Miller, "Distributive Justice" at 562, 590. See also Griffin, *Well-Being* at 285, 289.

[93] See Michael J. Sandel, "Introduction" to *Liberalism and Its Critics* 1, 6 (Michael J. Sandel ed. 1984); Sandel, *Liberalism* at 179; Charles Taylor, *Sources of the Self: The Making of the Modern Identity* 27 (1989); Alasdair MacIntyre, *After Virtue: A Study in Moral Theory* 220 (2nd edn. 1984); Clifford Geertz, "The Impact of the Concept of Culture on the Concept of Man," in *The Interpretation of Cultures: Selected Essays* 33 (1973). See also Richard Rorty, "The Priority of Democracy to Philosophy," in *Objectivity, Relativism, and Truth* (Philosophical Papers 1) 175 (1991); Nagel, *Equality* at 53; Galston, *Liberal Purposes* at chapter 10. *Cf.* Stephen Macedo, *Liberal Virtues: Citizenship, Virtues, and Community in Liberal Constitutionalism* 220–21, 259 (1990); Raz, *The Morality of Freedom* at 291, 426; Bruce A. Ackerman, *Social Justice in the Liberal State* 345 (1980); Lukes, *Individualism* at 78, 86, 146–47, 151–52; Amy Gutman, "Communitarian Critics of Liberalism," 14 *Philosophy and Public Affairs* 308, 316 (1985).

[94] See Mansbridge, "On the Relation of Altruism and Self-Interest" at 138. *Cf.* Amelie Oksenberg Rorty, "Relativism, Persons, and Practices," in Krausz, *Relativism: Interpretation and Confrontation* at 418, 424.

[95] See Geertz, "Impact" at 218–19.

regarding and the other-regarding standpoints of the agents in the relevant legal community.[96]

From these premises, we see that the relationship between people's dispositions and the values ingrained in their society's institutional design is one of reciprocity: social institutions – the law included – both reflect the prevailing system of belief of their constituents and at the same time shape it. Our attitudes towards one another and the prescriptions of our legal regime are embedded in one holistic web, each inculcating, and inculcated by, the other.[97] This conclusion may explain the empirical works respecting people's beliefs about distributive justice which demonstrate that national identity is by far the most influential personal attribute which accounts for a divergence in such beliefs.[98] Another important implication of this conclusion is that a change of our doctrinal rules can also bring about – rather than simply mirror – ethos reformation[99] (this aspect is highlighted in my discussion of the development in the rules governing our paradigm in international law).

But if indeed there is reciprocity between law and ethos, then any attempt to accommodate conflicting distributive values (like public law egalitarianism and private law libertarianism) within one legal regime is bound to be self-defeating. It seems artificial, even naive, to expect that the same person who is not required to pay (almost) any attention to the fate of others in every private-law-affected action – i.e., in the numerous interpersonal interactions she encounters daily with other people of her legal community – will recognize the legitimacy of the claims of others (equally strangers) to fragments of her resources when the tax-collector asks his due.[100] If our attitudes towards one another are, to some extent, the product

[96] *Cf.* Cass R. Sunstein, "Preferences and Politics," 20 *Philosophy and Public Affairs* 3, 8–10 (1991).

[97] *Cf.* J. M. Balkin, "Ideology as Constraint," 43 *Stanford Law Review* 1,133, 1,137, 1,142, 1,168–69 (1991). [98] See Miller, "Distributive Justice" at 581–88.

[99] Indeed, the social construction thesis should be distinguished from the arcane theory of "organistic historicism," which claims that law is embedded in the national spirit, nature, or character, and hence excludes any possibility of social (and legal) change and any utility in the borrowing or adaptation of social or legal institutions of one people by another nation. Thus, one can agree that we are partly defined by our communities and still endorse the view that we also partly define the values which shape our community. The latter view would be an empty addition if our community values were all-encompassing and if communities were wholly self-contained. But neither of these conditions obtains and therefore social change – *via*, for example, internal criticism or inter-cultural influences – is possible. This rejection of organistic historicism should caution us against identifying ethos without giving proper consideration to the possibility of ethos reformation.

[100] See Ignatieff, *The Needs of Strangers* at 13, 17, 137, 141.

of the prescriptions of our legal regime, then the completely self-regarding attitude generated by private law libertarianism cannot reasonably be expected to produce radically egalitarian policies (that is, policies which are supported by the other-regarding side of the self) when we come to shape our public law institutions. While exact correspondence between these two realms is not required, complete divergence is impossible.

Where does this leave the retrodictive strategy advocated above? The preceding paragraphs are not an abstract refutation of the challenge of private law libertarianism. I actually doubt if such a challenge can be ruled out by pure theoretical deliberations of any sort, let alone of the sketchy nature suggested above. Still, I think that this preliminary argument renders my theory of the link between the distributive values underlying private law and those of society's larger normative ethos plausible. In order to make such a theory persuasive, one cannot be content with philosophical speculations alone: some empirical support is needed. This is my plan for the following chapters. But before I embark on such a task, a final theoretical step remains.

Unjust enrichment and the resource involved

The socio-economic ethos of a legal community is a necessary, even principal, input for my positive theory, but it still does not furnish us with sufficient data. In this section, I demonstrate the necessity of considering the resource in question to explain the applicable doctrinal rules.

A consideration of resources implies that one can expect a variety of applicable rationales and corresponding measures of recovery in most societies. The distribution of the applicable rationales is not, to be sure, unrelated to the relevant socio-economic ethos. On the contrary, in most cases the normative ethos will correspond to the rationale which applies to an "average" resource in any given legal community and hence its primary importance. However, considering the resource at issue allows us to account for the outcome of cases in which the law provides resource-holders greater (or lesser) control than the ethos prescribes.

This continuum of entitlements in resources is neither accidental nor irrational. Synthesizing neo-Hegelian accounts of "property as personhood"[101] with a body of literature from psychology and the social sciences, I

[101] This section builds on the Hegelian theme of property as the embodiment of its holder's self. However, Hegel's theory of property (herein termed resource) is complex, multi-faceted, and somewhat obscure, and I have no intention of providing an account of it here, nor do I make any pretense to loyalty to Hegel's original ideas.

claim that the expected variability derives from the differing degrees to which a community views various resources as constitutive of their possessors' identity.[102] Thus, the more closely a resource is attached to its holder's identity in her society, the greater emphasis that society is expected to place on negative liberty, and therefore the more probable it is that the applicable rationale will be located somewhere to the *control* pole of the spectrum of available rationales. In contrast, as resources are viewed merely as valuable assets that have no direct bearing on the identity of their holder, the more likely that the focus will shift towards the other-regarding standpoint of the agent, and correspondingly the applicable rationale will be closer to the *sharing* pole.

People and their resources

Commentators often point to the subjective dimension of our relationships with the resources we hold. They suggest that at times we feel that a thing is so intimately connected with ourselves that it becomes a part of our very self. Being deprived of such a resource transcends the financial set-back involved; it is experienced as a violation and lessening of self.[103]

Perceiving resources as an extension of the self is not necessarily object-fetishism;[104] it may have important moral significance. Consider Jeremy Waldron's account of a case in which one works to bring about some change in the physical object she holds.[105] Changing an object, Waldron explains, precipitates a dual relation of will and object. On the one hand, the person's

On the contrary, my account consciously departs from the Hegelian roots in some important aspects. Moreover, I do not address the question Hegel and some neo-Hegelian writers deliberated on, i.e., the initial assignment of things to persons. Instead, I utilize the Hegelian perspective for a related but somewhat more modest task: given the fact that various people possess various resources, what can this perspective recommend regarding the rationales which should apply with respect to these holdings.

102 For a very different account of this variability see Richard A. Epstein, "On the Optimal Mix of Private and Common Property," in *Property Rights* 17 (Ellen F. Paul *et al.* eds. 1994).

103 See, e.g., Karl Olivecrona, "Locke's Theory on Appropriation," 24 *Philosophical Quarterly* 220, 224 (1974); Helga Dittmar, *The Social Psychology of Material Possessions: To Have Is To Be* 47 (1992).

104 See Margaret J. Radin, "Property and Personhood," 34 *Stanford Law Review* 957, 985–87 (1982).

105 See Jeremy Waldron, *The Right to Private Property* 353, 364–65, 369–70, 372–73, 378, 385 (1988). See also Peter G. Stillman, "Property, Freedom, and Individuality in Hegel's and Marx's Political Thought," in *Property: Nomos XXII* 130, 135 (J. Roland Pennock and John W. Chapman eds. 1980).

will has made a difference to the object: there is something in the object which may now be explained only in terms of the working of her will. On the other hand, and more significantly, the object itself, affected in that way by the will, makes a difference in turn to the person: her willing at one point of time can only be explained by reference to the external object of her labor. Thus, modifying something in the external world demonstrates a kind of responsibility, since the product of her will is thereby registered.

In other words, people's will is *reflected* in the object in as much as there is this dual line of effect from the will to the object and back to the will. Hence the moral significance of such relations of will and object: laboring on materials imposes some sort of consistency, permanence, and stability on the resolutions, plans, and projects of the will. Thus, one's moral development is fostered: her will becomes more self-disciplined and mature, and her abilities and self-conceptions sustained and developed.

Waldron limits his account of holdings as reflections of the self to cases in which one physically changes an object.[106] But this is too restrictive. The resources we hold without changing may also be affected by our wills – and thus express our personalities – in myriad ways. They may be integrated into our lives by being shaped or organized in line with our conception of self and our private needs, inclinations, and desires, our own life-plans. Thus, by merely living with an object or in a place for a period of time, one may become attached to it since it has become a medium through which she identifies herself, an essential element of her self-consciousness.[107]

This sense of attachment to our possessions is the heart of Margaret Radin's theory of property. In line with the notion of a situated self implied in the previous section, Radin sees persons as concrete selves whose situation in an environment of objects and other persons is constitutive. In particular, she insists that personhood requires "a continuity of memory and anticipation," and that our relations with things may be important to maintaining this sense of continuity: because they often represent our past experiences, possessions can be reminders and confirmers of our identity.[108] Hence, external things are part of the way we constitute ourselves:

[106] See Waldron, *The Right to Private Property* at 374.

[107] See Dudley Knowles, "Hegel on Property and Personality," 33 *Philosophical Quarterly* 45, 52, 56–57 (1983); C. Edwin Baker, "Property and Its Relation to Constitutionally Protected Liberty," 134 *University of Pennsylvania Law Review* 741, 746–47 (1986).

[108] See Russell W. Belk, "Possessions and the Extended Self," 15 *Journal of Consumer Research* 139, 148, 160 (1988); E. Doyle McCarthy, "Toward a Sociology of the Physical World: George Herbert Mead on Physical Objects," 5 *Studies in Symbolic Interaction* 105, 116–17 (1984).

"individuality and selfhood become intertwined with a particular object."[109]

Indeed, our attachment to the resources we hold is explicated and justified to the extent that they reflect our identity. Our resources can be reflections of our past and present; external projections of our personality;[110] or symbols of the unique place we have established for ourselves in our communities.[111] In so far as the resources we hold express our selves, we are attached to them, and thus experience a sense of personal violation when they are taken from us.[112]

This account has been empirically verified. Helga Dittmar has compiled and consolidated pertinent research from psychology and the social sciences. Her data confirms that people perceive their possessions as symbolically extending their sense of identity beyond the boundaries of their physical bodies: we really express who we are – both to ourselves and to others – through material possessions; and therefore we indeed often find it difficult to draw a clear line between the "me" and the "mine."[113]

Explaining our relations to our resources in these terms suggests that resources may be classified along a continuum. Self-investment in external things tends to be a matter of degree, rather than an either/or question.[114] Therefore, one's attachment to a resource, and the corresponding sense of personal loss she experiences in the case of invasion or deprivation thereof,

[109] See Radin, "Property and Personhood" at 959, 977; Margaret J. Radin, "Residential Rent Control," 15 *Philosophy and Public Affairs* 350, 362–63 (1986).

[110] *Cf.* Stephen R. Munzer, *A Theory of Property* section 4.3 (1990).

[111] *Cf.* Waldron, *The Right to Private Property* at 378.

[112] *Cf.* Andrew Reeve, *Property* 142 (1986).

[113] See Dittmar, *The Social Psychology* at chapters 3 to 5.

[114] But see Ernest J. Weinrib, "Right and Advantage in Private Law," 10 *Cardozo Law Review* 1,283, 1,286–87, 1,289–94, 1,303 (1989). In Weinrib's account of property as personhood, property is perceived as the embodiment of the agent's freedom of the will. Hence, the limits of one person's embodiment are the limits of another person's freedom. But, following Waldron and Radin, I propose to discard the obscure notion of a containment relation between resources and selves, and with it abandon the metaphor of an absolute and uniform presence of the self in each and every resource one holds. In its stead, we should adopt the view that the intensity of our connection of reflection-and-attachment with resources we possess varies according to the particular resource. This explains why in most societies – where some institutional significance is allocated to the other-regarding standpoint of the self – Weinrib's monolithic design will not do, and some variability in the rationales applicable to the various resources can be safely predicted. *Contra* Weinrib, his account is but one possible (and, I might add, not especially probable) contingent design of our area of law; it cannot be regarded as a constant, inherent, or natural characteristic of private law in general, or of unjust enrichment law in particular.

is also not constant across resources, but instead varies according to the circumstances; notably according to the nature of the relationship between the holders and the resource at issue. Not every resource is necessarily an expression of the self in the same degree. Hence, there is a spectrum of resources ranging from resources which are constitutive to people's identity to things which are held merely instrumentally and are thus wholly fungible.[115]

Accordingly, one can expect a differentiation of the doctrinal rules of our paradigm corresponding to the relationship of reflection and attachment between the specific resource and its holder: the more closely a resource is connected with personhood – i.e., the closer it is to the personal, rather than the fungible, pole of the continuum just described – the stronger its possessor's entitlement.

The significance of the social meaning of resources

I believe that the account offered above of the role our resources play in our lives captures a deep and universal human need to reflect oneself in the external world, and a resulting attachment to things that thus express their holders' personality.[116] Yet, I wish to be more precise regarding the way the continuum of resources is constituted. I want to argue that this continuum is neither universal, nor subjective, but instead primarily socially constituted.

More particularly, I believe that the significance of resources as symbolic reflections of the self turns mainly upon social processes. The social meaning of such resources in our society determines in which resources we are expected to invest our personalities; therefore, this social meaning also regulates, in a significant way, our attachment to the various resources we hold.[117] Social meanings, in short, prescribe the configuration of the continuum of resources and are thus of significant importance for my positive theory.[118]

115 See Radin, "Property and Personhood" at 959, 985–87; Radin, "Residential Rent Control" at 362–64; Olivecrona, "Locke's Theory" at 224. *Cf.* Justin Hughes, "The Philosophy of Intellectual Property," 77 *Georgetown Law Journal* 287, 339 (1988). Russell Belk suggested six characteristics of things that can be classified in the upper portions of the continuum: unwillingness to sell for market value, willingness to buy with little regard for price, non-substitutability, unwillingness to discard when utilitarian functions are lost, feelings of elation and depression due to the achievement of the object or its loss/damage, respectively, and personification. See Russell W. Belk, "The Ineluctable Mysteries of Possessions," in *To Have Possessions: A Handbook on Ownership and Property* 17, 35–37 (F. W. Rudmin ed. 1991).

116 *Cf.* Waldron, *The Right to Private Property* at 429.

117 *Cf.* Margaret J. Radin, "Introduction" to *Reinterpreting Property* 1, 18 (1993).

118 A normative analysis may, however, insist on challenging the propriety of the

This claim rests on two grounds. The first is the social construction thesis introduced in the previous section. This thesis insists that the communities we inhabit partly define or constitute our identity; that we are situated selves, encumbered by the social ethos of our environment; and that our self-understanding derives to some extent from the social processes that surround us.

There is no reason to believe that the phenomenon of reflecting one's personality in external objects is any exception to those processes of social construction. On the contrary, we use certain objects as reflections of our personalities – and are therefore attached to them in a particular way – in a *human* world. Put another way, the phenomenon of reflection-and-attachment is itself a social process, and as such can be expected to yield social – and not universal or subjective – products. People perceive certain resources as more reflections of their selves than others since others – to whom the external image of the self is communicated – also share with them the same symbolic meaning.[119] Hence, it is the social meaning of the resources which is all-important. Once again, we find no escape from a particularistic social investigation.[120]

This theoretical consideration is substantially supported by Dittmar's empirical survey.[121] Dittmar argues that possessiveness is not merely an

reference to prevailing social meanings. See Stephen J. Schnably, "Property and Pragmatism: A Critique of Radin's Theory of Property and Personhood," 45 *Stanford Law Review* 347 (1993).

119 *Cf.* Waldron, *The Right to Private Property* at 377.

120 My claim of the significance of the social meaning of resources resembles an aspect of Michael Walzer's particularistic theory of justice. Walzer claims that the conception and creation of all the (heterogeneous) goods with which distributive justice is concerned (from membership through money and commodities to kinship and love) are social processes. Hence, all such goods are social goods with shared meanings. Therefore, he concludes that, first, different goods have different shared social meanings and are accordingly subject to different distributive criteria, and, second, that the meaning of the same good may change as society changes and with it the appropriate distributive criteria of such good. See Walzer, *Spheres of Justice*. My emphasis on the significance of the social meaning of the resources coincides with Walzer's latter conclusion. However, in my account such meaning merely points to the relative attachment of the resources to their holder's identity, and hence prescribes the strength of her moral claim to each such resource. Therefore, resources are not subject to qualitatively different distributive criteria, but are merely quantitatively differentiated. Accordingly, my working image is not of spheres of justice, but of concentric circles of control. See pp. 47–49 below. It appears to me that the reason for this difference is that the various resources discussed herein are much more homogeneous than the goods Walzer considers. In a sense, this book can be read as providing a detailed (and still more particularistic) account of only one sphere of justice (although none of the spheres Walzer considers exactly coincides with the realm of resources our paradigm regulates).

121 See Dittmar, *The Social Psychology* at chapters 1 to 4.

innate urge. To be sure, the claim to an acquisitive instinct is not denied as inherently untenable. However, Dittmar claims – and establishes with a multitude of evidence – that biology can only postulate an underlying potential for investigating property-related behavior at a very abstract level. In contrast, the actual manifestation of this potentiality varies considerably cross-culturally. Hence, in order to provide a more meaningful and rich account of the way people are attached to their resources, attention must be turned to the specific socially transmitted and socially shared meaning system.

Dittmar demonstrates that the social and cultural context has a profound effect on the strength of possessiveness or materialism, and that it also significantly influences how people relate to their possessions. More to the point, she emphasizes that material objects have socially shared symbolic meanings – rather than merely instrumental or utilitarian functions – through which various aspects of identity are shaped, perceived, expressed, and communicated. Such meanings are transmitted through direct social interaction, as well as through social processes and institutions, such as schools, the media, and (I contend) the law. Hence, they vary historically and socio-culturally.

Following Dittmar's powerful evidence, it seems only plausible that the social meanings of resources are also helpful, indeed crucial, in an area that she does not discuss but is the focus of our attention, that is, the degree to which people are attached to the various resources they hold.

A conclusion is emerging from both the theoretical and the empirical fronts regarding the social construction of the continuum of resources. And yet, I do not deny the existence of instances of universal convergence and idiosyncratic preferences: one can plausibly imagine, for example, that most people in most societies are most closely attached to their bodies and probably also to their reputation and homes; by the same token, it cannot be denied that the connection of reflection-and-attachment with any given resource can vary within the same society across the various people who may hold it (compare, for example, the significance of a wedding ring at the hands of a jeweler with its significance for a loving wearer).[122]

[122] See Radin, "Property and Personhood" at 987; See also Radin, "Residential Rent Control" *passim*. In essence, Radin advocates a legal regime which would be even more particularistic than the one suggested by this section; a regime which will inquire into the specific relations of the holder to the object in question in each and every case. In addition to the consideration mentioned in the text below, one can raise additional grounds for rejecting this alternative, notably, the need for a legal regime to work on a fairly high level of generality due to considerations of both the

Still, I believe that a crucial point is missed if we look at the phenomenon of reflection-and-attachment either universally or personally. Our attachment to resources derives from our perception of them as being reflections of ourselves, symbols of our identity; and – as we have just learned – the way we constitute such symbols of identity is, to a considerable extent, through social processes; our resources gain their significance as reflections of the self *socially*. Hence, the social meanings of resources have a decisive bearing upon the set of resources to which people are typically attached, i.e., on the composition and order of the continuum of resources which is, by and large, applicable to the people of any particular society.

Circles of control

The personhood perspective explains why certain interests people have in their resources may give rise to stronger moral claims than others even within a given society. A legal regime responsive to its constituents' dispositions[123] is expected to afford correspondingly divergent degrees of protection to such intrinsically divergent holdings.[124] Entitlements in resources are thus expected to employ different rationales, which entail different measures of recovery in case of invasion or appropriation, according to the place of the specific resource in the particular continuum of attachment of the society in question.

This section's conclusions can be restated in terms that will help integrate them with the account of the previous sections. Recall the metaphor of a divided self, torn between its self-regarding and other-regarding standpoints. Recall also the hypothesis that the final equilibrium on which such self is settled is, to a large extent, a product of the social processes and institutions which help constitute it. In most societies, such an equilibrium is a mixture of the two standpoints of the self; only in pure libertarian regimes the other-regarding standpoint of the self is, by definition, institutionally muted.[125] Given the story of this section, this working image can be fine-tuned. If indeed a typical self in a given society is

rule of law and the ensuing administrative costs Radin's design would entail. However, these are factors external to our philosophical common-ground, and therefore beyond the scope of this section.

123 Decision-makers' responsiveness in the context of the social meanings of resources, as well as with respect to other aspects of an ethos, may come about through cultural constructs. *Cf.* Geertz, "Common Sense as a Cultural System," in *Local Knowledge* at 73.

124 *Cf.* Radin, "Property and Personhood" at 960.

125 In contrast, in "true" communist regimes the self-regarding standpoint of the self is supposedly muted (at least institutionally). Hence, there is no proprietary protection to any holding – and reflection-and-attachment – in any resource.

attached (in the strong sense detailed above) to different resources in different degrees, then it seems plausible that – *vis-à-vis* third parties who wish to share such resource with its holder[126] – the self-regarding standpoint of such a holder will be stronger, and her other-regarding standpoint weaker, with respect to resources which rank high in the continuum of attachment.[127] Similarly, when resources on the lower part of the continuum are at issue, the other-regarding standpoint of the self can be expected to be relatively more operative (the exact degree of the influence of the other-regarding standpoint of the self depends, of course, on the particular socio-economic ethos which broadly prescribes the equilibrium between the two standpoints).

Thus, it seems plausible that one would be most anxious to *control* her most precious resources – those external things that more than any others are constitutive of her identity. In fact, the relation of attachment and control seems more complex: it is not only that more attachment calls for more control, but it is also that our selves seem to be attached more closely to objects over which they exert more control.[128] This is another manifestation of the significance of the particular social environment in shaping the spectrum of attachment to the resources we hold.

On the other hand, in so far as one has any appreciation for the mandates of *sharing*, she is more likely to be ready and willing to share in resources that are relatively remote from her center of selfhood. In short, the

[126] The claim of intrinsic connection between core resources and the self-regarding standpoint of their holder needs to be refined. I do not deny that we may characterize some of our core resources as resources we care about for their own sake, and for which we are thus willing to sacrifice. In this respect, core resources give rise to the application of our other-regarding standpoint, and not to its self-regarding counterpart. But notice that in such cases our other-regarding standpoint is directed at the very resources we care about, and not at third parties who wish to share these resources with us. Hence, this connection between core resources and the other-regarding standpoint does not challenge my account relating core resources with self-regarding attitude towards such third parties. (To be sure, I do not deny that there may be cases in which our other-regarding attitude respecting a resource may entail an other-regarding attitude to third parties, but this attitude is, in such cases, derivative and contingent. Moreover, in other cases – and the empirical evidence collected above may indicate that these are the more frequent ones – our other-regarding attitude towards the resource we hold will reinforce, rather than weaken, our self-regarding attitude with respect to third parties who wish to share it with us.)

[127] Correspondingly, as the resource in question is more closely connected – in the reflection-and-attachment sense – to its holder's identity, any potential invader can be expected to employ more and more his other-regarding standpoint, and accordingly acknowledge the law's claim to refrain from the invasion.

[128] See Dittmar, *The Social Psychology* at 58–59.

competing values within the self do not apply with equal intensity across resources. And, again, in so far as the law both reflects and shapes its constituents' self, this variability can be expected to be mirrored in the legal doctrine of our paradigm.

What emerges from these observations is that – in the typical case – the control human actors are accorded by the doctrinal rules of our paradigm is not absolute but rather occurs along a continuum of diminishing interests: from core interests (protected against almost any kind of invasion or infringement) through less protected interests to least protected interests. More precisely, one can imagine that our doctrine draws concentric circles of diminishing control (and attachment) around the self.[129] This working image can help illustrate the significance of the socio-economic ethos on the one hand, and the social meaning of resources on the other.

Consider first the socio-economic ethos. Given two societies, in which the degree to which each resource is attached to the actor's identity is identical, the employment of a more other-regarding ethos would enlarge the radii of the various circles, and thus decrease the relative control each actor can exert over the resources at her disposal in favor of extended private responsibility.

Now consider the social meaning of the resource. Given one society with a stable socio-economic ethos, any resource which is considered relatively constitutive of people's identity will be placed in a relatively inner circle.

This illustration elucidates the minimalist characteristic which I claim to be universal respecting our paradigm and highlights its structural or schematic nature: the law of unjust enrichment is (or, at least, can be) a sophisticated, sensitive, and flexible framework which balances conflicting claims regarding various resources people hold, taking into account the specific socio-economic ethos of the pertinent society and the particular social meanings of the resources in question.

Indeed, when we come to account for the specific doctrinal rules we must resort to these two bodies of social data (which, for convenience, are both termed "the ethos" below). Like the socio-economic ethos, the social meanings of resources cannot be precisely identified and easily studied. Ethos talk is often messy and subject to disputes, but it is still the most helpful in formulating a positive theory for this segment of the law.

[129] *Cf.* Belk, "Possessions" at 152.

3 Retrodictions

Now that I have outlined my thesis, I will attempt to demonstrate its potential power. This chapter illustrates the way the tools developed thus far can be used to account for the doctrinal rules of our paradigm in any given society in two stages. First, I concentrate on the primary input one needs for this task: the socio-economic ethos. Thus, the American and Judaic socio-economic ethoses are summarized in the first and second sections respectively of this chapter, and the two ethoses are compared in the third section of this chapter, where some conclusions are reached regarding the expected differences between these two legal regimes, followed by some more specific conjectures as to the content of the specific rules that Talmudic civil law can be expected to employ. Then, in the fourth section of this chapter, the focus turns to the secondary input, which fine-tunes the broad prescriptions dictated by the socio-economic ethos, i.e., the social meaning of the resources at issue. Here, our attention will be directed solely on the contemporary American context, and our task will be to study the social meanings of the various resources which the contemporary doctrine regulates, and to infer the rationales (and measures of recovery) which the American doctrine can be expected to accord these resources.[1]

[1] With respect to both the socio-economic realm and the social meaning of resources, I rely on myriad sources which can be arranged in two broad categories: (i) "direct" data – as drawn from empirical research – of the prevalent perceptions of the pertinent group of people; and (ii) "indirect" information from certain public rhetoric and social practices and institutions (including the law) which express and "codify" the ethos. I blend the sources from these two categories, and pay little attention to the nature of the source from which ethos is deduced. I do so not merely as a matter of expositional convenience, but rather for substantive reasons: it is my belief that both methods of investigation stand on the same footing, and that the "indirect" information is not necessarily second best. Recall our working assumption that decision-makers, who prescribe the doctrinal rules, respond to what they think people in their culture perceive as the proper balance of the self-regarding and the

Chapters 4 and 5 examine the conclusions of this chapter in some detail against the actual doctrinal rules of contemporary American law and Talmudic civil law.[2] It is my claim that the explanatory power of this book's thesis, as demonstrated by this exercise, lends empirical support to the plausibility of my theory which has been thus far only theoretically defended.

The American socio-economic ethos

Although Americans come from numerous different traditions, and American politics is saturated with many ideological conflicts, commentators frequently claim that Americans form a "distinctive human product"; that they have an individualistic-liberal "national identity"; that beneath their sharp disagreements, "there is more than a little consensus about the relationship between the individual and society"; and that most such disagreements are still taking place, to a striking degree, within the boundaries of the democratic and capitalist traditions, to which the major constituents of the American civic culture are deeply committed.[3]

The underlying theme which runs through most of these characterizations and the most profound ethical attachment of "the American person"

other-regarding standpoints of the self, as well as to the relative attachment of any one resource to the self. These decision-makers, however, are affected by both categories of information. Hence, in attempting to account for the actual choices such decision-makers are expected to make, the observer should also attempt to utilize both sources of information. More importantly, recall that my theory presupposes a contextualized self which is continuously shaped by, and at the same time reshaping, her social environment. Correspondingly, it perceives the personal attitudes and the institutional design which reflects and shapes them as a holistic web: neither people's attitudes nor the social design can be said to be the foundation of one another; but both are, none the less, strongly embedded in a web, and each of them inculcates – and is inculcated by – its counterpart. Hence, calling the public rhetoric and social practices "indirect" data is, in an important way, misleading: it is not derivative; rather, data from group (ii) is just as informative as that from group (i).

2 Chapter 6 further discusses the development of the rules of international law with regard to restitution as a result of the expropriation of alien-owned property. This apparently remote situation is explored as a supplementary examination of the explanatory power of the theory, as well as in order to enrich it in some important aspects.

3 See Martin Diamond, "Ethics and Politics: The American Way," in *The Moral Foundations of the American Republic* 75, 99 (Robert H. Horwitz ed. 3rd edn. 1986); Stephen Macedo, "Liberal Virtues: Citizenship, Virtues, and Community" in *Liberal Constitutionalism* 5–6, 9 (1990); Robert N. Bellah *et al.*, *Habits of the Heart: Individualism and Commitment in American Life* 20 (1985); Herbert McClosky and John Zaller, *The American Ethos: Public Attitudes toward Capitalism and Democracy* 3–4 (1984).

is individual (negative) liberty.[4] Liberty, Herbert McClosky and John Zaller report, is more deeply embedded in the nation's ethos than any other value. America is "a nation obsessed with liberty"; individual liberty has always been the object of political authority, the measure of its worth.[5]

Indeed, several commentators observe that individualism lies at the very core of American culture. Both the American institutional design and the American people celebrate personal independence and self-reliance and enshrine the right of every individual to choose his or her own way and live their lives as they see fit.[6] Michael Walzer, for example, depicts the American people as "continually in motion," separating themselves from one another and hence "relatively dissociated." For Walzer, the obsession with mobility in contemporary American life represents the constant pursuit in America of private or personal happiness; the American belief that association should always be voluntary and that each member should always reserve "the right of rupture and withdrawal." Hence, the American self, for Walzer, is a "post-social" self, "free at last from all but the most temporary and limited alliances."[7]

Coinciding with this strong sense of individualism is the central place accorded to property in American constitutionalism and in American life as well as the "bourgeois virtues" which characterize the American people. Consider first the role of property. Jennifer Nedelsky has recently claimed that private property has shaped the structure of the American political system; that both the framework of our political institutions and the categories through which we understand politics developed around the task of providing security to property. Nedelsky maintains that "those who won the formative contest over the nature of the new republic were

[4] See, e.g., Bellah, *Habits of the Heart* at 23; Lawrence Friedman, *The Republic of Choice* 2 (1990).

[5] See McClosky and Zaller, *The American Ethos* at 18. When asked whether personal freedom or equality is more important, Americans preferred freedom over equality by a margin of 72 percent to 20 percent. In Western Europe, by comparison, only 49 percent chose freedom while 35 percent chose equality.

[6] See Bellah, *Habits of the Heart* at 142; McClosky and Zaller, *The American Ethos* at 111, 113, 270–71; Walter Berns, "Equally Endowed with Rights," in *Justice and Equality: Here and Now* 151, 157 (Frank S. Lucash ed. 1986); Ronald Beiner, "What's the Matter with Liberalism?" in *Law and Community: The End of Individualism* 36, 51 (Allan C. Hutchinson and Leslie J. M. Green eds. 1989); Mary Ann Glendon, "Individualism and Communitarianism in Contemporary Legal Systems: Tensions and Accommodations," (1993) *Brigham Young University Law Review* 385, 405.

[7] Michael Walzer, "The Communitarian Critique of Liberalism," 18 *Political Theory* 6, 11–16, 21 (1990). See also, e.g., Bellah, *Habits of the Heart* at 23, 167. *Cf.* Stephen Macedo, "Capitalism, Citizenship and Community," 6(1) *Social Philosophy and Policy* 113, 119, 137 (1988).

preoccupied with the protection of private property" as "the central instance of rights at risk in a republic,"[8] and that therefore they accorded property (implicit) priority over other rights. She acknowledges (even applauds) the constitutional shift of the New Deal and the modern welfare state it established. None the less, Nedelsky insists that the Madisonian legacy of property as "the quintessential instance of rights as boundaries," the symbol and source of a protected and sacred sphere, is still with us. Hence, for Nedelsky, while we engage in redistribution to ameliorate social ills, we have not accepted property as mere social construct to be redefined and redistributed without constraint; we have no consensus on a vision of the state that clearly defines redistribution as a legitimate goal.[9]

I return shortly to the question of redistribution in outlining the American distributive scheme. What is essential here, however, is the sense conveyed by Nedelsky – and undisputed even by those who criticize other parts of her work – of the powerful force of the concept of property in the American heritage, its central, almost emotional importance.[10] Property achieved such a high value, Nedelsky further suggests, due to the heavy weight the framers of the Constitution put on protecting individual liberty. Protecting liberty – at least in the negative sense – requires security of the concrete means every individual has for controlling his or her life; expressing oneself in a sphere which is untouchable by others; shielding oneself from the power of individual or collective others.[11]

Empirical surveys of public attitudes in the United States seem to support both the importance of property and its symbolic content. As McClosky and Zaller report, popular support in the United States for the institution of private property remains strong, and Americans still view property as a bulwark of individual freedom and independence and the source of personal economic well-being.[12]

The pursuit of personal independence is manifested also in what Martin Diamond terms as "bourgeois virtues" which characterize the "American

[8] For an account of the losing side of the formative debate, i.e., the Republican conception of property, which emphasizes duties, participation, and equality, see Elizabeth V. Mensch, "The Colonial Origins of Liberal Property Rights," 31 *Buffalo Law Review* 635, 646–52 (1982).

[9] Jennifer Nedelsky, *Private Property and the Limits of American Constitutionalism: The Madisonian Framework and its Legacy* 1–4, 6–9, 186 (1990). But see Thomas W. Merrill, "American Legal History: Zero-Sum Madison," 90 *Michigan Law Review* 1,392, Part II (1992) (book review).

[10] See, e.g., Laura S. Underkuffler, "On Property: An Essay," 100 *Yale Law Journal* 127, 129 (1990).

[11] See Nedelsky, *Private Property* at 186, 205, 207–08. But *cf.* Underkuffler, "On Property."

[12] See McClosky and Zaller, *The American Ethos* at 139–43.

person." America's commercial society, says Diamond, unleashes acquisitiveness: a desire for getting the (material) fruits of one's own exertions or qualities. Acquisitiveness, unlike avarice or covetousness, carries with it valuable qualities: "frugality, economy, moderation, labor, prudence, tranquility, order, and rule."[13] Indeed, the American political system was intended to rest, and still rests, on "the aggressive private pursuit by all of immediate personal interests." It fosters industriousness and entrepreneurship; encourages competition; and ennobles the drive towards economic gain.[14]

Appreciating the place of liberty, property, and bourgeois ethics in the American way of life explains the importance Americans attach to the distributive principle of desert. David Miller has recently published a comprehensive compilation of empirical materials regarding the beliefs about distributive justice prevailing in advanced industrial societies, chiefly in the United States. He concludes that the evidence highlights popular support for desert – loosely defined as reward in proportion to contribution[15] – as the major criterion for income distribution. He adds that this preference is prevailing also among working-class subjects (especially in the United States).[16]

Such an emphasis on desert does not seem accidental; rather, it appears to be the product of the American institutional design. American democracy, Martin Diamond observes, never denied the unequal existence of human virtues or excellences. On the contrary, the American political order presupposed that an inequality of virtues and abilities is rooted in human nature and that this inequality would manifest itself and flourish in the private realm of society;[17] its founders perceived "the protection of different and unequal faculties of acquiring property" as the first object of government.[18]

The relative inegalitarianism which is entailed by adherence to desert is also empirically affirmed.[19] While overwhelmingly supporting the principle of an equal start in the race ("equal opportunity"), most Americans reject

[13] See Diamond, "Ethics and Politics" at 99–101.

[14] See McClosky and Zaller, *The American Ethos* at 101–11, 117–19; Berns, "Equally Endowed" at 160–61; Diamond, "Ethics and Politics" at 94–95.

[15] Miller says it is difficult to define more carefully what exactly is to be rewarded according to the American ethos – ability, effort, or performance.

[16] See David Miller, "Distributive Justice: What the People Think," 102 *Ethics* 555, 560, 564, 567, 580, 582–84 (1992).

[17] Diamond, "Ethics and Politics" at 103.

[18] See Berns, "Equally Endowed" at 158. See also, e.g., Nedelsky, *Private Property* at 2, 205.

[19] Recall that egalitarianism is here understood to favor the worse off over the better off; giving preferential weight to improvements in the life of the former as against the advantages of the latter.

equality of economic rewards ("equal outcome") and regard "earned" or "deserved" inequalities as natural to democratic life.[20]

None the less, Miller, who highlights the American commitment to the inegalitarian distributive principle of desert, also insists that this commitment is moderated by some degree of attachment to egalitarianism (the popular view that "the current spread of incomes is too great, and that a fair distribution would compress this range somewhat"), and to needs-based convictions (the prevalent concern that "people at the bottom end of the scale are not earning a 'living-wage,' that is, one that is adequate to maintain a decent way of life"). And yet Miller emphasizes that these countervailing factors are quite weak. This finding of relative weakness of egalitarian and needs-based convictions in America is especially conspicuous when viewed through the lenses of the whole international community. The international comparisons Miller cites show that the preeminence of desert, and the relative weakness of equality and needs, characterize Western societies more than any others. Moreover, these preferences especially distinguish the American people, even as compared to other Westerners.

Furthermore, Miller adds two important comments regarding the egalitarian and needs-based concerns: (i) both seem to be more readily analyzed by Americans as a popular perception of market distortions of the "appropriate" reward to various occupational groups; and (ii) the second, needs-based commitment (and the popular support to the American welfare state) is not widely accepted as a means for achieving "justice"; instead, Miller suggests that significant portions of the population may perceive it more as a matter of generosity[21] or of long-term self-interest. As he concludes, the Western – notably American – beliefs about distributive justice reflect "the predominantly instrumental and competitive nature of social relations in contemporary Western societies."[22]

The socio-economic ethos of Judaism

Judaism establishes a unique social structure embedded in its own value system which is quite dissimilar from the American ethos.[23] There is a

[20] See McClosky and Zaller, *The American Ethos* at 63, 81–82, 94, 121. See also, e.g., Miller, "Distributive Justice" at 565–66; Bellah, *Habits of the Heart* at 25–26. But see, e.g., Aaron Wildavsky, "Resolved, that Individualism and Egalitarianism be made Compatible in America: Political-Cultural Roots of Exceptionalism," in *Is America Different?: A New Look at American Exceptionalism* 116, 118–19, 128 (Byron E. Shafer ed. 1991). [21] See also Nedelsky, *Private Property* at 262, 328 note 170.

[22] See Miller, "Distributive Justice" at 567–70, 574–76, 586–88, 591.

[23] See Robert M. Cover, "Obligation: A Jewish Jurisprudence of the Social Order," 5 *Journal of Law and Religion* 65 (1987).

dispute regarding the relationship between the Judaic social vision and its theological underpinnings.[24] I cannot of course resolve this controversy. But for the purposes of this discussion, suffice it to indicate that even adherents of the view which emphasizes the theocentric quality of Judaism admit that "even if it is assumed that the ultimate and overriding aim of Judaism is service of the Creator, the welfare of the individual and of society are important – albeit mediate – goals of religious law."[25] Hence, both attitudes acknowledge the importance of the social vision of Judaism – as an end in itself or as a prerequisite for the achievement of the ultimate calling – and this is the only claim necessary for the development of my argument.

Judaism shapes a distinct "Jewish economic person" and a particular socio-economic system different from both capitalism and socialism.[26] The Judaic ethos aims at balancing the individual's independence and well-being with the bonds of fellowship and mutual responsibility. Community-wise, this platform is far more ambitious than the more individualistic program of modern Western civilization. It rejects the clearly delineated approach of absolute – yet minimal – rights and favors in its stead a scheme of open-ended, but therefore necessarily relative, entitlements.[27]

Like individualism, Judaism emphasizes the significance of each and every person. Each was created in the divine image, and hence each is equally and uniquely sanctified; each represents in himself a world of importance; each individual's well-being and independence are of major concern to many of the laws and regulations Judaism prescribes.[28]

At the same time, Judaism posits a concept of membership which is natural; it perceives human life as intrinsically social and the individual's

[24] Compare Izhak Englard, "The Interaction of Morality and Jewish Law," 7 *Jewish Law Annual* 114, 119–20 (1988); Suzanne L. Stone, "In Pursuit of the Counter-Text: The Turn to the Jewish Legal Model in Contemporary American Legal Theory," 106 *Harvard Law Review* 813, 821–22, 834, 849–55, 868–69, 872, 893–94 (1993) with Shubert Spero, *Morality, Halakha and the Jewish Tradition* 63, 90 (1983); Ze'ev W. Falk, *Legal Values and Judaism: Towards a Philosophy of Halakha* 52 (1980); Isadore Twersky, "Some Aspects of the Jewish Attitude Toward the Welfare State," in *A Treasury of Tradition* 221, 225, 227 (Norman Lamm and Walter S. Wurzburger eds. 1967).

[25] See Englard, "The Interaction of Morality" at 123.

[26] See Meir Tamari, *With All Your Possessions: Jewish Ethics and Economic Life* 1–5, 59 (1986).

[27] See, e.g., Lenn E. Goodman, *On Justice: An Essay in Jewish Philosophy* 29 (1991).

[28] See, e.g., Myer S. Lew, *The Humanity of Jewish Law* 109, 111, 130 (1985); Boaz Cohen, "Law and Ethics in Light of the Jewish Tradition," in *Law and Tradition in Judaism* 182, 231 (1959); Lenn E. Goodman, "The Individual and the Community in the Normative Traditions of Judaism," in *Autonomy and Judaism: The Individual and the Community in Jewish Philosophical Thought* 69, 104–05 (Daniel Frank ed. 1992).

identity as largely socially defined.[29] As Lenn Goodman observes, the Torah aims at the construction not only of a society, but of a community. "Its central, thematic interpersonal law is that of fellowship – *love thy fellow* – from which all the rest are said to be derived" as mere applications or interpretations. The communal bonds of fellowship, respect, concern, reverence, and generosity are perceived as prerequisites to the human accommodation. "As members of a community, others become second selves, their interests integrated."[30]

This Judaic vision of community does not, however, entail complete benevolence or self-sacrifice. Judaism gives priority to the self over the other. It acknowledges each person's proximity and relatedness to himself; recognizes that each is usually in the best position to help himself; and accepts that if one does not give oneself priority, one will end up truly deprived and disadvantaged.[31]

Hence, Judaism presents a dualistic social vision which finds intrinsic significance in both the individual *and* the community. Therefore, it prescribes a social equilibrium distinguished from both individualism and communitarianism, the two extremes of a spectrum the mean of which Judaism seeks to reach. Rather, it gives paramount importance to a unique notion of mutual responsibility. This notion acknowledges both the importance of each person and the interdependence of human existence. It provides that we all have obligations towards one another even apart from any formal undertakings we may make.[32]

In particular, Judaism prescribes as an axiomatic principle the maxim of mutual responsibility for the *material needs* of each and every fellow member.[33] This dimension of the Judaic ethos is the most germane for our purposes here. It is manifested in the Judaic conceptions of property and of charity, and in the unique linkage Judaism finds between these two conceptions.

Judaism recognizes the legitimacy and importance of private property. None the less, it never sanctifies property rights, nor does it consider such

[29] See, e.g., Falk, *Legal Values and Judaism* at 14, 117, 119; Goodman, *On Justice* at 17; Goodman, "The Individual and the Community" at 102–03.

[30] Goodman, *On Justice* at 6, 8, 29, 42. See also, e.g., Goodman, "The Individual and the Community" at 80; Lew, *The Humanity of Jewish Law* at 29, 117.

[31] See Spero, *Morality, Halakha and the Jewish Tradition* at 225. See also, e.g., Cohen, "Law and Ethics" at 226.

[32] See, e.g., Goodman, *On Justice* at 15–16.

[33] See Tamari, *With All Your Possessions* at 210–11, 240. See also, e.g., Kaufman Kohler, "The Historical Development of Jewish Charity," in *Hebrew Union College and other Addresses* 229, 234–35 (1933).

rights absolute or natural.[34] On the contrary, the central principle of the Jewish economic philosophy is the divine origin of wealth. Property was entrusted to us by God for our well-being; but property-owners are mere custodians of the resources they hold. Hence, "the same Jewish law which protects the rights of the individual to his own property in turn limits those rights and grants others, the community and other individuals, moral claims to that property."[35]

The Judaic concept of charity – which is the manifestation of the Jewish distributive scheme – is based upon this perception of property: something which is given to its possessor by God as a form of custody partly for charity. Therefore, justice requires that the "haves" share their property with the "have nots"; providing the needs of individuals in the community is for Judaism no more than what is just and right. The Hebrew name given to charity, *tzedakah*, means justice and righteousness. *Tzedakah* is not an act of special kindness, mercy, grace, or one based on personal pangs of conscience, but is rather giving the needy their due. *Tzedakah* – one of the hallmarks of Jewish life – is the fulfillment of a legal obligation; a manifestation of the rights of the community and its less fortunate members in the property of other members.[36] That *tzedakah* is the receiver's right corresponds with one of the most important features of this institution: preserving the recipient's dignity and minimizing his shame. A *right* to *tzedakah* coincides with a tactful approach to the needy which eliminates or deftly camouflages humiliation and degradation.[37]

An important attribute of *tzedakah* is the criterion of distribution. Michael Walzer explains that the starting point of the Judaic distributive outlook is the Talmudic maxim that the needs of the poor must be met. This injunction, Walzer emphasizes, entails an important negative thrust: that

[34] See, e.g., Tamari, *With All Your Possessions* at 2, 54; Edward Zipperstein, *Business Ethics in Jewish Law* 25, 81 (1981); Aaron Lichtenstein, "Towards an Understanding of Coercion over Sodom Qualities," in I *Hagut Ivrit Be'Amerika* 362, 380–81 (M. Zohori *et al.* eds. 1972).

[35] Tamari, *With All Your Possessions* at 36–37, 51. See also Ephraim Frisch, *An Historical Survey of Jewish Philanthropy* 77 (1924); Kohler, "The Historical Development" at 236; Zipperstein, *Business Ethics in Jewish Law* at 71–72, 76–77, 84.

[36] See Cohen, "Law and Ethics" at 208; Frisch, *An Historical Survey* at 22, 77–80, 114–15; George Horowitz, *The Spirit of Jewish Law* 142 (1973); Lew, *The Humanity of Jewish Law* at 126, 191; Tamari, *With All Your Possessions* at 52, 211, 242–43, 245. See also Howard L. Adelson, "The Origins of the Concept of Social Justice," in *Social Justice in the Ancient World* 25 (K. D. Irani and Morris Silver eds. 1995).

[37] See Aaron Levine, *Free Enterprise and Jewish Law: Aspects of Jewish Business Ethics* 156 (1980); Tamari, *With All Your Possessions* at 246–47; Meyer Waxman, *Judaism: Religion and Ethics* 297–99 (1958); Twersky, "Some Aspects of the Jewish Attitude" at 234.

"all other criteria, beyond need itself, are experienced as distortions and not as limitations of the distributive process."[38]

The criterion of need in distribution shapes the doctrinal rules of *tzedakah*: It determines the eligibility requirements for receiving charity, i.e., level of wealth and liquidity position;[39] it explains the persistent efforts of Jewish communal organization to eliminate beggary; to tighten the link between need and provision by freeing the distributive process from all extraneous factors for which beggars are rewarded;[40] finally, it defines the goal for the Judaic social scheme: *tzedakah* aspires to achieve relief for the needy, and not an equal distribution of wealth; it seeks to provide the means for breaking the poverty cycle, the basic necessities that would rehabilitate, retrain, and ultimately set the poor on their own.[41] Although *tzedakah* is based on need, in contrast to the American concept of desert, it is still not a radically egalitarian idea; it is a manifestation of Judaism's attempt to reach the mean along the individual-community spectrum.

The obligations of individuals to make *tzedakah* have been rigidly defined, institutionalized, and regulated by the setting up of a coercive tax system.[42] But as Isadore Twersky explains, Judaism still "hoped to combine the thesis of free spontaneous giving with the anti-thesis of soulless, obligatory contribution and produce a composite act which is subjective though quantified, inspired though regular, intimate yet formal." Hence, there is a constant interplay between the individual and the community respecting the responsibility for and the awareness of the needs of the disadvantaged: The commandments of charity are addressed to the individual, who is envisioned as "the hero of philanthropy, seeking exposure to needy people and responding effusively to their requests"; but, at the same time "the Halakha has assigned an indispensable, all-inclusive role to the community" which appears as "a modified welfare city-state"; and still, finally, "according to the social ethos of Judaism, the individual can never isolate himself from the needy." Corporate responsibility does not eclipse individual awareness and should not dull individual sensitiveness; individual obligations of *tzedakah* never cease.[43]

[38] See Michael Walzer, *Spheres of Justice: A Defense of Pluralism and Equality* 75 (1983). See also, e.g., Frisch, *An Historical Survey* at 118.

[39] See, e.g., Levine, *Free Enterprise* at 155–57.

[40] See Walzer, *Spheres of Justice* at 75.

[41] See, e.g., Aaron Levine, *Economics and Jewish Law* 135 (1987); Tamari, *With All Your Possessions* at 277; Walzer, *Spheres of Justice* at 92.

[42] See, e.g., Tamari, *With All Your Possessions* at 211, 256; Twersky, "Some Aspects of the Jewish Attitude" at 228.

[43] Twersky, "Some Aspects of the Jewish Attitude" at 228–29, 232–33. See also, e.g., II Salo W. Baron, *The Jewish Community: Its History and Structure to the American Revolution* 319–20 (1942); Kohler, "The Historical Development" at 252.

In spite of this, Judaism does not require complete benevolence and acknowledges the priority of the self over the other. The obligation to satisfy the needs of the poor is thus subject to a means constraint, and over-generosity in the giving of charity is limited by an interdict against donating more than 20 percent of one's income to charity.[44] Once again, the goal is to reach a delicate equilibrium between one individual and another, between a community and its members.

Socio-economic ethos-based retrodictions

Although both the American and the Judaic socio-economic ethos include both individualistic and communitarian concerns, the differences between these two value systems are not very difficult to highlight. While the American ethos emphasizes individual negative liberty, freedom to choose one's associates, independence, and self-reliance, the Judaic ethos perceives membership as natural, and puts heavy weight on fellowship, collective solidarity, and mutual responsibility; whereas the American ethos is preoccupied with the notion of private property as the central instance of rights as boundaries, a symbol of the individual protected sphere, Judaism downplays the significance of private property, insisting that all wealth belongs to God, and that possessors of property are mere custodians; and, finally, while Americans are committed to the distributive principle of desert – reward in proportion to contribution – which corresponds to their bourgeois virtues of industry, entrepreneurship, and competition, the Judaic distributive scheme evolves around the notion of *tzedakah*: the legal *right* of each and every member of the community to be helped – by the community, as well as by others as individuals – in proportion to her needs.

One basic claim of this book is that appreciating the particular ethos of any one society is a crucial step for understanding the doctrinal rules which govern our paradigmatic case. If this claim is solid, then one can expect that the differences between the doctrinal rules of the American legal regime and those of the Judaic one would be as conspicuous as the differences between the two ethoses.

More particularly, one can expect that the rules of the American doctrine will be concentrated mainly between *control* and *well-being* (and the typical measures of recovery will be, correspondingly, *profits*, *fair market value*, or any intermediate or combined measure thereof). The American commitment to the individualistic values of desert and negative liberty is

[44] See, e.g., Levine, *Free Enterprise* at 156; Spero, *Morality, Halakha and the Jewish Tradition* at 221.

moderated by some – albeit fairly weak – egalitarian and needs-based convictions. Therefore, we should not expect to find the American doctrine dominated by a monolithic libertarian vision, but instead by the usual heterogeneous continuum of resources as introduced in the fourth section of chapter 2. None the less, individualistic (that is, self-regarding) values rank high in the American ethos, and thus we can conclude that – at least relative to the Judaic doctrine – the American doctrine will afford a significant measure of *control* to holders of many sorts of resources (and will certainly promote their *well-being*).

In contrast, it seems safe to conjecture that the Judaic doctrinal rules are more of the *sharing* type. In the third section of chapter 2, I concluded that legal communities that adopt strong needs-based social programs are likely to employ also *sharing*. The Judaic concept of *tzedakah* suits well the category of strong needs-based platforms: it perceives the claim to supply the needs of the "have-nots" as a right rather than a matter of generosity; it does not limit that right to the prerequisites for individual free choice; and it is premised on the communitarian maxim of mutual responsibility. Moreover, *tzedakah* applies both on the community level and on the individual level. *Tzedakah* may thus be an obvious example of a convergence between the distributive values promoted in private law and public law, which supports the implausibility of complete divergence advocated by "private law libertarians."[45] This attribute of *tzedakah* reassures the conclusion that the needs-based values it represents will be at work also with respect to our (private law) doctrine. Hence, *sharing* can be expected to dominate Judaic law.

The retrodictions of the last two paragraphs are significant, but are still fairly general and require some refinement. In so far as the American doctrine is concerned, such refinement is provided in the next section, based on an analysis of the social meanings of the various resources which this doctrine regulates. The following paragraphs focus on the Judaic doctrine, restating two central features of the Judaic distributive scheme – as manifested in the fundamental concept of *tzedakah* – and conjecturing about some doctrinal rules which stem from these ethical commitments.

Recall the characteristics of *tzedakah*. *Tzedakah* is not an institution for equal distribution of wealth, but rather a needs-based practice of provision. Hence, one can expect that the defendant's claim to share the plaintiff's entitlement will be vindicated if, and only if, the defendant is indeed in need. This conclusion is reinforced, as may be recalled, by the close relation between the grounds which support needs-based and equality-based

[45] See pp. 35–40 above.

programs and the theoretical premise of *sharing*.[46] While it is difficult to speculate how this is actually implemented, it is plausible to expect some sort of a doctrinal assurance that the defendant is needy as a prerequisite to his right to invoke *sharing*.

A second proviso can also be expected. In cases like our paradigm where *harm* is less than *gain*, *sharing* – which limits the plaintiff's remedy to her *harm* – encourages non-consensual invasions. Resource-holders would undoubtedly find such an incentive troublesome, and in so far as a legal regime tries to afford (even some) protection to the self-regarding standpoint of such resource-holders it also is expected to share (some of) these worries.

The Judaic socio-economic vision indeed seeks to accommodate individualistic concerns within its communitarian thrust. It acknowledges the priority of the self-regarding over the other-regarding standpoint of the agent. It accordingly puts limits on the "call of duty" and does not require self-sacrifice. Moreover, although the Judaic ethos is much more communitarian than the American, it none the less seeks to protect and promote individual well-being.

These concerns suggest that the individual (resource-holder) should be supplied with some assurance. To be sure, a legal system which attempts, as its main theme, to promote other-regarding values will probably make some fine distinctions respecting the complaints resource-holders raise against *sharing*. It may reject a resource-holder's claims whenever she did not actually lose anything – i.e., whenever the value of her resource was not diminished and she herself could not make any gain therefrom (or was unwilling or uninterested to use it in a fashion that would produce such a gain). Accepting the demands of resource-holders in such circumstances would significantly curtail the communitarian strain of the Judaic scheme.

But the force of the more individualistic values may be more significant in an opposite case, where actual *harm* is inflicted by the invasion. In order to discourage any potential invader from considering the infliction of such a harm, a legal system which attempts to incorporate some individualistic values within its communitarian framework may accept the complaint of resource-holders whenever actual *harm* is caused (but again, only in such cases).

Given the aspiration to a *dualistic* vision that does not neglect the self-regarding aspect of its constituents, the Judaic doctrine can be expected to adopt this compromise solution and to qualify, accordingly, the

[46] See pp. 29–31 above.

applicability of *sharing* to cases in which the appropriation of the plaintiff's resource does not actually harm her in the sense of diminishing the value of her estate or preventing her from capturing any part of the expected gains she would have secured but for the invasion.

The contemporary social meaning of some resources

Thus far our discussion has focused on the first and primary input my theory requires: the socio-economic ethos. This section attempts to produce certain conclusions based on the second, fine-tuning, input of the theory, i.e., the social meaning ascribed to the resources regulated by the doctrine. Here, we focus exclusively on contemporary America, examining the meaning American society ascribes to the resources that are regulated by the American doctrine of our paradigm, i.e., identity, body, reputation, commercial attributes of personality, land, chattels, copyright, trademark, patent, information, contractual relations and performances, and pre-contractual expectations. Through an examination of the perceived connections between each of these resources and their holders' personhood, we seek to generate some clues as to the American continuum of resources and hence to the pertaining legal rules.

One disclaimer is appropriate at the outset. I examine the existing categories the law employs, and do not – at least not explicitly – challenge the way it is currently divided. Obviously, a doctrinal division which is not necessarily informed only by the personhood perspective[47] generates some categories whose social meanings are ambiguous or which accommodate heterogeneous resources. Fortunately – but not unexpectedly – this disappointing phenomenon is relatively marginal. Alongside these fields of law – and to a surprisingly significant extent – other doctrinal areas are circumscribed in a way that responds to my theory, and thus enable my retrodictive strategy to yield some fruitful results.

Let us begin with three relatively clear cases: one's identity, one's body, and one's land. Appropriating B's identity (by, for example, presenting oneself as B) is an obvious case of invasion of a resource closely connected to

[47] I believe that it is wrong to suggest that the law perceives resources merely in terms of their connection to personhood. Surely the law appreciates also other virtues – notably utilitarian – in the private holding of certain resources. I need not – and do not – deny this anticipated rejoinder since my theory does not require that the personhood perspective would be the exclusive social viewpoint on the regulated resources. All I claim is that "personhood-oriented" social meanings of such resources can be detected and that such meanings importantly inform the applicable rules of our paradigmatic case.

B's self. My identity is what I am, it is my self, and not merely a reflection of my personality (it *is* my personality!).[48] Hence, people's identity can be expected to be well protected in most communities; and surely to be closely secured in America's individualistic society.

Similar conclusions seem to follow respecting the body, "the most precious possession that most of us own."[49] Thus, research conducted with Brooklyn College subjects found out that body parts are considered to be parts of the self with greatest frequency and certainty, and concluded that "the body is frequently considered to be the core of the self."[50] These findings are hardly surprising. Our bodies are not merely the physical embodiments of our selves, but are also the utmost reflections of who we are; they are literally external projections of our personalities; the ultimate resource in which Waldron's metaphor of a dual relation of effect from the will to the object and back to the will, indisputably exists.[51] Our body is undoubtedly a resource we are most anxious to control.

One final "easy case" is land, one of the most traditional objects of property rights in American jurisprudence.[52] Land, as a clear external resource, is obviously qualitatively different from identity or body. Nevertheless, Americans tend to accord land a unique status. Land is linked closely to personal freedom, rank, and power, and thus to the American way of life. It is deeply ingrained as a symbol of self in the American ethos, echoing cultural images from the frontier.[53] Therefore, it would not be at all

[48] See, e.g., Helga Dittmar, *The Social Psychology of Material Possessions: To Have Is To Be* 5 (1992).

[49] Russell W. Belk, "The Ineluctable Mysteries of Possessions," in *To Have Possessions: A Handbook on Ownership and Property* 17, 19 (F. W. Rudmin ed. 1991).

[50] See Ernst Prelinger, "Extension and Structure of the Self," 47 *Journal of Psychology* 13, 18 (1959). See also, e.g., Russell W. Belk, "Possessions and the Extended Self," 15 *Journal of Consumer Research* 139, 157 (1988). A scale of the various body parts in terms of "selfness" is drawn in Belk, *ibid.* at 142.

[51] *Cf.* Margaret J. Radin, "Market-Inalienability," 100 *Harvard Law Review* 1,849, 1,880–81 and note 117 (1987); Margaret J. Radin, "Property and Personhood," 34 *Stanford Law Review* 957, 966 (1982).

[52] See Donald W. Large, "This Land is Whose Land? Changing Concepts of Land as Property," 1973 *Wisconsin Law Review* 1,039, 1,040. Large points out a certain diminishment in the status of land as subject to exclusive private ownership due to the environmental revolution. This may well be true (and far beyond my agenda), but it would certainly take some time for the entrenched images to which I allude to be overturned, or even deteriorate.

[53] *Cf.* Lynton K. Caldwell, "Land and the Law: Problems in Legal Philosophy," 1986 *University of Illinois Law Review* 319, 320; McClosky and Zaller, *The American Ethos* at 138; Belk, "Possessions and the Extended Self" at 153; Clare Cooper, "The House as Symbol of the Self," in *Environmental Psychology: People and Their Physical Settings* 435, 437–38 (Harold M. Proshansky *et al.* eds. 2nd edn. 1976); E. Doyle McCarthy, "Toward a

surprising to find that land ranks high – maybe lower than identity and body, but surely relatively high – in comparison to other external resources in the American continuum of resources governing our paradigm.[54]

These are indeed relatively clear cases. But along with these cases there are also resources whose social meaning is more difficult to pinpoint. Some require a more delicate investigation of their social meaning in contemporary America. Respecting others, an even more discriminating exploration is not fruitful since their social meaning turns out to be ambiguous. As we will see in chapter 4, the law is ambiguous precisely in relation to resources whose social meaning is also ambiguous.

Consider, for example, one's reputation. Robert Post conducted a careful study of American defamation law which yields an informative account of the social meaning of reputation in contemporary America. Post claims that this meaning is informed by two distinct conceptions: (i) reputation as (mere) property, an object in the marketplace which is separate from its holder's identity; and (ii) reputation as dignity, that is the intrinsic, constitutive sense of self-worth, inclusion, and belonging as a full and respected member of society; a sense which is "perpetually dependent upon the ceremonial observance by those around us of rules of deference and demeanor" and is therefore not convertible to money.[55]

Corresponding to these two social meanings, I suggest that we distinguish between two types of cases which implicate reputation in importantly differing ways. The first is of defamation, where both conceptions of reputation as property and as dignity are at work.[56] In such a case, the idea of dignity can be expected to give the deprivation of reputation a highly personal flavor: dignity denotes one's place in one's community which is an important component of one's self-worth and personality. It seems plaus-

Sociology of the Physical World: George Herbert Mead on Physical Objects," 5 *Studies in Symbolic Interaction* 105, 116–17 (1984); Radin, "Property and Personhood" at 992, 1,013.

54 One may insist on a distinction between the family home (or farm land) and land which is used for commercial purposes, and claim that treatment under the law of the latter should not be influenced by the social meaning of the former. But, as indicated above, this claim (and similar challenges to other existing legal categories) is beyond the scope of this book.

55 See Robert C. Post, "The Social Foundations of Defamation Law: Reputation and the Constitution," 74 *California Law Review* 691, 693–94, 699–701, 707–08, 710–12, 715, 720 (1986).

56 The claim that defamation involves both conceptions of reputation as property and as dignity is reinforced by some empirical data which suggest that monetary and dignitary considerations are blended together as motivating factors in libel litigations: see Randall P. Bezanson, "The Libel Suit in Retrospect: What Plaintiffs Want and What Plaintiffs Get," 74 *California Law Review* 789, 794–95 (1986).

ible to conjecture that in so far as cases of defamation are concerned reputation is ranked high in the American spectrum of resources.

But the American doctrine deals also with another kind of case which may initially be confused with defamation. In this second category, the resource appropriated is a commercial attribute of the personality of the plaintiff (usually a celebrity), like her name, picture, voice, etc. By utilizing such a commercialized attribute of personality, the invader deprives her of a valuable asset. Moreover, it does not seem farfetched to assume that one is attached to every attribute of one's personality, the commercial ones included, since they all reflect – to some extent, at least – one's self. Hence, it is reasonable to expect some protection to the holding of commercial attributes of one's personality. Yet, in so far as the appropriation does not involve any degradation, the mere utilizing of the pertinent attribute – which is, by definition, commercialized regardless of the appropriation – does not affect the plaintiff's place in society, and thus her self-worth. Put another way, in this second category the plaintiff's dignity – the most personal component of reputation – remains intact. Therefore, relative to reputation in cases of defamation, commercial attributes of personality would be expected to rank low in the American continuum of resources.[57]

Similarly careful discrimination seems to be necessary when we consider copyrights and patents. Justin Hughes' helpful distinction between these two categories of intellectual property does much of our work here.[58] Hughes starts with the intuitive appeal of the personhood perspective to intellectual property: "an idea belongs to its creator because the idea is a manifestation of the creator's personality or self." But as he correctly mentions, intellectual products are not homogeneous: while some categories of intellectual property seem to be receptacles for personality, others do not seem so closely tied to their creator's identity.

Fortunately, this diversity occurs, by and large, along the doctrinal lines that arrange the internal division of intellectual property law in America. A major distinction can thus be drawn between copyrights and patents. Counter examples – such as atlases and maps – notwithstanding, copyright usually protects "personality-laden categories" like poems, stories, novels, musical works, sculptures, paintings, and prints – works that can all be characterized as "the personal reaction of an individual upon nature."[59] In contrast, technological categories of intellectual property, notably patent-

[57] But *cf.* Justin Hughes, "The Philosophy of Intellectual Property," 77 *Georgetown Law Journal* 287, 340–41 (1988). [58] See *ibid.* at 330, 339–43.

[59] Here Hughes quotes Justice Holmes in *Bleistein* v. *Donaldson Lithographing Co.* 188 US 239, 250 (1903).

able inventions, embody purely utilitarian solutions to specific needs, and hence seem to be "characterless and without personality." "We tend not to think of them as manifesting the personality of an individual, but rather as manifesting a raw, almost generic insight."

This dichotomy should not be taken too far. As Hughes correctly mentions, the difference between these genres of intellectual property is not unqualified. On the one hand, the personal expression which is no doubt reflected in works of art is in fact constrained to some extent – even respecting these resources – by economy, efficiency, and physical environment. On the other hand, although chiefly utilitarian in purpose – and hence more subject to the sorts of external constraints mentioned above – technological inventions are not literally characterless. They still reflect personal ingenuity, and furthermore allow some space for personal choice – and thus personal style – among equally effective solutions.

Moreover,[60] in discussing the categories of copyrights and patents, we are not necessarily considering cases in which the resource-holder is the creator or the inventor, but also cases in which she is their transferee. To be sure, a transferee of a work of art – to take a clear case of a personal object of copyright – may still invest her personality in the object, perceive the object as the reflection of her self, and hence be intrinsically connected to it. Works of art seem especially prone to such a sense of reflection-and-attachment regardless of the identity of their holder.[61] None the less, it should still be conceded that this sense of intrinsic connection is usually milder than the sense of attachment felt by the artist herself.

Hence, given both the plurality of holders and the (minimal but still existent) external constraints creators face, copyrighted works may be somewhat inferior in rank to the "clear" cases of identity and body, as well as those of reputation and land. None the less, the personhood perspective clearly prescribes their relatively high position along the spectrum of resources, and certainly justifies their ranking as higher than patents.[62] In

[60] The second qualification of the copyright–patent dichotomy is not Hughes', but instead derives from a general conclusion of my thesis that social meanings of resources are determined in categories, irrespective of the holder's identity.

[61] *Cf.* Tom G. Palmer, "Are Patents and Copyrights Morally Justified? The Philosophy of Property Rights and Ideal Objects," 13 *Harvard Journal of Law and Public Policy* 817, 844–45 (1990).

[62] See Hughes, "The Philosophy of Intellectual Property" at 351–53. Some commentators insist that the principal historical purpose of copyright in America was to protect the public and promote learning, and not to reflect personality. See, e.g., L. Ray Patterson and Stanley W. Lindberg, *The Nature of Copyright: A Law of Users' Rights* (1991). Others complain against the hold of authorship on the American legal imagination questioning the "naturalness and inevitability of Romantic ideas about creativity,"

contrast, while our first qualification clarifies that patents are not devoid of personality and hence justifies their protection from a personhood perspective, their strong utilitarian characteristics none the less prescribe a relatively low place along the continuum of attachment employed by American law.

Whereas copyrights and patents have gained reasonably definite social meanings in contemporary America, the meaning of trademark – the third branch of intellectual property law – is highly ambiguous. From the standpoint of a personality analysis, two conflicting meanings seem to co-exist. The first social meaning is relatively personal. American courts have consistently emphasized that a trademark is a symbol of the reputation of its owner; her goodwill or "commercial identity."[63] Reputation in this context surely, in Post's classification, is reputation as property, rather than reputation as dignity. Hence, the rules governing the appropriation of a trademark can be expected to be akin to those governing the private taking of commercial attributes of personality.

But other understandings of trademarks co-exist alongside this relatively personal social meaning. A persistent perception of trademarks has been and continues to be as warranties of quality to be expected from a particular source; "liability marks" whose primary purpose is not to bear individual goodwill but rather to allow defective works to be traced back to their origins. Moreover, in recent times another non-personal understanding of trademarks has emerged. According to this meaning, trademarks identify and distinguish the goods rather than their producers, so that the commercial reputation of the product and the goodwill of its maker may be dissociated.[64] Neither of these meanings seems to have a personal aspect. Hence, in so far as trademarks are perceived in one or the other of these

and suggesting instead a more realistic, collaborative model of composition. See, e.g., Peter Jaszi and Martha Woodmansee, "Introduction" to *The Construction of Authorship: Textual Appropriation in Law and Literature* 1 (Martha Woodmansee and Peter Jaszi eds. 1994). These claims call for a serious normative debate, but they do not contradict Hughes' insistence that the personal aspect of copyright is deeply ingrained in the American thinking regarding copyright law. See, e.g., Jane C. Ginsburg, "Creation and Commercial Value: Copyright Protection of Works of Information," 90 *Columbia Law Review* 1,865, 1,866–67 (1990).

[63] See I J. Thomas McCarthy, *Trademarks and Unfair Competition* (permanent edn. revised vol. 1994) § 2.07.

[64] See Thomas D. Drescher, "The Transformation and Evolution of Trademarks – From Signals to Symbols to Myth," 82 *Trademark Reportet* 301, 319–20, 323–24 (1992). Drescher also addresses a third, emerging, meaning to trademarks, i.e., as myths designed to identify the consumer: see *ibid.* at 328–38.

ways, a personhood perspective does not afford them any special protection against the mere appropriation of trademarks.

A similar conclusion – of an ambiguous social meaning – also characterizes the category of chattels. On the one hand, certain chattels are frequently and justifiably described as classic examples of "personal property" since they are considered to be closely connected to their holder's identity in our culture. This is how commentators often speak of (somewhat atypical resources such as) people's wedding rings, portraits, and heirlooms, as well as (the more usual example) of people's – notably Americans' – cars.[65] However, on the other hand, many conventional chattels seem to have no personal attribute. Many mass-produced consumer goods – especially disposable goods – lack any symbolic function in contemporary America and serve solely for utilitarian purposes.[66] Given this high diversity which characterizes the contemporary social meanings of chattels, it seems hard to anticipate the place this category holds in the American spectrum of resources.

Thus far, I have examined the cases where a sense of reflection-and-attachment is clearly found, the cases where a more careful discrimination is required, and the cases of ambiguous categories of resources. There is also a fourth group within the list of resources the American doctrine regulates. The remainder of these resources – information, contractual relations and performances, and pre-contractual expectations – seem to have almost no personality association with their holders: while information and contracts are indeed significant forms of wealth – and are hence primary economic commodities – in modern industrialized societies, they are clear examples of characterless goods. The fungible nature of contractual rights[67] is perhaps best illustrated by the prevailing rule in American jurisprudence which permits – even encourages – efficient breaches;[68] the commodified quality of information is one of the main distinctions

[65] See, e.g., Belk, "The Ineluctable Mysteries" at 21–22, 25, 27–35; Radin, "Property and Personhood" at 959, 1,001.

[66] I do not deny that other consumer goods – notably durable goods – do serve as reflections of the American person's identity: see, e.g., Dittmar, *The Social Psychology* at 7–8, 14, 60–61, 98–101. All I seek to establish is the great variance currently found in the chattels category.

[67] Note that contractual rights are promises given to resource-holders by promisors. Hence, if they can be said to be at all connected to someone's identity, it is to the promisor's, rather than to the promisee's, who is the resource-holder.

[68] See generally Richard A. Posner, *Economic Analysis of Law* 117–20 (4th edn. 1992). But see Daniel Friedmann, "The Efficient Breach Fallacy," 18 *Journal of Legal Studies* 1, 18–23 (1989).

between this resource and the categories of resources grouped under intellectual property law.

Hence, the personhood perspective does not warrant any protection against the mere taking of such resources as it does with regard to the resources which were analyzed thus far and which we have found to be connected – in varying degrees – to their holders' identity. Since the doctrinal rules of our paradigm none the less accord some protection to these resources, a personhood perspective would dictate a showing of something more than their mere appropriation. One such additional component can be found in the impropriety of the invader's demeanor. If, but only if, the appropriation is effected in a way which is considered by the predominant social norms as a showing of disrespect towards the possessor of the pertinent resource, then the insult involved in the appropriation – rather than the mere taking – may trigger the personhood perspective that seeks to guard people's interests in their most closely connected (in the reflection-and-attachment sense) resources, including – as we have seen – their dignity.

With these retrodictions in hand – both regarding the continuum of resources in contemporary America, and respecting the thrust of Talmudic civil law – we can now check if my theory yields the actual doctrinal rules.

4 Contemporary American law

Two general conclusions regarding the rules governing our paradigm in American law emerge from the preceding chapter. First, that, by and large, American law will apply the more individualistic rationales of *well-being and/or control*, and will seldom, relative to Talmudic civil law, apply *sharing*. Second, that within the confines of the individualistic side of the *control–sharing* spectrum, the various resources regulated by contemporary American law are still importantly different from one another, and that this variability can be expected to be manifested in the applicable rationales.

More specifically, I suggested that the sphere of control American law is expected to confer on its constituents will not be absolute, but rather will occur along a continuum of diminishing interests: from core interests (one's identity, physical integrity, reputation as dignity, and land) through less-protected interests (copyright, and to a lesser degree, commercial attributes of one's personality and patents) to least-protected interests (contractual relations and performances and information). As may be recalled, it was somewhat more difficult to decide where to locate trademarks and chattels along this spectrum of resources.

The first group includes interests which are perceived in contemporary America as personal. Hence, one can expect that the agent's control over any of these resources is the primary social goal to be promoted by the applicable doctrinal rules. The second, intermediate group includes less personal resources, and can thus be expected to be dominated by relatively weaker rules than its predecessor. Finally, I concluded that the mere appropriation of resources from the third group – which includes the least personal resources – will not trigger liability. Instead, liability can be expected to apply only if the invasion occurs by resorting to improper means.

This chapter examines the validity of these retrodictions by surveying the doctrinal rules which are applicable to various resources. The resources are divided into four categories: interests in tangible property, interests in intangible property, interests in self, and other interests. Although interests in self are the core interests as defined by chapter 3, I turn first to tangible and intangible property because these are the most conventional – and the most litigated – categories of the law of remedies.

My consideration of each resource focuses exclusively on one aspect of its holder's entitlement: the available measure of recovery. Using the translation scheme of the first section of chapter 2, I seek to employ this datum to uncover the applicable rationale. This exercise demonstrates the power of these tools in helping to decipher some of the internal logic and consistency, and to expose certain dominant patterns, tendencies, and inclinations in a complicated set of cases and statutes prescribed by a host of social decision-makers.

Furthermore, the following account (the findings of which are summarized in table 2[1]) supports the claim that a harmonious mosaic can be made from such diverse data. Constructing such a mosaic is indeed a complicated process. Not surprisingly, only a few of the materials reported below echo my theory and thus reinforce it directly. Most of the materials, as might be expected, merely assign a certain measure of recovery to the appropriation of a certain resource. Hence, we need to implement my translation scheme. However, as the sections below develop, it becomes clear that the application of this scheme in practice is by no means trivial in itself. There are cases in which the available remedy is not easily translatable into a corresponding rationale. These cases demonstrate the subtleties of the seemingly technical tools of the first section of chapter 2 and thus sharpen our understanding of the functioning of these devices. Occasionally, even improved skills do not suffice and some judgment is called for. This additional judgment must then be based both on the reasoning of the cases and on the emerging pattern which springs from the systematic review of the doctrine as a whole.

The emerging mosaic is, to be sure, blemished by some gaps and uncertainties, and even – although in surprisingly fewer occasions than might have been expected – by inconsistencies and anomalies. Still, by and large, this chapter tells a fundamentally coherent story. It thus shows that the intuitions of the myriad social decision-makers do reflect and shape a homogeneous cultural and social ethos. It also verifies the pertinence of the personhood theory and the correspondence between most of the norms it recommends and the actual legal rules governing the paradigm.

[1] See p. 107 below.

Interests in tangible property

Land

Consider first the case of land, one of the classic resources which is described as closely connected to its holder's identity. A typical example of the appropriation of this resource would be a case in which A severs a fixture, crop, timber, minerals, earth, or other component from B's land. When B learns about this "trespass and conversion," she sues A for his resultant benefit, and in most cases prevails.[2]

Many commentators who discuss the applicability of the restitutionary doctrine to land pay little or no attention to this simple scenario, turning quickly to the case of "bare use" of B's land.[3] The latter category raises some interesting questions and will be considered shortly. But I submit that the vast body of case law which has evolved regarding the category of "trespass and conversion" deserves some close scrutiny. Such an inquiry is especially informative for identifying the applicable measure of recovery for land and the corresponding rationale behind it.

Consider, for example, a case where A cuts down timber from B's land. Subsequently, A removes, loads, hauls, and manufactures the timber into a finished product, a costly process to be sure. The value of the standing timber is usually termed "stumpage value," and the value of the timber following its improvement by A is termed "enhanced value." Typically, the enhanced value is greater than the stumpage value. In any case, the latter is said to be the minimal recovery to which B is entitled.[4] But can she recover more than this?

This question, and analogous questions in connection with oil and minerals and regarding earth, sand, and gravel, have often been litigated.[5]

2 See *Restatement of Restitution* § 129(3) and comment d (1937); II *Restatement (Second) of Restitution* § 45(4) and comment i (Tentative Draft, 1983–84). The proposed new *Restatement* mentions that A's liability in restitution is conditioned upon a component of "wrongfulness," as distinct from a belief in the rightfulness of the invasion. The materials that follow refine this observation.

3 See, e.g., I George E. Palmer, *The Law of Restitution* § 2.5 (1978 and Supplement 1995).

4 See, e.g., *Crofoot Lumber Inc.* v. *Ford*, 191 Cal. App. 2d 238, 250 (Ct. App. 1961); *Burbridge* v. *Bradley Lumber Co.*, 239 SW 2d 285, 288 (Arkansas 1951). See also *Bowen* v. *Detroit United Railway*, 180 NW 495 (Michigan 1920) (minerals).

5 Cases are collected in "Annotation, Measure of Damages for Destruction of or Injury to Trees and Shrubbery," 69 ALR 2d 1,335 §§ 5–8 (1960) (hereinafter "Trees Annotation"); "Annotation, Right of Trespasser to Credit for Expenditures in Producing, As Against his Liability for Value of, Oil or Minerals," 21 ALR 2d 380 (1952) (hereinafter "Minerals Annotation") ; R. A. Vinluan, "Annotation, Measure of Damages for Wrongful Removal of Earth, Sand, or Gravel from Land," 1 ALR 3d 801 (1965).

Three rules seem to emerge respecting these types of cases, and are illustrated below by reference to the timber case.[6]

1. Where the timber is cut and removed willfully or in bad faith, B – the landowner – is entitled to recover the enhanced value, without any deduction of A's – the trespasser's – costs or any part thereof.[7]
2. On the other hand, where the timber is cut and removed inadvertently, by mistake, or without knowledge of B's adverse claim, courts generally limit B's remedy to the stumpage value.[8] However, where the landowner in such a case proves also that she herself intended to cut the trees and sell them, she is none the less entitled to her lost profits, which is part of her *harm*.[9]
3. Finally, courts have recently observed a need for a third category which falls between the willful trespass and the innocent one. This category encompasses cases in which A knows of B's adverse claim (or is negligently unaware thereof), but none the less acts *bona fide*, based on a reasonable – although mistaken – belief of his superior claim. In such cases, courts felt that both the measure of stumpage value and that of enhanced value are flawed: on the one hand, there is no apparent justification to punish A by disallowing the deduction of his expenses; on the other hand, however, it seems inadequate to limit recovery to the stumpage value, thus prescribing a forced retroactive sale of B's property at the market price although A knew (or should have known) that B did not want to sell. Hence, the emerging rule for this type of case is to allow the landowner to recover the greater of (i) the stumpage value; and (ii) the enhanced value less the reasonable expenses of the knowing but *bona fide* trespasser.[10]

[6] The notes which follow include some reference to materials regarding the mineral category. The gravel cases are somewhat less sophisticated, and have yet to develop the third rule formulated below.

[7] See, e.g., *Masonite Corp.* v. *Tate*, 404 So. 2d 565, 568 (Mississippi 1981); "Trees Annotation," § 8. See also "Minerals Annotation," § 5; Dan B. Dobbs, *Handbook on the Law of Remedies: Damages – Equity – Restitution* § 5.3(3) (2nd edn. 1993).

[8] See "Trees Annotation," § 5. See also "Minerals Annotation," § 3. The "Trees Annotation" contends that although the stumpage value is the measure of recovery which is most frequently available, some courts have permitted the landowner in type (2) cases a more favorable measure of recovery: *ibid.* §§ 6–7. Most of the cases referred to, however, are not of unconscious invaders, who cut the trees inadvertently, but rather of knowing converters, who none the less acted in good faith, as defined by rule (3).

[9] See *Pearce* v. *G. R. Kirk Co.*, 602 P 2d 357, 360–61 (Washington 1979).

[10] See *D. B. Frampton and Co.* v. *Saulsberry*, 268 SW 2d 25 (Kentucky Ct. App. 1954); *Crofoot Lumber Inc.* v. *Ford*, 191 Cal. App. 2d 238 (Ct. App. 1961). The third rule originated in several Arkansas cases, and applied there even with regard to defendants unconscious of their breach. See, e.g., *Burbridge* v. *Bradley Lumber Co.*, 239 SW 2d 285 (Arkansas 1951). None the less, it seems erroneous to treat it – as "Trees Annotation," § 7 does

This set of rules seems coherent to me, and furthermore informative as to the translation of measures of recovery to rationales. The first rule prescribes that a *proceeds* measure of recovery applies where the trespasser's expenses were not incurred in good faith. Not allowing him to deduct such expenses penalizes him for his willfulness or bad faith.[11] The second rule applies where "the matter is not to be treated as a case of a forced sale but as a case of sale which has taken place by inadvertence."[12] This rule brings to fore the muteness of *control* in the case of an infringer who is certain of his own entitlement to the invaded resource. Such an unsuspecting – although mistaken – infringer cannot be deterred by a *profits* (or any other, for that matter) measure of recovery. Hence, even where the applicable rationale is aimed at vindicating the resource-holder's control, one can suspect that it will hardly ever affect the measure of recovery imposed on such a trespasser.[13] A's unconsciousness of B's claim nullifies any deterrence goal, which is otherwise operative as the third rule demonstrates. Hence, the only relevant goal in type 2 cases is the preservation of the landowner's *ex ante* level of welfare, which dictates an essentially *fair market value* measure of recovery. (Notice also that this goal is at work throughout the three rules, since *fair market value* is said to be the minimal measure of recovery and would apply in cases 1 and 3 if it exceeds the measures they prescribe.) Finally, the third rule prescribes a *profits* measure of recovery, applying where punishment is inappropriate but deterrence is still relevant. Denying the knowing trespasser any net profit vindicates the landowner's control over her property.

In sum, it emerges that cases of "trespass and conversion" *per se* (type 3 above) are not subject to the *proceeds* retributive rule, nor are they intended to vindicate only the landowner's well-being. The applicable rationale with respect to land in these cases is hence *well-being and control*.

Does this rationale apply regarding the other major category of the

– as an exception to the stumpage-value rule respecting innocent trespassers. The annotation itself cites a line of Louisiana cases, in addition to the Kentucky and California cases cited above, which confine the rule's applicability to cases of knowledge or negligent unawareness of the plaintiff's title. See also "Minerals Annotation," § 4.

11 See, e.g., "Minerals Annotation," § 2.

12 *Livingstone* v. *Rawyards Coal Co.*, 5 App. Cas. 25, 34 (House of Lords 1880) (Appeal taken from Scotland) (*per* Lord Hatherley).

13 See Peter K. Huber, "Mistaken Transfers and Profitable Infringements of Property Rights: an Economic Analysis," 49 *Louisiana Law Review* 71, 103, 108 (1988). But see John P. Dawson, "Restitution Without Enrichment," 61 *Boston University Law Review* 563, 614, 617 (1981).

appropriation-of-interests-in-land cases, the "bare-use"-of-land type? This latter type has given rise to considerable controversy. None the less, I believe that the leading case of "bare use" alludes precisely to this rule.

Consider the famous case of *Edwards* v. *Lee*.[14] The surface of land overlying a cave is owned by A and B; the line between their separate tracts bisects that surface. The only practicable access to the cave is through A's tract. A opens the cave as a tourist attraction, charging admission, and exhibiting all of it.[15] B files a claim that A is wrongfully profiting from her resource.

In response to B's claim, A maintains that B's property has not in any way been injured by the use, and was restored, as a result of a separate injunction sought and granted, to its original condition. Moreover, the cave was of no practical use to B since it could only be entered through A's land. The Kentucky Supreme Court rejected these claims, holding that as a knowing trespasser A is accountable for "the benefits, or net profits, received by [him] from the use of the property of the [plaintiff]."[16]

At that time, allowing B to recover A's generated profit from the "bare use" of her land, without him removing any of its physical substance, was deemed a "welcome departure" from the traditional view.[17] The traditional view – which originated in a much-cited English case of *Phillips* v. *Homfray*[18] – disallowed any restitutionary claims in cases of "bare use." *Edwards* notwithstanding, at the time of the compilation of the *Restatement of Restitution*, its reporters felt constrained by contrary authority, and stated the traditional view to be the law.[19] However, since that time, American courts have joined the literature that almost unanimously condemned the traditional view as anachronistic and have either disapproved of it or ignored it altogether.[20] A proposed draft of a new *Restatement* rejects this limitation as well.[21]

14 96 SW 2d 1,028 (Kentucky 1936).

15 This summary of the case's facts derives from II *Restatement (Second) of Restitution* § 46(1) illustration 3 (Tentative Draft, 1983–84).

16 *Edwards* v. *Lee*, 96 SW 2d 1,028, 1,032 (Kentucky 1936). *Cf. Don* v. *Trojan Construction Co.*, 2 Cal. Rptr. 626, 628 (1960).

17 See "Reporters' Notes" to *Restatement of Restitution* 194–95 (1937).

18 24 Ch. 439 (Court of Appeal 1883).

19 See *Restatement of Restitution* § 129(1)–(2) (1937).

20 See II *Restatement (Second) of Restitution* § 46(1) comment a (Tentative Draft, 1983–84); *Raven Red Ash Coal Co.* v. *Ball*, 39 SE 2d 231, 236–38 (Virginia 1946); *Monarch Accounting Supplies Inc.* v. *Prezioso*, 368 A 2d 6, 10 (Connecticut 1976); *Phillips Petroleum Co.* v. *Cowden*, 241 F 2d 586 (5th Cir. 1957); I Palmer, *The Law of Restitution* § 2.5.

21 See II *Restatement (Second) of Restitution* § 46(1) (Tentative Draft, 1983–84). In England, the traditional view has never been explicitly overruled. See *Morris* v. *Tarrant*, [1971] 2 QB 143, 162. However, it is most severely criticized in the literature (see, e.g., Lord Goff of Chieveley and Gareth Jones, *The Law of Restitution* 717–19 (4th edn. 1993)), and

In any case, *Edwards* prescribes a *profits* measure of recovery. The court repeatedly emphasized that "profits rather than rent form the basis of recovery." Accordingly, it held that the landowner is entitled to a share of the net profit proportionate to the footage of the cave on his land and to the relative value of the particular points of interest featured in advertising the cave as well as their possible appeal in drawing visitors. The trespasser's profits of the adjoining hotel were excluded from the calculation.[22]

Edwards' formula illuminates the fine distinction between *profits* and *proportional profits*. The Kentucky court isolated A's profits from the trespass to B's land from those which would have accrued to A's enterprise even if he would not have invaded B's entitlement as he did (the latter category encompasses both the hotel revenues and a relative portion of the net profits of the part of the cave that was below the surface of A's land). By doing so, the court neutralized any possible confiscatory component from its award and set the recovery at A's *profits*. On the other hand, the court did not allow A to further prorate the profits attributable to B's part of the cave, i.e., to keep some additional amount of the net profits that represents the fruits of the expenses he incurred in securing the net profits that are attributable to B's part of the cave. Indeed, the *proportional profits* measure of

a recent Law Commission has recommended its reconsideration (see Law Commission Consultation Paper No. 132 on Aggravated, Exemplary and Restitutionary Damages 160 (1993)). Other countries, which generally follow the English restitutionary doctrine, seem to reject *Phillips*. See *Daniel* v. *O'Leary*, 14 NBR 2d 564 (QB 1976) (Canada); Daniel Friedmann, *The Law of Unjust Enrichment* §§ 285–86 (2nd edn. 1982 and Supplement 1988) (Israel). Furthermore, the significance of the traditional view has been somewhat ameliorated by certain tort law subterfuges: (i) the Anglo-American tort doctrine of mesne profits applies in cases of use and occupation of real property during the time it was held by one in wrongful possession; (ii) in cases where the defendant has used the plaintiff's underground ways to his benefit, the "way-leave rule" makes him liable for a reasonable wayleave rent: see, e.g., *Whitwham* v. *Westminster Brymbo Coal and Coke Co.*, [1896] 2 Ch. 538 (Court of Appeal); (iii) where a money judgment is awarded as a substitute for a mandatory injunction, English courts are unwilling to award merely nominal damages even where the plaintiff's estate has not been diminished. See *Wrotham Park Estate Co.* v. *Parkside Homes Ltd.*, [1974] 1 WLR 798, 814–16 (Chancery). These tort law pecuniary remedies should not, however, be conflated with the measure of recovery available in restitution since they limit the available remedy to the *fair market value* of the rent for the relevant period, and do not provide an alternative *profits* measure of recovery. See *Van Ruymbeke* v. *Patapsco Industrial Park*, 276 A 2d 61 (Maryland 1971); *Quality Excelsior Coal Co.* v. *Reeves*, 177 SW 2d 728, 732 (Arkansas 1944); *Wrotham Park Estate Co.* v. *Parkside Homes Ltd.*, [1974] 1 WLR 798, 814–16 (Chancery). See also *Swordheath Properties Ltd.* v. *Tabet* [1979] 1 WLR 285 (Court of Appeal). For the most recent (and perplexing) developments on this front of English Law see Elizabeth Cooke, "Trespass, Mesne Profits and Restitution," 110 *Law Quarterly Review* 420 (1994).

22 *Edwards* v. *Lee*, 96 SW 2d 1,028, 1,031, 1,033 (Kentucky 1936).

recovery – which was implicitly rejected in *Edwards* – would allow a defendant to deduct not only his material contribution to the gain, but also a relative portion of any profits created by his expenditures. In contrast, cases like *Edwards*, where profits that were generated from the appropriated resource are isolated from other profits of other independent parts of the defendant's enterprise, should be interpreted as employing the *profits* measure of recovery. In other words, if a certain portion of the invader's profits would have been secured even if the invaded resource would not have taken part in the invader's enterprise, separating such profits from the recovery available to the plaintiff is consistent with an application of a *profits* measure, since it does not compromise the incentive effects that such a measure is supposed to generate.

No authority suggests that *profits* should be awarded even where it is lower than the *fair market value*;[23] and one case explicitly rejects such a possibility.[24] Thus, the emerging measure of recovery for the "bare-use" cases is the greater of *fair market value* and *profits*; the corresponding rationale is *well-being and control*.

While in general *Edwards* has been widely praised, the literature is somewhat equivocal respecting its formula for pecuniary recovery.[25] On balance, however, I believe that *Edwards* does represent the state of the law, reflected to some extent in subsequent cases.[26] Furthermore, the *Edwards* formula confers upon landowners the same sort of protection accorded to them in connection with the "trespass and conversion" cases. At the outset of its discussion, the *Edwards* court emphasized the law's policy to protect the landowner's legal right.[27] This premise explains the rigid *well-being and control* rationale pertaining to land as evidenced by both "trespass and conversion" cases and "bare use" ones. It also reinforces the recommendations of a personhood perspective which explains such an ethical impulse.[28]

23 See Dawson, "Restitution Without Enrichment" at 613.

24 See *Mederacke* v. *Becker*, 205 NE 2d 519, 524 (Illinois App. Ct. 1965). See also Friedmann, *The Law of Unjust Enrichment* § 391.

25 See Dawson, "Restitution Without Enrichment" at 613.

26 See *Monarch Accounting Supplies Inc.* v. *Prezioso*, 368 A 2d 6, 10 (Connecticut 1976); *King County* v. *Odman*, 111 P 2d 228, 230 (Washington 1941). *Cf. Granchelli* v. *Walters S. Johnson Building. Co.*, 446 NYS 2d 755, 756 (App. Div. 1981). But see *Phillips Petroleum Co.* v. *Cowden*, 241 F 2d 586, 594 (5th Cir. 1957).

27 *Edwards* v. *Lee*, 96 SW 2d 1,028, 1,030 (Kentucky 1936).

28 An interesting question arises in connection with nuisance cases. An early English case, *Kirk* v. *Todd*, 21 Ch. 484, 488 (Court of Appeal 1882), implies that a restitutionary claim will be denied since (in the circumstances there) the dumper does not get any benefit by fouling the landowner's stream. *Kirk* has been criticized as an unwarranted application of the debatable traditional view. See, e.g., Goff and Jones, *The Law of Restitution* at 721. And indeed, in *Evans* v. *City of Johnstown*, 410 NYS 2d 199 (Supreme

Chattels

One of the earliest restitutionary cases in Anglo-American jurisprudence, *Lamine* v. *Dorrell*, holds that "[i]f a man takes goods to which he has no right, and sells them, the owner may waive the tort and recover the price for which they were sold."[29] Thus, the *Lamine* rule, still applicable today, prescribes that the amount realized on the sale by a "knowing converter" is the applicable measure of recovery.[30] On the other hand, where the converter was unconscious of the plaintiff's ownership – so that deterrence cannot be a relevant goal of the law – his liability is limited (as it is in the land cases) to *fair market value*, i.e., the value of the chattel at the time of the sale.[31]

The *Lamine* rule, which is used by plaintiffs where the knowing converter sells the chattel for a price above its *fair market value*, entails a *proceeds* measure of recovery. Practically, however, most cases deal with a converter who merely sells the item converted so that his material contribution is minimal.[32] Hence, *Lamine* cannot distinguish among *proceeds*, *profits* and

Court 1978), revised on other grounds, 470 NYS 2d 451 (App. Div. 1983), recovery in a sewage-dumping case was based on an unjust enrichment theory. See also *Carr-Saunders* v. *Dick McNeil Associates*, [1986] 1 WLR 922, 931 (Chancery) (England). None the less, the prevailing view seems to limit monetary recovery where an injunction is denied to the *fair market value* of the right to pollute. See I Palmer, *The Law of Restitution* § 2.10 at 137. Given the possible motive of denying injunctions in such cases, i.e., the excessive transaction costs and holdout difficulties that may impede socially desirable activities, this limitation seems reasonable. See Daniel Friedmann, "Restitution of Benefits Obtained Through the Appropriation of Property or the Commission of a Wrong," 80 *Columbia Law Review* 504, 509 note 28 (1980). In fact, nuisance may be one important example with regard to which an economic explanation seems more convincing than any ethical one. Another variant of infringing upon the entitlement of landowners may arise in cases when the defendant physically intrudes into the solitude or seclusion of the plaintiff at her living quarters. If the intrusion is intentional and "highly offensive to a reasonable person," a tort liability arises. *See Restatement (Second) of Torts* § 652B (1977). The proposed *Restatement of Restitution* states that unless such an intrusion is "occasional," a gain-based remedy is also available. See II *Restatement (Second) of Restitution* § 46(1) (Tentative Draft, 1983–84). See also *E. I. duPont deNumours and Co.* v. *Christopher*, 431 F 2d 1,012 (1970), cert. denied, 400 US 1,024 (1971), discussed at note 138, p. 99 below.

29 92 Eng. Rep. 303, 303 (KB 1705) (the citation is of the reporter's syllabus).

30 See, e.g., II *Restatement (Second) of Restitution* § 45(1) comment b and illustration 1 (Tentative Draft, 1983–84).

31 See *Restatement of Restitution* § 154 comment a (1937). See also, e.g., Graham Douthwaite, *Attorney Guide to Restitution* § 8.2 at 329 (1977). But see I Palmer, *The Law of Restitution* § 2.12 at 158.

32 In the rare case of a converter who has improved the misappropriated property prior to its sale, a question arises as to whether to allow him to deduct his costs (or, alternatively, the costs plus any profit that should be attributed to them). The proposed new *Restatement* suggests that if the defendant was not aware that he had acquired the property wrongfully when making the improvement, he will not owe

proportional profits. In any case, subsequent cases hold that if the invader's gain is less than the *fair market value* of the chattel appropriated, the plaintiff can "ignore the subsequent sale and recover the reasonable value of the property taken."[33] Unlike an actual gain-based recovery, the recovery of *fair market value* is not conditional on the defendant's consciousness.[34]

Chattels may also be appropriated temporarily. In this category of cases, the plaintiff's claim will be for the use of her chattel, rather than for the amount realized on its sale. A typical defendant's strategy would then be to argue that the plaintiff's remedy should be limited to her out-of-pocket expenses (i.e., her *harm*) as a result of his unauthorized use of her chattel. This claim, however, is doomed to fail. An appropriation of a chattel enables its owner to pursue the appropriator's gain independently of her own loss.[35] Although the minimal measure of recovery is indeed the fair market value of the use,[36] in the typical case – where the defendant is a "knowing converter" – the plaintiff may elect to recover his generated gain.[37] It is only where the defendant is unaware of the plaintiff's ownership in the chattel – i.e., where deterrence is irrelevant – that the measure of recovery is limited to the use value of the property, that is its *fair market value*.[38]

A more difficult question is whether this "gain" alludes to *proceeds*, *profits* or *proportional profits*, that is whether the defendant will be allowed to deduct the costs he incurred in securing his gain, and whether any proportional profit should also be attributed to these costs. Both the

restitution to the extent that "an ascertainable part of the price is attributable to the improvement." See II *Restatement (Second) of Restitution* § 45(1) comment c (Tentative Draft, 1983–84). On the other hand, G. H. L. Fridman and James G. McLeod, *Restitution* 556 (1982) (Canada) would allow only a deduction of the value of any improvement. Since deterrence is not a factor in the case of an unconscious invader, I prefer the former view, which allows the plaintiff to resort only to a *proportional profits* measure of recovery.

33 See *Felder* v. *Reeth*, 34 F 2d 744, 746–47 (9th Cir. 1929); *Restatement of Restitution* § 128 comment k (1937).

34 See Dawson, "Restitution Without Enrichment" at 611.

35 See *John A. Artukovich & Sons* v. *Reliance Truck Co.*, 614 P 2d 327, 329 (Arizona 1980). See also, e.g., *Restatement of Restitution* § 128 comment i (1937); II *Restatement (Second) of Restitution* § 45(2) and comment f (Tentative Draft, 1983–84); *Ablah* v. *Eyman*, 365 P 2d 181, 191 (Kansas 1961).

36 I Palmer, *The Law of Restitution* § 2.2(a) at Supplement 34. See also *Strand Electric and Engineering Co.* v. *Brisford Entertainments Ltd.*, [1952] 2 QB 246 (England).

37 See *John A. Artukovich & Sons* v. *Reliance Truck Co.*, 614 P 2d 327 (Arizona 1980). See also *Ablah* v. *Eyman*, 365 P 2d 181 (Kansas 1961); *Olwell* v. *Nye & Nissen Co.*, 173 P 2d 652 (Washington 1947). But *cf. Strand Electric and Engineering Co.* v. *Brisford Entertainments Ltd.*, [1952] 2 QB 246 (England, Court of Appeal).

38 See *Restatement of Restitution* § 128 comment k (1937); II *Restatement (Second) of Restitution* § 45 comment c and illustrations 5 and 6 (Tentative Draft, 1983–84).

Restatement and the commentators recognize the deductibility of the invader's costs. There is however some disagreement among these authorities regarding the second question. Whereas the *Restatement* seems to prefer a *profits* measure of recovery, commentators who discuss this question refer to a *proportional profits* remedy.[39] This debate has not yet been resolved by any court decision.

In conclusion, in the sale cases, where the distinction between the different gain-based remedies is rarely relevant, the applicable measure of recovery is the greater of *fair market value* and *gain*. In contrast, in the use cases, where this distinction seems cardinal, the law is still surprisingly unsettled. The best that can be said at this time is that the rationale governing chattels is either *well-being and control* or *well-being and hypothetical consent*. This uncertainty and the elasticity it engenders may be attributable to the inherent diversity within the chattels category, as has been noted in chapter 3.

Sui generis: private necessity

A third type of appropriating tangible property – private necessity – compliments our exploration of measures of recovery thus far. A, a shipowner, keeps his ship at B's dock through a storm without B's consent or permission. A is perfectly aware of the fact that B's property may be damaged. None the less, he believes that the preservation of the ship and the lives of his crew justify his deed. Consequently, as the ship beats against the dock, it damages the dock, and B, the dockowner, seeks remedy.[40] The *Restatement of Restitution* limits A's liability to "the amount of harm done."[41] Thus, B is not entitled to A's resultant benefit which is, in this circumstance, the value of the lives saved and of the property salvaged. Moreover, A seems to be further exempted from paying for the rental value for the use of B's dock.[42] The only available measure of recovery is *harm*.

The conventional explanation of this rule is that saving life or property is so privileged an act as to deprive the resource-holder of her entitlement to

39 Compare *Restatement of Restitution* § 128 comment k (1937) with I Palmer, *The Law of Restitution* § 2.12 at 161 and Friedmann, *The Law of Unjust Enrichment* §§ 390, 393.

40 This hypothetical is based on the famous case of *Vincent* v. *Lake Erie Transp. Co.*, 124 NW 221 (Minnesota 1910).

41 *Restatement of Restitution* § 122 (1937). See also *Restatement (Second) of Torts* §§ 197, 263 (1965). Similar results seem to occur in maritime jettison cases. See, e.g., Friedmann, "Restitution of Benefits" at 530 note 135.

42 There is some confusion in the *Restatement of Restitution* in this respect, but the *Restatement of Torts*, to which the *Restatement of Restitution* refers, seems to exclude not only an actual gain-based recovery, but also an award of the fair rental value.

terminate or prevent the invasion, but still not so privileged as to relieve the invader from liability to pay any material harm he does thereby.[43] This explanation indeed embodies the rationale corresponding to the available remedy: cases of (extreme) private necessity are the main – the only – example in American restitutionary doctrine for a *sharing* rationale. The applicable rule for such cases vindicates the claim of a person in a state of emergency or extreme need to share another's entitlement. A's claim is limited, however, to the exclusion of B's otherwise protected claims to both control her resource and receive the *fair market value* of the contract imposed on her. It does not extend to a claim to sacrifice the level of welfare embodied in the resource-holder's estate.

Interests in intangible property

Copyright

The Copyright Act of 1976 prescribes that a prevailing copyright owner in an infringement action is entitled to recover either "the owner's actual damages and any additional profits of the infringer," or "statutory damages." The profits component includes:

> any profits of the infringer that are attributable to the infringement and are not taken into account in computing the actual damages. In establishing the infringer's profits, the copyright owner is required to present proof only of the infringer's gross revenue, and the infringer is required to prove his or her deductible expenses and the elements of profit attributable to factors other than the copyrighted work.[44]

This formula alludes to a *proportional profits* measure of recovery. And indeed, since the leading case of *Sheldon* v. *Metro-Goldwyn Pictures Corp.*,[45] this complicated and elusive measure has been most intensely exercised and explored in the context of copyright.

Consider the following hypothetical copyright case.[46] A, a new hotel owner plans to conduct a revue as part of the many attractions of his hotel.

[43] See Francis H. Bohlen, "Incomplete Privilege to Inflict Intentional Invasions of Interests of Property and Personality," 39 *Harvard Law Review* 307, 313 (1926).

[44] 15 USC § 504.

[45] 309 US 390 (1940).

[46] The hypothetical is a mixture of the facts in *Sheldon* v. *Metro-Goldwyn Pictures Corp.*, 309 US 390 (1940) and those of *Frank Music Corp.* v. *Metro Goldwyn Mayer Inc.*, 772 F 2d 505 (9th Cir. 1985).

He tries to purchase B's copyright to a certain play, parts of which he wants to include in his revue. The price around which the negotiations are conducted is $X. But the talks do not ripen into an agreement. None the less, A bases one segment of his revue on B's play. A incurs considerable expenses in producing the infringing portion, which is directed, performed, and decorated by top professionals, and is advertised as such. The revue and the hotel are a great success, and both generate significant profits. B files a complaint, seeking an accounting of all these gains.

According to the Copyright Act and the accompanying case law, our hypothetical case will probably be resolved along the following lines:

1. B is not limited to her actual damages or to her lost profits (i.e., to her *harm*), even if A can demonstrate that his profits exceed B's lost profits either because his production is more efficient than the production she could have made or since the environment in which he sells the entertaining product is more receptive to it than hers.[47]
2. Similarly, B is not limited to the sum of $X discussed between the parties prior to the unilateral appropriation. Courts are unwilling to counter-factually ascribe B with consent to sell at what probably represented the *ex-ante fair market value* of the appropriated copyright.[48]
3. On the other hand, B will not be entitled to the entire *proceeds* earned by A on the infringing revue, but only to such profits as remain after A reduces them by proof of allowable elements of cost.[49]
4. Furthermore, where it is clear that A's net profits from the revue are also attributable to what he himself supplied, "and the evidence is sufficient to provide a fair basis of division so as to give the copyright proprietor [B] all the profits that can be deemed to have resulted from the use of what belonged to [her]," the profits will be apportioned accordingly. This rule applies even in cases of deliberate plagiarism.[50]

[47] See *Taylor* v. *Meirick*, 712 F 2d 1,112, 1,120 (7th Cir. 1983). See also, e.g., *Blackman* v. *Hustler Magazine Inc.*, 800 F 2d 1,160, 1,163 note 6 (DC Cir. 1986).

[48] See *Sheldon* v. *Metro-Goldwyn Pictures Corp.*, 106 F 2d 45, 50 (1939), affirmed, 309 US 390 (1940). See also Douglas Laycock, *Modern American Remedies: Cases and Materials* 567 (2nd edn. 1994); II Paul Goldstein, *Copyright* 12:4 (2nd edn. 1996). But see Wade R. Keeton, "Monetary Recovery under the Copyright Act," 65 *Oregon Law Review* 809, 825 (1986).

[49] See, e.g., *F. W. Woolworth Co.* v. *Contemporary Arts Inc.*, 344 US 228, 233 (1952). See also Alois V. Gross, "Annotation, Measure of Damages and Profits to which Copyright Owner is Entitled under 17 USCS § 504(b)," 100 ALR Fed. 258 §§ 39–71 (1990); Goldstein, *Copyright* § 12.1.2.1; III Melville B. Nimmer and David Nimmer, *Nimmer on Copyright* § 14.03[B] (permanent edn. revised vol. 1996).

[50] See *Sheldon* v. *Metro-Goldwyn Pictures Corp.*, 309 US 390, 402, 405 (1940). See also, e.g., *Schroeder* v. *William Morrow & Co.*, 566 F 2d 3, 6–7 (7th Cir. 1977); *Rogers* v. *Koons*, 960 F 2d 301, 313 (2nd Cir. 1992).

5. Any doubt as to the computation of costs or in the apportionment of net profits is to be resolved in favor of the plaintiff, B.[51] None the less, "what is required is not mathematical exactness but only a reasonable approximation," which may be attained with the aid of expert testimony.[52] Confronted with the inevitable imprecision of computing expenses and disentangling the contributions of inherently incommensurable factors, courts do not deny deduction and apportionment altogether. Instead, they "make an award which by no possibility shall be too small," preferring to err on the side of the plaintiff.[53] In so far as our hypothetical is concerned, this guideline directs the court to make a qualitative comparison
of the infringing segment in A's revue to the other segments thereof.[54]
6. Indirect profits can be taken into account if, but only if, they are not too remote and speculative.[55] The question of whether specific profits were made from an infringement is causative in nature, looking for a "sufficient nexus" between the infringement and the profit. Thus, in so far as the revue had a promotional value for A's hotel, B is also entitled to a proportional part of A's hotel's net profits, taking into account the other available attractions it offers.[56]
7. The cases reveal – but do not discuss from a policy standpoint – some dispute as to the availability of the *fair market value* of the infringing segment as an alternative measure of recovery.[57] Therefore, it is not clear whether the measure of recovery is *proportional profits* or the greater of *fair market value* and *proportional profits*. However, since awarding *proportional profits* where it is smaller than *fair market value* cannot be explicated in any principled fashion,[58] I prefer the latter

[51] See, e.g., *Eales* v. *Environmental Lifestyles Inc.*, 958 F 2d 876, 881 (9th Cir. 1992); *Cream Records Inc.*, v. *Joseph Schlitz Brewing Co.*, 864 F 2d 668, 669 (9th Cir. 1989); *Lottie Joplin Thomas Trust* v. *Crown Publishers Inc.*, 592 F 2d 651, 657 (2nd Cir. 1978).

[52] *Sheldon* v. *Metro-Goldwyn Pictures Corp.*, 309 US 390, 408–09 (1940). See also, e.g., *Orgel* v. *Clark Boardman Co.*, 301 F 2d 119 (2nd Cir. 1962), cert. denied, 371 US 817 (1962).

[53] See, e.g., *Sheldon* v. *Metro-Goldwyn Pictures Corp.*, 106 F 2d 45, 48, 51 (1939), affirmed, 309 US 390 (1940); *Sygma Photo News Inc.* v. *High Soc'y Magazine Inc.*, 778 F 2d 89, 95 (2nd Cir. 1985). But *cf. Walker* v. *Forbes Inc.*, 28 F.3d 409, 411–14 (4th Cir. 1994) convincingly criticized by Goldstein, *Copyright* at 12:29–12:30.

[54] See *Frank Music Corp.* v. *Metro Goldwyn Mayer Inc.*, 886 F 2d 1,545, 1,548–50 (9th Cir. 1989). See also, e.g., *Blackman* v. *Hustler Magazine Inc.*, 800 F 2d 1,160, 1,164–65 (DC Cir. 1986).

[55] See Goldstein, *Copyright* § 12.1.2.3; Nimmer, *Nimmer on Copyright* § 14.03[A].

[56] See *Frank Music Corp.* v. *Metro Goldwyn Mayer Inc.*, 772 F 2d 505, 516–17 (9th Cir. 1985); *Frank Music Corp.* v. *Metro Goldwyn Mayer Inc.*, 886 F 2d 1,545, 1,550, 1,553–54 (9th Cir. 1989). See also *Business Trends Analysts Inc.*, v. *Freedonia Group Inc.*, 887 F 2d 399, 404, 407 (2nd Cir. 1989). But *cf.* Edwards v. Lee, 96 SW 2d 1,028 (Kentucky 1936), discussed at pp. 76–78 above, in which indirect profits were excluded.

[57] Compare *Deltak Inc.* v. *Advanced Systems Inc.*, 767 F 2d 357, 362 (7th Cir. 1985) with *Business Trends Analysts Inc.*, v. *Freedonia Group Inc.*, 887 F 2d 399, 405–07 (2nd Cir. 1989).

[58] See pp. 20–21 above.

alternative which represents the rationale of *well-being and hypothetical consent*.[59]

8. Finally, although innocent intent does not derogate from liability, unconsciousness has some bearing on the available remedies.[60] In particular, where there has been no notice of copyright and the defendant is an innocent infringer, a court may deny recovery of profits.[61] As explained above, this exemption does not derogate from the *hypothetical consent* prong of the rationale, since deterrence is irrelevant to unconscious infringers.

As the following subsections demonstrate, this entitlement encompasses the most rigid rationale in the realm of intangible property. This phenomenon seems to be explicated by reference to the uniqueness of copyright as the most personal work of intellectual property in which the artist – or, to a lesser degree, her transferee – invests a part of herself.[62]

Trademark

Section 35 of the Trademark Act of 1946 prescribes that a trademark owner is entitled, "subject to the principles of equity," to the infringer's profits. In assessing profits, the plaintiff is "required to prove defendant's sales only; defendant must prove all elements of cost or deduction claim." If the monetary award is found by the court "either inadequate or excessive," the court has power to increase or decrease it, as it "shall find to be just," as long as such adjusted sum constitutes "compensation and not penalty."[63]

Not unlike this statutory prescription, the case law on monetary recovery in trademarks infringement cases is deeply unsettled and uncertain.[64] If there is any consistency in this body of law, it may be detected by referring to two conflicting trends. The competition between these trends – which may explicate the doctrinal confusion – is currently reflected in two unresolved questions: (i) is the trademark owner (B) entitled to an accounting of A's gains in non-competitive relationships? Or, will an accounting be available only in competitive ones, where A's gain approxi-

[59] For similar conclusions (on different grounds) see Goldstein, *Copyright* at 12:12–12:16; Andrew W. Coleman, "Copyright Damages and the Value of the Infringing Use: Restitutionary Recovery in Copyright Infringement Actions," 21 *AIPLA Quarterly Journal* 91 (1993).

[60] See Nimmer, *Nimmer on Copyright* § 13.08.

[61] Copyright Act of 1976, 15 USC § 405(b).

[62] *Cf.* Dawson, "Restitution Without Enrichment" at 616–17.

[63] 15 USC § 1,117.

[64] See III J. Thomas McCarthy, *Trademarks and Unfair Competition* § 30:24[2] (permanent edn. revised vol. 1994); James M. Koelemay, Jr., "Monetary Relief for Trademark Infringement under the Lenham Act," 72 *Trademark Reporter* 458, 525 (1982).

mates B's lost profits (her *harm*)? (ii) What is the state of mind of the infringer (A) the proof of which is a prerequisite to such recovery?[65]

One view regarding the first question conceives of any gain-based recovery as merely another (indirect) way of measuring B's loss and thus limits the trademark-owner's recovery to her *harm*. Hence, where the parties are not in direct competition – so there can be no actual diversion of B's trade to A – any lost profits recovery is said to be speculative, and is for that reason denied.[66] Against this view – which is considered "traditional" but still prevails in many jurisdictions – stands a long-time adversary which is gaining more support as time passes. The more modern approach bases the recovery of profits on "an unjust enrichment theory."[67] It perceives B's entitlement as important enough to deter potential infringers from bypassing the market and unilaterally appropriating the trademark. Therefore, it rejects the limitation to lost profits[68] and allows a gain-based recovery even if the parties operate in different geographical territories[69] notwithstanding the lack of any product competition.[70] More particularly, this approach prescribes that a trademark owner is entitled to the relatively stringent remedy of the greater[71] of *fair market value*[72] and *proportional profits*.[73]

The second question which concerns the trademark infringement cases touches on the "requirement of wrongful intent." Here, too, there seem to be two rival attitudes. The first insists on the equitable nature of the

[65] See generally II McCarthy, *Trademarks and Unfair Competition* §§ 30:25–30:28; Koelemay, "Monetary Relief" at 458–525; James M. Koelemay, Jr., "A Practical Guide to Monetary Relief in Trademark Infringement Cases," 75 *Trademark Reporter* 263 §§ II.A and II.C (1995).

[66] See, e.g., *Raxton Corp.* v. *Anania Assoc. Inc.*, 668 F 2d 622, 625 (1st Cir. 1982); *George Basch Co. Inc.* v. *Blue Coral Inc.*, 968 F 2d 1,532, 1,538–39 (2nd Cir. 1992).

[67] The first hint of this theory can be found in *Hamilton-Brown Shoe Co.* v. *Wolf Bros. & Co.*, 240 US 251, 259 (1916).

[68] See *Mishawaka Rubber & Woolen Manufacturing Co.* v. *S. S. Kresge Co.*, 316 US 203, 207 (1942).

[69] See, e.g., *Blue Bell Co.* v. *Frontier Refining Co.*, 213 F 2d 354, 363 (10th Cir. 1954).

[70] See, e.g., *Maier Brewing Co.* v. *Fleischmann Distilling Corp.*, 390 F 2d 117 (9th Cir. 1968), cert. denied, 391 US 966 (1968); *W. B. Bassett Co.* v. *Revlon Inc.*, 435 F 2d 656, 664 (2nd Cir. 1970).

[71] See, e.g., *Playboy Enterprises Inc.* v. *Baccarat Clothing Co.*, 692 F 2d 1,272, 1,274–75 (9th Cir. 1982).

[72] For the availability of a "reasonable royalty" (i.e., *fair market value*) alternative see Koelemay, "A Practical Guide" at § III.B.

[73] The defendant can deduct any reasonable expenses he incurred in securing the gross revenues from the infringing trademark. See, e.g., *W. B. Bassett Co.* v. *Revlon Inc.*, 435 F 2d 656, 665 (2nd Cir. 1970). He can also retain any portion of the profits which is not attributable to the infringement. See, e.g., *Mishawaka Rubber & Woolen Manufacturing Co.* v. *S. S. Kresge Co.*, 316 US 203, 206–07 (1942). See generally *Restatement (Third) of Unfair Competition* § 37 comments d and g–h (1995); Koelemay, "A Practical Guide" at § IV.

accounting remedy[74] and accordingly denies actual gain-based recovery where the "character of [the defendant's] conduct" does not call for such a "stringent control."[75] As a prerequisite to recovery, it requires some showing of bad faith or egregious conduct; where there was no deliberate intent to fraudulently cause confusion, even a knowing use does not justify an accounting of profits.[76] On the other hand, other courts have emphasized that subjective intent is not determinative, so that where the defendant knowingly appropriates the plaintiff's mark the requirement of wrongful intent is "conclusively presumed."[77]

The co-existence of these competing approaches – which represent different measures of recovery and hence different rationales – seems puzzling at first glance. My own speculation with respect to this bifurcation connects it to the ambiguity of the social meaning of trademarks which has been observed in chapter 3: trademarks are currently perceived as symbols of their holders' commercial identity, on the one hand, but also as mere liability marks or symbols of the goods involved, on the other hand. Whereas the former meaning gives the protected interest a personal flavor and thus warrants a relatively stringent protection, the latter meaning is purely commercial and may thus involve much milder rationale.

Patent

According to the Patent Act of 1952, a successful patentee in a patent infringement case is entitled to "damages adequate to compensate for the infringement, but in no case less than a reasonable royalty for the use made of the invention by the infringer."[78] This clause prescribes that only compensatory damages, as measured by the patentee's lost profits or by a reasonable royalty, are recoverable by the patent owner.[79] The infringer's profits as such cannot be recovered, so that actual gain-based recovery is excluded.[80] Hence, evidence of the infringer's profits may be relevant only to

[74] See, e.g., *Fuller Prods. Co.* v. *Fuller Brush Co.*, 299 F 2d 772, 777 (7th Cir. 1962), cert. denied, 370 US 923 (1962).

[75] *Champion Spark Plug Co.* v. *Sanders*, 331 US 125, 130–31 (1947). See also, e.g., *Sands, Taylor & Wood Co.* v. *Quaker Oats Co.*, 978 F 2d 947, 961–63 (1992).

[76] See, e.g., *Restatement (Third) of Unfair Competition* § 37(1)(a) and comment e (1995); *Nalpac Ltd.* v. *Corning Glass Works*, 784 F 2d 752 (6th Cir. 1986); *George Basch Co. Inc.* v. *Blue Coral Inc.*, 968 F 2d 1,532, 1,539–40 (2nd Cir. 1992).

[77] See, e.g., *WSM Inc.* v. *Tenn. Sales Co.*, 709 F 2d 1,084, 1,087 (6th Cir. 1983).

[78] 35 USC § 284.

[79] See, e.g., *Georgia-Pac. Corp.* v. *US Plywood Corp.*, 243 F Supp. 500, 516 (SDNY 1965).

[80] See *Aro Manufacturing* v. *Convertible Top Replacement Co.*, 377 US 476, 502–13 (1964); I Palmer, *The Law of Restitution* § 2.7(b) note 25. According to the legal regime prior to the 1952 Patent Act, actual gain-based recovery was recognized and the doctrines of cost deduction and apportionment of profits applied. Hence, the previous doctrine

the extent that they are of some probative value to either: (i) the ascertainment of the lost profits the patentee suffered and can now pursue as part of her *harm* recovery; to qualify as relevant under this prong it has to be shown that but for the infringement the profits would have been made by the patentee;[81] or (ii) the computation of royalties the patentee would have charged the infringer had the latter not circumvented the negotiations table;[82] the determination under this alternative still leaves the infringer with part of his profits.[83] In any case, either of these evidentiary positions is a far cry from a rule which makes the patentee entitled, as a matter of substantive law, to the infringer's profits.[84]

The fact that actual gain-based recovery is not allowed does not mean, however, that the patentee may only recover for her *harm*. On the contrary, an award of reasonable royalty is not conditioned upon a showing that, but for the infringement, the patentee would have secured the infringer's profit or any profit whatsoever. The mere deprivation of the license fee which the patentee is entitled to collect from the infringer suffices to trigger the reasonable royalty measure of recovery.[85]

A dominant method of determining the reasonable royalty is by imagining a fictitious situation in which the patentee and the infringer would have "willingly" negotiated a royalty agreement at the time infringement began, and then imagining what the royalty in such situation would have been, taking into account all the relevant circumstances.[86] The most significant fact for such a determination is the *fair market value* of a

alluded to a *proportional profits* measure of recovery. For a thorough study of the successive statutory schemes see *Georgia-Pac. Corp.* v. *US Plywood Corp.*, 243 F Supp. 500, 516–46 (SDNY 1965).

81 See, e.g., *Kori Corp.* v. *Wilco Marsh Buggies & Draglines Inc.*, 761 F 2d 649, 655 (Fed. Cir. 1985), cert. denied, 474 US 902 (1985); *Georgia-Pac. Corp.* v. *US Plywood Corp.*, 243 F Supp. 500, 516 and note 4 (SDNY 1965). For an elaborate discussion of the lost-profits alternative, see Laura B. Pincus, "The Computation of Damages in Patent Infringement Cases," 5 *Harvard Journal of Law and Technology* 95, 100–18 (1991).

82 See, e.g., *Zegers* v. *Zegers Inc.*, 458 F 2d 726, 728 and note 8 (7th Cir. 1972), cert. denied, 409 US 878 (1972).

83 See Pincus, "The Computation of Damages" at 125–26.

84 See *Georgia-Pac. Corp.* v. *US Plywood Corp.*, 243 F Supp. 500, 528 (SDNY 1965).

85 See, e.g., *Zegers* v. *Zegers Inc.*, 458 F 2d 726, 729 (7th Cir. 1972), cert. denied, 409 US 878 (1972); *Foster* v. *American Machinery & Foundry Co.*, 492 F 2d 1,317, 1,321 (2nd Cir. 1974), cert. denied, 419 US 833 (1974).

86 See, e.g., *Rite-Hite Corp.* v. *Kelley Co.*, 774 F Supp. 1,514, 1,543 (Eastern District of Wisconsin 1991). Cases are collected in V Donald S. Chisum, *Patents* § 20.03[3] (permanent edn. revised vol. 1993 and Supplement 1994); Wesley Kobylak, "Annotation, Factors to be Considered in Determining a 'Reasonable Royalty' for Purposes of Calculating Damages for Patent Infringement Under 35 USCS § 284," 66 ALR Fed. 186 (1984).

license to the infringed patent. Royalty rates previously charged by the patentee are thus of decisive importance.[87]

Needless to say, such hypothetical negotiations are a fiction. "[T]he reasonable royalty device conjures a willing licensor and licensee, who like Ghosts of Christmas Past, are dimly seen as negotiating a license. There is, of course, no actual willingness on either side, and no license to do anything."[88] Indeed, as may have been expected given the utilitarian characteristics of patents as discussed in chapter 3, this is a typical example of the relatively lenient measure of recovery which is aimed at vindicating the resource-holder's *well-being*, but in fact vindicates neither her *control* over the resource nor even her *hypothetical consent* to its transfer.

Interests in self

Individual reputation and dignity

Now we turn to those cases involving resources most closely connected to the self. The first type of such case regards individual reputation and dignity. When A publishes, or otherwise communicates, a false statement (or implication) which tends to diminish B's reputation, esteem, respect, goodwill or the confidence in which B is held, and to expose B to contempt, hatred, ridicule, or obloquy, B has, subject to certain privileges, a valid cause of action in defamation against A.[89] A closely related, and at times indistinguishable, cause of action is known as "false light." The latter seems to be a less demanding claim to pursue as it has been indicated that the false representation does not have to be "defamatory." Rather, it is enough that B was given "unreasonable and highly objectionable publicity that attributes to [her] characteristics, conduct or beliefs that are false, and so is placed before the public in false light."[90] The interest protected by both causes of action is the same – one's reputation, which as we have seen reflects in such circumstances one's dignity and worth, a highly personal interest indeed. The distinction between defamation and false light is often blurred[91] and is

[87] See, e.g., *Nickson Industries Inc.* v. *Rol Manufacturing Co.*, 847 F 2d 795, 798 (Fed. Cir. 1988).

[88] *Panduit Corp.* v. *Stahlin Bros. Fibre Works Inc.*, 575 F 2d 1,152, 1,159 (6th Cir. 1978).

[89] See *Black's Law Dictionary* 417 (6th ed. 1990).

[90] *Restatement (Second) of Torts* § 652E comment b (1977).

[91] See J. Thomas McCarthy, *The Right of Publicity and Privacy* § 5.12[c] (permanent edn. revised vol. 1994).

at any rate insignificant for our purposes; I therefore discuss both claims jointly.[92]

It is often indicated that defamation is not a wrong which may give rise to a restitutionary claim, i.e., that currently a plaintiff is limited to recover only damages for the *harm* she has suffered.[93] The basis of this contention is one case of New York's lowest instance: *Hart* v. *E. P. Dutton & Co.*[94] The ostensible importance of this case – which in my opinion no longer represents the true state of the law – justifies its consideration in some detail.

Hart claimed that a book the defendant had published contained defamatory statements which falsely depicted him as a traitor or agent of the enemy Axis powers during World War II. Since the statute of limitations barred a libel cause of action, Hart turned to a restitutionary claim seeking to recover the profits derived from the publication of the libel, a considerable sum of money. The court dismissed the complaint holding that it failed to state any cause of action other than libel, which as indicated was barred. Certain parts of the opinion may suggest a narrow rationale for its holding, i.e., that the circumvention of the prescription of the statute of limitation should be prevented. However, *Hart* seems to prescribe also the broader rule which limits recovery to the plaintiff's *harm*.

92 An additional cause of action which is sometimes discussed by restitution scholars together with claims of defamation and false light is the "private facts" branch of the right of privacy. This tort of public disclosure of embarrassing private facts by private parties is intended to vindicate an entitlement "to be let alone." See Samuel D. Warren and Louis D. Brandeis, "The Right to Privacy," 4 *Harvard Law Review* 193, 195 (1890). In this connection, many commentators criticize *Cason* v. *Baskin*, 20 So. 2d 243 (Florida 1944) in which the Florida Supreme Court was unwilling to allow recovery of profits obtained through invasion of the right of privacy. See, e.g. Kenneth H. York, "Extension of Restitutional Remedies in the Tort Field," 4 *UCLA Law Review* 499, 502–03, 539 (1957). I share the underlying sentiments of such authors according to which, in so far as the law recognizes the individual's right to control the dissemination of true information concerning her person, restitution of profits generated from an infringement of such right should be allowed. But constitutional First Amendment concerns seem to curtail the entitlement to be let alone, and the corresponding tort of public disclosure, to such a degree that makes it at best anecdotal and at worst a sham. See, e.g., Diane L. Ziemmerman, "Requiem for a Heavyweight: A Farewell to Warren and Brandeis's Privacy Tort," 68 *Cornell Law Review* 291 (1983). Hence, discussing in detail the appropriate remedy to vindicate an entitlement that hardly ever exists seems somewhat redundant. *Cf. Young* v. *That Was The Week That Was*, 312 F Supp. 1,337, 1,341–42 (Northern District of Ohio 1969).

93 See Peter Birks, *An Introduction to the Law of Restitution* 328 (paperback edn. with revisions 1989). See also, e.g., Russell G. Donaldson, "Annotation, False Light Invasion of Privacy – Defenses and Remedies," 57 ALR 4th 244, § 25 (1987).

94 93 NYS 2d 871 (Supreme Court 1949), affirmed, 98 NYS 2d 773 (App. Div. 1950), appeal denied, 3|01 NY 814 (1950).

In support of this broader holding, the court focused on the fact that the profits derived are due in large measure to elements outside of the printed matter, i.e., to the expenses and efforts incurred for a period of years by the publisher. To require the defendant to account to the plaintiff for profits derived from the publication of the book is thus said to result in an "inequitable" situation – the "unjust enrichment of the plaintiff." Such a remedy would avail the plaintiff of "the fruits of the defendant's labor and investment even beyond that which may flow from the alleged libel."[95]

Admittedly, one's reputation is not an interest which can be valued by market standards,[96] and therefore *fair market value* cannot be used as the appropriate remedy. Furthermore, where the profit is not derived from a pamphlet which consists entirely of the defamatory statements, but rather from an integrated piece such as a book, it is unlikely that a feasible method of apportioning profits can be readily identified[97] so that calculating *proportional profits* is a burdensome task (even in comparison to the parallel task in the context of copyright).

None the less, many commentators who discuss *Hart* are critical of this broad holding[98] and the proposed draft of the new *Restatement of Restitution* describes its rule as "an apparent anomaly."[99] Thus, it has been pointed out that the *Hart* court does not explain satisfactorily "[w]hy it should be unjust for the plaintiff, at whose expense [a] benefit was acquired, to reclaim the benefit resulting from the wrongful act."[100] More specifically, it has been suggested that "the plaintiff in such a case is entitled to [her] good name, even if this interest is one which [she] is unlikely to market. Where a defendant profits from a libel, he in effect sells it and thus makes the interest a salable one. He should thus be liable in restitution."[101] The difficulty raised by the court – that such a remedy gives the plaintiff the fruits of years of expenses incurred by the defendant – should be addressed, says one final commentator, "by recognized limitations built into the relief, [such as] the defense of laches."[102]

95 *Hart* v. *E. P. Dutton & Co.*, 93 NYS 2d 871, 877 (Supreme Court 1949), affirmed, 98 NYS 2d 773 (App. Div. 1950), appeal denied, 301 NY 814 (1950).

96 I Palmer, *The Law of Restitution* § 2.9 at 130.

97 See *ibid.* § 2.10 at 139.

98 See, e.g., Goff and Jones, *The Law of Restitution* at 722 and note 64.

99 II *Restatement (Second) of Restitution* 139 (Tentative Draft, 1983–84).

100 Fridman and McLeod, *Restitution* at 550.

101 Friedmann, "Restitution of Benefits" at 511. See also Gareth Jones, "A Topography of the Law of Restitution," in *Essays in Restitution* 1, 10 (P. D. Finn ed. 1990) (Australia).

102 York, "Extension of Restitutional Remedies" at 543.

Hence, the emerging opinion rejects *Hart* and seems to suggest that the appropriate remedy should be based on the defendant's actual gains. One Canadian book has even suggested that "libel must now be included among the torts capable of being [remedied by a restitutionary measure]."[103] This view was supported by reference to some English decisions where punitive damages have been awarded in circumstances where a defendant has published defamatory statements, calculating that his profits will outweigh the defamed party's loss.[104]

Resorting to punitive damages in such circumstances is no doubt aimed at effectively deterring such a well-calculated invader. But employing the blunt instrument of punitive damages leaves the amount of damages to the discretion of any particular decision-maker. This seems inappropriate when in fact we know that the desired deterrence can be effectuated if a *profits* measure of recovery is available. Punitive damages are only a subterfuge; a *profits* measure of recovery is a more sensitive remedy which best reflects the inclination of the legal community in Anglo-American jurisdictions.[105]

This seems to have been recognized by Judge Posner. In considering a false-light claim, he held that an award of punitive damages should be based on the profits attributable to the defendant's violation of the plaintiff's rights. And he further added that:

> Should it prove infeasible to disentangle the various factors that contributed to the profitability of the [relevant] issue of the magazine and to determine the effect that [the false-light portion thereof] may have had on the profitability of subsequent issues, the profits of the entire ... issue might be a reasonable starting point for assessing punitive damages.[106]

[103] See Peter D. Maddaugh and John D. McCamus, *The Law of Restitution* 514 note 44, 526–29 (1990). See also Law Commission Consultation Paper No. 132 on Aggravated, Exemplary and Restitutionary Damages 158 (1993); G. H. L. Fridman, *Restitution* 361–62 (2nd edn. 1992). But see Dobbs, *Handbook on the Law of Remedies* § 2.7(13).

[104] See, e.g., *Cassell & Co* v. *Broome*, [1972] AC 1,027, 1,079, 1,088, 1,094, 1,101, 1,130, 1,132 (House of Lords).

[105] *Cf.* Jeff Berryman, "The Case for Restitutionary Damages over Punitive Damages: Teaching the Wrongdoer that Tort Does not Pay," 73 *Canadian Bar Review* 320 (1994); Peter Birks, "Civil Wrongs: A New World," 1990–91 *Butterworth Lectures* 55, 86.

[106] *Douglass* v. *Hustler Magazine Inc.*, 769 F 2d 1,128, 1,145 (7th Cir. 1985), cert. denied, 475 US 1,094 (1986). Arguing that Judge Posner's opinion leads to outright adoption of a *profits* measure of recovery is an overstatement. The quotation in the text may be interpreted as searching for proxies to either *profits* or *proportional profits*, and demonstrates again the evasiveness of both terms. Nevertheless, I tend to believe that *Douglass* calls for the approximation of *profits*, the measure of recovery which best vindicates the plaintiff's *control*. This is based on another part of the opinion in which Judge Posner discusses the plaintiff's right to control the dissemination of the nude photographs which were the subject of the controversy. See *ibid.* at 1,138–39.

Indeed, the demanding *profits* measure of recovery (and the corresponding *control* rationale) – and not the lenient measure of *harm* (and its corresponding *sharing* rationale) – best suits an entitlement in the personal resource of one's reputation.

Commercial attributes of personality

A person's entitlement regarding the use of commercial attributes of her identity has been titled by American jurisprudence "the right of publicity."[107] In the last four decades the right of publicity was recognized, shaped, and discussed by courts and legislators, and a fairly substantial body of legal materials has evolved in the elaboration of its parameters.[108]

The typical case in which the right of publicity is invoked is that of a celebrity whose attribute was used to enhance the commercial value of an enterprise.[109] The case may involve the appropriation of the plaintiff's name, picture, personal characteristics, voice, or any other attribute (whether it is invoked directly, or by using more subtle identifiers) which generates an associative value, or economic impact, upon the marketability of a product.[110]

The ordinary measure of recovery which was employed in a considerable number of right-of-publicity cases is the *fair market value* of the appropriated attribute which the defendant has used without the plaintiff's permission.[111] Such a pecuniary remedy is regularly not conditioned upon the

See also *Taylor* v. *Meirick*, 712 F 2d 1,112, 1,120 (7th Cir. 1983) (a copyright case in which Judge Posner explains the connection between *profits* and *control*). It may be added that, in order to succeed in either a defamation or a false-light claim, a plaintiff may have to satisfy a burden of demonstrating "actual malice" on behalf of the defendant, meaning knowledge of falsity or reckless disregard for truth. For securing a punitive damages award, she is probably required to show a higher degree of fault: personal ill-will towards her or reckless or wanton disregard of her rights. See generally Rodney A. Smolla, *Law of Defamation* §§ 3, 9.08 (permanent edn. revised vol. 1991); Donaldson, "Annotation, False Light Invasion of Privacy" § 31. In *Douglass*, however, Judge Posner seems to suggest that these requirements can be quite easily discharged, by showing that the defendant knew, or did not care, that he was acting without authorization: *ibid.* at 1,139.

107 The term "right of publicity" was coined and that right first recognized by Judge Frank in *Haelen Laboratories Inc.* v. *Topps Chewing Gum Inc.*, 202 F 2d 866, 868 (1953), cert. denied, 346 US 816 (1953).

108 See McCarthy, *The Right of Publicity*.

109 See, e.g., Sheldon W. Halpern, "The Right of Publicity: Commercial Exploitation of the Associative Value of Personality," 39 *Vanderbilt Law Review* 1,199, 1,200 (1986).

110 See *Restatement (Third) of Unfair Competition* § 46 comment d and § 47 (1995). See also, e.g., Halpern, "The Right of Publicity" at 1,242–55.

111 Cases and commentaries are collected in McCarthy, *The Right of Publicity* § 11.8[B].

making of any net actual profit by the defendant.[112] Alternatively, "if the defendant's unpermitted use is in a context which will damage plaintiff's future professional career expectations or the publicity value of plaintiff's identity, the court may award as damages the projected loss of income."[113] That is, where *harm* is greater than *fair market value*, the measure of recovery will be the former.

Notwithstanding the intensity of the litigation in this category, the data concerning the possibility of awarding the defendant's profits is relatively scarce. In only three reported cases have courts considered the availability of such a remedy. However, none of them advances any theoretical reasoning to support its conclusion. Two of the cases are from the same District Court which – applying New York law in both cases – has reached opposite results.[114] The third is a dissenting opinion in a California Supreme Court case which suggests that a plaintiff should be awarded the defendant's actual gain.[115] On the legislative front, only three of the fourteen states which have enacted specific statutes pertinent to the right of publicity provide for recovering the infringer's profits.[116] Both the cases and the statutes which do call for an actual gain-based remedy are not very clear in whether they refer to *profits* or *proportional profits*. Finally, the *Restatement of Unfair Competition* suggests that in addition to *fair market value*, a measure of *proportional profits* is also available, unless the case is of "an innocent infringer."[117]

More informative grounds for allowing an actual gain-based remedy are found in the literature. Thus, a leading commentator claims that limiting recovery to *fair market value* is "inherently unfair," since:

[112] At times, however, profits have been a consideration in determining the amount of damages. See *Hogan* v. *A. S. Barnes & Co.*, 114 *United States Patents Quarterly* 314, 321 (Pennsylvania Trial Ct. 1957); *Athans* v. *Canadian Adventure Camps Ltd.*, 17 OR 2d 425, 436–38 (HC 1977) (Canada).

[113] McCarthy, *The Right of Publicity* § 11.8[C].

[114] Compare *Price* v. *Hal Roach Studios Inc.*, 400 F Supp. 836, 847 (SDNY 1975) with *Factors Etc. Inc.* v. *Pro Arts Inc.*, 496 F Supp. 1,090, 1,104 (SDNY 1980), revised on other grounds, 652 F 2d 278 (2nd Cir. 1981).

[115] *Lugosi* v. *Universal Pictures*, 603 P 2d 425, 452 (California 1979) (Bird CJ, dissenting). The dissent reasoned this view by drawing an analogy to intellectual-property law. The analogy is somewhat troubling since, as we have seen, this wide body of law does not apply the same rules regarding the availability of an actual gain-based recovery. Moreover, the dissent does not explain what is the relevant "resemblance" between these two categories of cases which calls for the drawing of such an analogy.

[116] For a collection and analysis of the state statutes see McCarthy, *The Right of Publicity* §§ 6.2–6.15.

[117] See *Restatement (Third) of Unfair Competition* § 49 and comments c–d (1995).

If all a defendant has to pay for the unauthorized use of plaintiff's identity is a reasonable royalty that would have been paid in a voluntary negotiation . . . then defendant is no worse off for its unpermitted taking . . . [Thus, the plaintiff loses] the right to make voluntary decisions about who is to make use of his or her identity, and when and where.[118]

This observation is no doubt solid, but it still begs the question: does American law intend to confer upon the holder of an entitlement to the commercial attributes of personality only the level of welfare embedded in these attributes, making *fair market value* the appropriate remedy? Or, alternatively, does the entitlement also expand to the control over the exploitation of associative value of the resource-holder's identity, availing her with an actual gain-based remedy?[119]

Although at times cases do express notions of control,[120] the above question still seems to be unsettled. In line with the analysis in chapter 3, I submit that the answer to this question – and the corresponding measure of recovery – is dependent upon the nature of the appropriation. More precisely, I suggest that the emerging doctrine distinguishes between cases of "mere" appropriation of the commercial attributes of one's personality and cases of a "degrading appropriation." The latter category includes cases in which the commercial exploitation can also be analyzed as defamation or false light, that is, where it involves also the appropriation of the "goodness" of the plaintiff's name, her reputation (as dignity).

The first category can be exemplified by the only right-of-publicity case which has been discussed thus far by the Supreme Court. In *Zacchini* v. *Scripps-Howard Broadcasting Co.*,[121] the plaintiff's "human cannonball" act was videotaped and broadcast in its entirety without his consent. In upholding the constitutionality of a State right-of-publicity law, the court emphasized that "[a]n entertainer such as petitioner usually has no objection to the widespread publication of his act so long as he gets the commercial benefit of such publication."[122] In such a case, the gravamen flowing from the unauthorized commercial use is simply the threat to the "economic value of the performance," since broadcasting the act free on television "goes to the heart of petitioner's ability to make a living as an entertainer."[123] Therefore, the court added in a note, if the broadcast increases, rather than decreases, the value of the performance, by

118 McCarthy, *The Right of Publicity* § 11.8[B].

119 McCarthy supports the latter alternative. See J. Thomas McCarthy, "Melville B. Nimmer and the Right of Publicity: A Tribute," 34 *UCLA Law Review* 1,703, 1,704, 1,710–11 (1987).

120 See *Lugosi* v. *Universal Pictures*, 603 P 2d 425, 440–41 (California 1979) (Bird CJ, dissenting).

121 433 US 562 (1977).

122 *Ibid.* at 573.

123 *Ibid.* at 575–76.

stimulating the public interest in seeing the act live, there will be no recovery.[124]

Thus, it seems that the entitlement in attributes of one's personality *that are already commercialized* focuses on the level of welfare of the resource-holder. This interpretation of *Zacchini* suggests that the only proper remedy for a case of the first category is what is indeed the ordinary remedy sought in right-of-publicity cases: *fair market value.*

On the other hand, where the appropriation degrades the plaintiff in any fashion, so that the invader appropriates the plaintiff's reputation (as dignity), the latter seems to be able to avail herself, as an alternative to *fair market value*, of the measure of recovery which vindicates her control, i.e., *profits*. This indeed was the case where the appropriation of the plaintiff's picture constituted a "false-light" tort.[125] Similarly, this may also be the appropriate remedy where the plaintiff does not want anyone – herself included – to make a profit from the associative value of the appropriated attribute.[126]

In sum, it seems that the available measure of recovery in pure right-of-publicity cases is *fair market value*; the parallel rationale is *well-being*. Only where commercializing an attribute of the plaintiff's identity is also degrading, does the appropriation of her reputation prescribe also a *profits* measure of recovery, so that the applicable rationale is *well-being and control.*

Identity

An obvious case of appropriating one's interest in oneself is the rare case where the defendant appropriates the whole of the plaintiff's identity, that is where he presents himself to a third party as the plaintiff or her agent while in fact he is neither. If such false pretense generates a benefit the defendant could not have reaped otherwise, the plaintiff's suit for such a profit comes fully within the scope of our paradigm.

Consider *English* v. *Dedham Vale Properties Ltd.*[127] A, without B's authority or knowledge, submitted to a local planning authority an application for permission to develop a plot that was thereafter sold by B to A. The application was made in B's name and was signed by A's employee as

124 *Ibid.* at 575 note 12. For a critical view of allowing the defendant to set off the *fair market value* of the appropriated performance against the uninvited benefit he conferred on the plaintiff, see Friedmann, "Restitution of Benefits" at 546–47.

125 See *Douglass* v. *Hustler Magazine Inc.*, 769 F 2d 1,128 (7th Cir. 1985), cert. denied, 475 US 1,094 (1986).

126 *Cf. Waits* v. *Frito-Lay Inc.*, 978 F 2d 1,093, 1,103–05 (9th Cir. 1992), cert. denied, 113 S Ct. 1,047 (1993). This category may also include cases of non-celebrities.

127 [1978] 1 WLR 93 (Chancery) (England).

"agent" for B. The court held that B was entitled to the profits which accrued to A from the granting of the planning permission. By using B's name without authority A was said to "assume the character of self-appointed agents for the plaintiffs" and "place themselves in a fiduciary relationship with the plaintiffs." Hence, A was held to be accountable to B for the generated profit.

On its face, the *English* case seems inconclusive for our purposes since the defendant's *profits* seem to have been equal to the *fair market value* of the application. None the less, the court's language appears broad enough to indicate a general rule according to which a plaintiff whose name and identity have been used by the defendant is entitled to take over the full generated benefit, presumably the greater of *fair market value* and *profits*.[128] It hence invokes the rationale of *well-being and control*.[129]

Physical integrity

I do not know of a single case from an Anglo-American jurisdiction in which a plaintiff has sought the profits that were derived from a non-consensual invasion to her body or appropriation of any part thereof.[130] The reason for

128 See *ibid*. at 106. A similar conclusion can be drawn from II *Restatement (Second) of Restitution* § 45 illustration 8 (Tentative Draft, 1983–84).

129 I do not know of an exact counterpart to the English scenario in American jurisprudence. A specific restitution case of the Florida Supreme Court deals, however, with a somewhat similar situation and reaches parallel results. See *Bell* v. *Smith*, 32 So. 2d 829, 832 (Florida 1947).

130 A type of case which seems at first sight pertinent is that of a slayer who attempts to inherit from his victim or take as beneficiary under his victim's will. Allowing him to do so is tantamount to allowing him to keep the profits of an appropriation of his victim's life, which seems by almost any account to be the most significant resource a person holds. Courts and legislators alike have long dealt with this case. The typical solution in American jurisdictions (known as the "slayer's rule") is to bar a felonious and intentional killer – as distinguished from a person who has been convicted of accidental manslaughter killing – from inheriting from his victim. See, e.g., Uniform Probate Code § 2-803, 8 ULA 172 (1983 and Supplement 1991). This type of case may be of some informative value for an effort to identify the rationale which governs one's body. None the less, it is importantly different from our paradigm, and raise issues and difficulties that are not relevant for our purposes. First, there are preexisting relationships between the parties: the victim is either an ancestor from whom the slayer would otherwise inherit under the laws of descent and distribution, or a beneficiary under the ancestor's will. Moreover, since the holder of the appropriated resource is dead, the typical plaintiffs are other legatees or inheritors, while our paradigm is confined to cases of direct conflict between a resource-holder and an invader to the exclusion of triangle situations such as this. Similarly, I do not discuss another type of case, where the body part – say certain cells – has been taken by a physician who failed to inform his patient of his intent to conduct research on such cells, and who subsequently uses the cells in potentially lucrative medical research. This scenario occurred in *Moore* v. *Regents of the University*

the idiosyncrasy of this type of case seems quite obvious: usually the *harm* inflicted on a victim of battery, or any other incident of infringing one's physical integrity, is at least equal to the gain secured by the invader.

Consider however the hypothetical case in which A, without B's consent, appropriates a part of B's body and sells it in a profitable transaction to C. One commentator who examines an example of cutting a prince's hair without permission and selling the locks for large sums, suggests that the invader would be accountable in such circumstances for any generated profit;[131] other commentators, as well as a recent English Law Commission consultation paper, share this view.[132]

In so far as this view is adopted as law, the measure of recovery in this type of case would presumably be either *proceeds* or *profits*, depending on whether the expenditures involved in contemplating and executing the invader's scheme are allowed to be deducted notwithstanding their illegality.[133] These measures, and their corresponding rationales (*control and condemnation* or *control*), are of course compatible with the obvious importance we attribute to our bodies, the utmost personal resource of all.

Other interests

Information

Our fourth and final category of resources includes all the other interests regulated by American law. Thus, the Uniform Trade Secrets Act ("UTSA"),

of California, 793 P 2d 479 (1990) where the California Supreme Court held that the patient is not entitled to any portion of the generated profits and that his sole remedy is under the cause of action of breach of the physician's disclosure obligation. It seems to me that *Moore* does not undermine the conclusions of the text. First, its scenario deviates from the contours of our paradigmatic case – it occurs on the back of a preexisting contractual relationship. Second, and more significantly, the primary reasoning of *Moore* – the policy consideration not to threaten medical research by restricting access to necessary raw materials – implicates the need to encourage socially useful activities, whereas our paradigm seeks to isolate the bilateral relations of resource-holder and (private) appropriator from any third parties' (or public) interests. These two distinctions are enough to justify my avoidance of directly attacking *Moore* as many commentators have done. See Jesse Dukeminier and James E. Krier, *Property* 86–87 and 88 note 46 (3rd edn. 1993).

131 See Harry Street, *Principles of the Law of Damages* 254 (1962).

132 See Friedmann, "Restitution of Benefits" at 512, 557; Laycock, *Modern American Remedies* at 557–59; Law Commission Consultation Paper No. 132 on Aggravated, Exemplary and Restitutionary Damages 158 (1993).

133 Friedmann, *The Law of Unjust Enrichment* § 397, opines that generally illegal expenditures should be deductible, unless the illegality is of a "high degree".

now adopted by forty-one states,[134] codifies the basic principles of the common law of trade secrets. It displaces and preempts any conflicting tort, restitutionary, or other doctrines protective of trade secrets.[135] The UTSA prescribes the rationale applicable to trade secrets, i.e., "information, including a formula, pattern, compilation, program, device, method, technique, or process, that: (i) derives independent economic value, actual or potential, from not being generally known to, and not being readily ascertainable by proper means by, other persons who can obtain economic value from its disclosure or use, and (ii) is the subject of efforts that are reasonable under the circumstances to maintain its secrecy."[136]

The UTSA protects a trade-secret-holder from *misappropriation*: the disclosure or use of her trade secret without her express or implied consent by a person who "used improper means to acquire knowledge of the trade secret."[137] The key concept of improper means "includes theft, bribery, misrepresentation, breach or inducement of a breach of a duty to maintain secrecy or espionage through electronic or other means."[138]

[134] Uniform Trade Secrets Act, 14 ULA 437 (1990 and Supplement 1996).

[135] See Uniform Trade Secrets Act, 14 ULA 434 (1990) prefatory note and § 7(a) at 463. See also, e.g., *Electro-Craft Corp.* v. *Controlled Motion Inc.*, 332 NW 2d 890, 898 (Minnesota 1983); *Sheets* v. *Yamaha Motors Corp.*, 849 F 2d 179, 183 and note 3 (5th Cir. 1988). For a comparison of the Uniform Act with the preexisting common law rules see, e.g., Peter B. Swann, "Maryland Uniform Trade Secrets Act," 49 *Maryland Law Review* 1,056 (1990). The restitutionary aspects of the pre-UTSA regime are addressed by I Palmer, *The Law of Restitution* § 2.8; H. O. Hunter, "Measuring the Unjust Enrichment in a Restitution Case," 12 *Sydney Law Review* 76, 85–89 (1989).

[136] Uniform Trade Secrets Act § 1(4), 14 ULA 437 (1990). For a comprehensive survey of the types of trade secrets see Don Wiesner and Anita Cava, "Stealing Trade Secrets Ethically," 47 *Maryland Law Review* 1,076, 1,084–95 (1988).

[137] Uniform Trade Secrets Act § 1(2)(ii)(A), 14 ULA 437 (1990).

[138] Uniform Trade Secrets Act § 1(1), 14 ULA 437 (1990). Commentators point out three pre-UTSA cases that are said to indicate the breadth of the "improper means" category:

1. The celebrated case of *International News Service* v. *Associated Press*, 248 US 215 (1918) – the first one to develop the misappropriation doctrine – has done so in the context of publicly disclosed trade values, i.e., news. But although some language used by the majority was indeed far-reaching, the case was decided upon the question of unfair competition (*ibid.* at 235), and over time was indeed interpreted as such. See, e.g., *Restatement (Third) of Unfair Competition* § 38 and comment c (1995).
2. Another famous case – *E. I. duPont deNumours & Co.* v. *Christopher*, 431 F 2d 1,012 (1970), cert. denied, 400 US 1,024 (1971) – holds that an aerial espionage is deemed improper notwithstanding the fact that the airspace in which the photographic expedition was conducted was a "no man's land," and therefore no trespass occurred. This case, which was explicitly endorsed by the UTSA, indeed signals an expansive approach of the "improper means" doctrine, especially when contrasted with its English counterpart, which is still limited

A successful claimant in a trade-secrets case is entitled to pecuniary remedies. Such remedies:

> can include both the actual loss caused by misappropriation and the unjust enrichment caused by misappropriation that is not taken into account in computing actual loss. In lieu of damages measured by any other methods, the damages caused by misappropriation may be measured by imposition of liability for a reasonable royalty for a misappropriator's unauthorized disclosure or use of a trade secret.[139]

In my terminology, this formula – together with the common law rules it codifies – embodies a measure of recovery of the greater of *proportional profits*[140] and *fair market value*.[141] This pecuniary remedy may be pursued irrespective of the loss the plaintiff may have suffered on account of the misappropriation.

Such a measure of recovery is supposed to indicate a *well-being and hypothetical consent* rationale. But one should not overlook the distinction from the seemingly parallel resources of intangible property, notably

to cases of breach of confidence. See, e.g., Goff and Jones, *The Law of Restitution* at chapter 36. None the less, this category still seems to me best explicated as one of the manifestations of the stringency of the rationale applicable to land, that makes cases of intrusion especially suitable to a well-protective legal rule.

3. Finally, some point to *Cablevision of Breckenridge Inc.* v. *Tannhauser Condominium Assn.*, 649 P 2d 1,093 (Colorado 1982), which provides remedy against an unauthorized reception of subscription television. But this case explicitly holds that the protected interest is not the broadcast signals, but rather the reception, processing, and distribution system the plaintiff has installed and the service it enables Cablevision to provide.

139 Uniform Trade Secrets Act § 3, 14 ULA 455 (1990). See also *Restatement (Third) of Unfair Competition* § 45 (1995). The exception to the plaintiff's right to these pecuniary remedies is not relevant to our paradigm since it refers to a transferee of the misappropriator. See *ibid.* at 457.

140 The permissibility of the deduction of the misappropriator's costs is clearly indicated in Uniform Trade Secrets Act § 3 comment, 14 ULA 455, 456 (1990). See also Michael A. Rosenhouse, "Annotation, Proper Measure and Elements of Damages for Misappropriation of Trade Secret," 11 ALR 4th 12, §§ 15–26 (1982); Roger M. Milgrim, *Milgrim on Trade Secrets* § 15.02 [3][c] (permanent edn. and Supplement 1995). The issue of the attribution of profits to the defendant's contribution is much less certain. The UTSA says nothing about it; and the surprisingly few common law cases which deal with the issue seem to follow the attribution rules shaped in the context of copyright and trademark law. See *USM Corp.* v. *Marson Fastener Corp.*, 467 NE 2d 1,271, 1,277 and note 3 (Massachusetts 1984); See also *Restatement (Third) of Unfair Competition* § 45 comment f (1995); Rosenhouse, *ibid.* at § 28a.

141 The "reasonable royalty" measure is a "general option," an "alternative" which "a complainant can request." See Uniform Trade Secrets Act § 3 comment, 14 ULA 455, 456 (1990). This was also the case prior to the UTSA. See, e.g., *Carter Products Inc.* v. *Colgate-Palmolive Co.*, 214 F Supp. 383, 394 (District of Maryland 1963).

copyright. Unlike intangible property, trade secrets are protected (in so far as our paradigmatic case is concerned) only from *improper* means of appropriation.[142] Thus, the holder of a trade secret has no rights against one who discovers the secret by "fair and honest means," which do not offend "standards of commercial ethics" of "good faith and honest, fair dealing."[143] Such "proper means" which preclude recovery include an independent discovery of the secret, a discovery due to public disclosure or failure to exercise reasonable care to maintain secrecy, and "reverse engineering," i.e., the analysis of publicly available products or information.[144] In each of these cases, a competitor can legitimately obliterate the plaintiff's entitlement.

Another manifestation of the "improper means" limitation of the trade-secret-holder's entitlement is the duration with regard to which the infringer's profits are recaptured. The accounting of profits is limited to the "lead time" it would otherwise have taken the misappropriator to discover the trade secret.[145] Moreover, profits that are not "tainted" by the improper means initially used are beyond the scope of the entitlement in a trade secret.[146]

Indeed, as chapter 3 explains, an entitlement to a trade secret, protected by a seemingly *well-being and hypothetical consent* rationale, is importantly different from the sorts of entitlements discussed thus far.[147] The mere appropriation – albeit a conscious one – of the entitlement is not actionable. A certain component of impropriety is also needed to render the invasion wrongful and therefore trigger liability.[148] A trade secret has some similarities to intellectual properties, but it is the least connected to its holder's identity, and it would appear that an entitlement to a trade secret is accordingly quite weak; as long as the defendant appropriates the trade

[142] See *Restatement (Third) of Unfair Competition* § 40(a) and comment b (1995). Similarly, according to the pre-UTSA law, the protection was "merely against breach of faith and reprehensible means of learning another's secret." See *Restatement (First) of Torts* § 757 comment b (1939).

[143] *Kewanee Oil Co.* v. *Bicron Corp.*, 416 US 470, 476, 481–82 (1974).

[144] See, e.g., Uniform Trade Secrets Act § 1 comment, 14 ULA 438 (1990); *Restatement (Third) of Unfair Competition* § 43 and comments b–c (1995); *Sheets* v. *Yamaha Motors Corp.*, 849 F 2d 179, 183–84 (5th Cir. 1988); *Kewanee Oil Co.* v. *Bicron Corp.*, 416 US 470, 476 (1974). See also Donald M. Zupanec, "Annotation, Disclosure of Trade Secrets as Abandonment of Secrecy," 92 ALR 3d 138 (1982); Wiesner and Cava, "Stealing Trade Secrets Ethically" at 1,121–25.

[145] See Uniform Trade Secrets Act § 3 comment, 14 ULA 456 (1990); I Palmer, *The Law of Restitution* § 2.8 at 111.

[146] See, e.g., *Winston Research Corp.* v. *Minnesota Mining & Mfg. Co.*, 350 F 2d 134, 144 (9th Cir. 1965).

[147] *Cf.* I Palmer, *The Law of Restitution* § 2.8 at 107.

[148] Uniform Trade Secrets Act, 14 ULA 434 (1990) (prefatory note).

secrets "ethically," the appropriation is legitimate and he is not subject to any legal sanction.[149]

Thus, it stands to reason that the applicable rationale deviates from those discussed thus far. Indeed, as suggested at the end of chapter 3, here we need a new rationale best termed *propriety of means*, underscoring the only claim a holder of such trade secrets has against potential appropriators.

Contractual relations and performances

A contracts to purchase from B 50,000 units of a certain article manufactured by B, at $10 per unit, for a total of $500,000. B's cost of production is $9 per unit; her expected profit is therefore $50,000. C induces A to break his contract with B and buy the same article at the same price from him. C's cost of production is $8 per unit. B is able to mitigate the loss and sell the goods at $9.60 per unit, for a total of $480,000. The reduction in profit to B is thus $20,000, while C has gained $100,000.[150] Is B entitled to C's actual gain (or any part thereof), or is her recovery limited to her own *harm*, i.e., her lost profits?

Although the law on this question is still evolving and not unequivocal,[151] it seems that in this hypothetical case – the case of a commercial contract which does not involve unique goods[152] – the plaintiff will not be able to reap any part of C's actual gain; her recovery will be limited to her own lost profit. One court explains that the aim of awarding damages in tortious interference cases is to preserve the plaintiff's economic position. It further defends the limitation of recovery to the plaintiff's loss even where doing so permits the tortfeasor to retain a portion of its profits: A contract party is permitted – even encouraged – when economically efficient to "buy out" a contract by paying the plaintiff's actual damages; and this is true even if making the plaintiff whole permits the breaching party to retain profits in excess of the plaintiff's loss. "It would be inconsistent to require the party inducing the breaching to disgorge its excess profits while permitting the breaching party to retain its excess profits."[153]

149 *Cf.* Wiesner and Cava, "Stealing Trade Secrets Ethically" at 1,127.

150 The hypothetical is Friedmann's. See Friedmann, "Restitution of Benefits" at 553.

151 A caveat to the *Restatement of Restitution* § 133 comment c (1937) states that "[t]he institute takes no position" as to the restitutionary duty in cases of profits from tortious interference with contractual relations. On the other hand, in II *Restatement (Second) of Restitution* 140 (Tentative Draft, 1983–84) an introductory note to chapter 4 states that "prospective § 56 [which thus far was not articulated] states a rule of liability [in restitution for such cases]." There is no hint as to what the contours of this liability are.

152 The analysis of this section is strictly confined to this sort of contract.

153 *Marcus, Stowell & Beye Government Sec. Inc.* v. *Jefferson Inv. Corp.*, 797 F 2d 227, 231–32 (5th Cir. 1986). See also *Gonzales* v. *Kentucky Derby Co.*, 189 NYS 783, 786 (App. Div.

None the less, some cases – which are frequently cited as evidence for an opposite rule – have allowed a recovery based upon the gain realized by the tortfeasor. Some of these cases use the defendant's profits merely as evidence of the plaintiff's lost profits which were diverted to the defendant who is, in most such cases, her sole competitor.[154] These cases cannot of course support an opposite conclusion to the one stated above.

More interesting cases which *do* qualify, but do not reverse, the broad rule which limits recovery to the plaintiff's loss implicate some element of reprehensible behavior of the defendant. Thus, in cases, but only in cases,[155] where the party inducing the breaching utilizes means such as intimidating tactics,[156] "flagrant commercial bribery,"[157] or fraudulent misrepresentations in abuse of governmental responsibilities,[158] a plaintiff was allowed to recover – alternatively to her own lost profits – the profits secured by the defendant due to the use of such means.[159] The focus of this sub-rule is the

1921), affirmed, 135 NE 938 (1922); *American Air Filter Co.* v *Michael J. McNichol and John F. Scanlan Inc.*, 527 F 2d 1,297, 1,300 (3rd Cir. 1975); *McRoberts Protective Agency Inc.* v. *Lansdell Protective Agency Inc.*, 403 NYS 2d 511, 513–14 (App. Div. 1978); *Ramona Manor Convalescent Hosp.* v. *Care Enterprises*, 225 Cal. Rptr. 120, 130 (Ct. App. 1986); *Dorsett Carpet Mills Inc.* v. *Whitt Tile & Marble Distributing Co.*, 734 SW 2d 322, 325 (Tennessee 1987); *Developers Three, A Partnership* v. *Nationwide Ins. Co.*, 582 NE 2d 1,130, 1,136 (Ohio App. 1990). An even weaker case for disgorging the profits of the party inducing the breach exists where the contract at issue is for personal services. Early decisions in Anglo-American jurisprudence support, however, such a remedy. See, e.g., *Lightly* v. *Clouston*, 127 Eng. Rep. 774, 775 (CP 1808); I Palmer, *The Law of Restitution* § 2.6 at 85–87. But such a view is not generally espoused. See R. M. Jackson, *The History of Quasi-Contract in English Law* 80 (1936); Sir P. H. Winfield, *The Law of Quasi-Contracts* 99 (1952); Frederic C. Woodward, *The Law of Quasi Contracts* § 285(4) (1913); Friedmann, "Restitution of Benefits" at 528. But see I Palmer, *The Law of Restitution*, *ibid.*

154 See *Automatic Laundry Serv. Inc.* v. *Demas*, 141 A 2d 497 (Maryland 1958); *Ramona Manor Convalescent Hosp.* v. *Care Enterprises*, 225 Cal. Rptr. 120, 130 (Ct. App. 1986); *Fleer Corp.* v. *Topps Chewing Gum Inc.*, 539 A 2d 1,060 (Delaware 1988); *Sandare Chem.* v. *Wako International Co.*, 820 SW 2d 21, 23–24 (Texas App. 1991). See also *Caskie* v. *Philadelphia Rapid Transit Co.*, 184 A. 17 (Pennsylvania 1936); *Second National Bank of Toledo* v. *M. Samuel & Sons Inc.*, 12 F 2d 963 (1926), cert. denied, 273 US 720 (1926).

155 *Cf.* Dobbs, *Handbook on the Law of Remedies* at § 6.6(3). But see *Colorado Interstate Gas Co.* v. *Natural Gas Pipeline Co. of America*, 885 F 2d 683, 691 note 12 (10 Cir. 1989); I Palmer, *The Law of Restitution* § 2.6. But *cf.* Friedmann, *The Law of Unjust Enrichment* at Supplement 60–61 (in jurisdictions where specific performance is a primary remedy – i.e., where the efficient breach theory is rejected – restitutionary damages should be available for tortious interference with contract).

156 See *Schechter* v. *Friedman*, 57 A 2d 251, 253 (New Jersey 1948).

157 See *Phillips Chemical Co.* v. *Morgan*, 440 So. 2d 1,292 (Florida App. 1983).

158 See the celebrated case of *Federal Sugar Refining Co.* v. *US Sugar Equalization*, 268 F. 575 (SDNY 1920), helpfully discussed in I Palmer, *The Law of Restitution* § 2.6 at 81–82.

159 *Cf.* Birks, *An Introduction to the Law of Restitution* at 336–38; Douthwaite, *Attorney Guide to Restitution* § 5.8 at 237–38; Friedmann, "Restitution of Benefits" at 554.

nature of the improper conduct;[160] its purpose is to deter such undesirable demeanor and not merely to protect the plaintiff's entitlement in her contractual relationships.[161]

Finally, *National Merchandising Corp.* v. *Leyden*[162] is often cited for its proposition that an unjust enrichment measure is appropriate as an alternative premise to a lost-profits award for willful interference with contractual relations. As the court explains, "an intending tortfeasor should not be prompted to speculate that his profits might exceed the injuring party's losses thus encouraging the commission of the tort."[163] None the less, it is far from clear whether the defendant's profits actually exceeded the plaintiff's loss, and the *Leyden* court noted that its conclusion was based in part on the difficulty in determining the plaintiff's loss. Thus, one subsequent case theorizes that *Leyden* may be "simply a case where the plaintiff's loss could not be accurately determined thereby requiring the court to look to the defendant's profits."[164] Moreover, *Leyden* also complies with the second group of cases just mentioned, since the defendants "knowingly abetted the violation of a decree and could very likely have been charged themselves with a civil contempt which can readily entail a disgorging of profits by the contemnor."[165]

To summarize, contractual relations and performances are perceived as pure economic resources with no unique flavor of their holder's personality. Correspondingly, the rationale pertaining to contracts seems to be bifurcated.

In the typical case, the measure of recovery is the resource-holder's lost profits. This certainly constitutes the plaintiff's *harm*. It is however hard to distinguish it from the *fair market value* of the plaintiff's entitlement especially since the cases emphasize the goal of preserving her level of welfare. Thus, the applicable rationale is *sharing/well-being*.

Alternatively, if the defendant's profits are tainted by certain condemnable behavior which deviates from the mere inducement of breaching her contract, the more rigorous remedy of *profits* applies. In the case of contracts

160 See *American Air Filter Co. v Michael J. McNichol and John F. Scanlan Inc.*, 527 F 2d 1,297, 1,300 note 8 (3rd Cir. 1975) (distinguishing *Certified Lab. of Texas Inc.* v. *Rubinson*, 303 F Supp. 1,014 (Eastern District of Pennsylvania 1969)).

161 *Cf. Marcus, Stowell & Beye Government Sec. Inc.* v. *Jefferson Inv. Corp.*, 797 F 2d 227, 232 (5th Cir. 1986); *Developers Three, A Partnership* v. *Nationwide Ins. Co.*, 582 NE 2d 1,130, 1,136 (Ohio App. 1990).

162 348 NE 2d 771 (Massachusetts 1976).

163 *Ibid.* at 776.

164 See *Marcus, Stowell & Beye Government Sec. Inc.* v. *Jefferson Inv. Corp.*, 797 F 2d 227, 231 note 5 (5th Cir. 1986).

165 *National Merchandising Corp.* v. *Leyden*, 348 NE 2d 771, 775 (Massachusetts 1976).

this measure is only aimed at deterring any potential invader from resorting to improper means. It points to the rationale first introduced in the discussion of trade secrets, i.e., *propriety of means.*

Pre-contractual expectations

As an extension to the tort of intentional interference with the performance of a contract, American law recognizes and protects certain reasonable pre-contractual expectations against certain types of interference.[166] As may have been expected, the entitlement attached by tort law to such prospective economic advantages is relatively thin, and the mere diversion of the plaintiff's trade does not suffice to trigger liability.[167] It is only "the right to do business in a fair setting that is protected."[168]

Application of unjust enrichment law to the circumstances under consideration is still in the initial stages of development. None the less, the importation of the restitutionary doctrine seems to lead the pertinent case law in two important directions: remedial and substantive.

The remedial prong supplements the tort harm-based remedies with a restitution profits-based remedy. Such supplementation underscores the impropriety of certain indecent tactics, notably false representation, and deters any potential defendant from overstepping the lines of fair competition.[169]

The substantive prong, on the other hand, broadens the contours of the tort claim by recognizing claims for takings of certain types of expectations – notably of the "new property" variety – although no improper conduct exists. Such a remedy was developed in the context of federal contract awards under the Small Business Act[170] where courts have vindicated the claim of the second-lowest bidder against the successful bidder who did not qualify as a small business.[171] Here, the decisions seem to be divided along the line of decisions regarding interference with contracts: where the defendant's misrepresentation as to his eligibility is fraudulent, a profits-based recovery may be awarded;[172] but where no malicious conduct is

166 See generally W. Page Keeton *et al.*, *Prosser and Keeton on the Law of Torts* 1,005–12 (5th edn. 1984).

167 See *International News Service* v. *Associated Press*, 248 US 215, 259 (1918) (Brandeis J, dissenting).

168 See, e.g., *Utah Foam Products Inc.* v. *Polytec Inc.*, 584 So. 2d 1,345, 1,353 (Alabama 1991).

169 See *Zippertubing Co.* v. *Teleflex Inc.*, 757 F 2d 1,401, 1,411 (3rd Cir. 1985).

170 Small Business Act of 1978, 15 USC § 631.

171 See *Iconco, A Corp.* v. *Jensen Construction Co.*, 622 F 2d 1,291 (8th Cir. 1980). Although there was initially some dispute with regard to *Iconco's* new cause of action, it seems that its rule does reflect an emerging consensus. See, e.g., *Fordice Construction Co.* v. *Central States Dredging Co.*, 631 F Supp. 1,536 (Southern District of Mississippi 1986).

proved, the plaintiff is entitled only to her lost profits.[173]

In conclusion, expectations are generally subject to a *propriety of means* rationale with a *profits* measure of recovery to deter any deviation therefrom. "New property" types of expectations, however, are increasingly considered as an essential part of their holder's well-being (although in many cases it would be farfetched to connect them with their holders' personality).[174] Hence, these types of expectations become favorably discriminated and are protected also against "non-degrading" invasions. Even where no improper means is utilized, the appropriator of such resource has to restore the plaintiff's *ex ante* level of welfare.

Summary

The materials of this chapter cover a wide array of resources and prescribe pecuniary remedies with regard to various sorts of invasions. The heterogeneity and diversity of the doctrine may be *a priori* perplexing. But once the doctrine is analyzed by the translation scheme of the first section of chapter 2, and explained by the personhood perspective of the fourth section of chapter 2, order comes to view. The measures of recovery are translated into a variety of rationales whose variety is explicated in turn by means of a personhood continuum.

Thus, resources such as one's identity, physical integrity, reputation (as dignity), and land, which are perceived as intrinsically attached to the actor's identity, rank high in the generated spectrum of protected interests. Other resources, like copyright, and (to a lesser degree) commercial attributes of personality and patents are less personal, and hence protected by relatively less stringent rationales. Finally, excepting the thin category of private necessity, only a relatively narrow variety of resources, which rank low in the protected-interests spectrum, are there to be shared. The mere appropriation of information or of "regular" pre-contractual expectation is

[172] See *Nationwide Roofing & Sheet Metal Inc.*, v. *Trotwood Heating Inc.*, 520 NE 2d 602 (Ohio Ct. App. 1987).

[173] See *Integrity Management International Inc.* v. *Tombs & Sons Inc.*, No. 83-4231-O, 1988 US District, Lexis 7,162 at *11 (District of Kansas June 20, 1988). *Cf.* I Palmer, *The Law of Restitution* § 2.6A. But see *Nationwide Roofing & Sheet Metal Inc.*, v. *Trotwood Heating Inc.*, 520 NE 2d 602, 604 (Ohio Ct. App. 1987). But *cf. Stoke-on-Trent City Council* v. *W. & J. Wass Ltd.*, [1988] 1 WLR 1,406, 1,418–19 (Court of Appeal) (England).

[174] Charles Reich, who introduced the concept of the New Property, acknowledged this heterogeneity. See Charles Reich, "The New Property," 73 *Yale Law Journal* 733, 785–86 (1964).

Table 2 *Measures of recovery and rationales applicable to various resources in American law*

The resource		Measures of recovery	Rationale
Identity		The greater of fair market value and profits	Well-being and control
Physical integrity		Proceeds/profits	Control [and condemnation]
Individual reputation and dignity		Profits	Control
Commercial attributes of personaltiy		Fair market value	Well-being
Land		The greater of fair market value and profits	Well-being and control
Chattels		The greater of fair market value and profits/ proportional profits	Well-being and [hypothetical consent/control]
Tangible property – private necessity		Harm	Sharing
Copyright		The greater of fair market value and proportional profits	Well-being and hypothetical consent
Trademark	as a symbol of commercial identity	The greater of fair market value and proportional profits	Well-being and hypothetical consent
	as a pure commercial attribute	Harm	Propriety of means
Patent		Fair market value	Well-being
Information		The greater of fair market value and proportional profits	Propriety of means
Contractual relations and performances		Harm/fair market value	Sharing/well-being
		Profits	Propriety of means
Pre-contractual expectations	'regular'	Profits	Propriety of means
	'new property'	Harm/fair market value	Sharing/well-being
		Profits	Propriety of means

legitimate, and the only entitlement of their holder is to the propriety of means utilized in the process of such an invasion.

The importance of the defendant's culpability was the subject of certain disagreement between George Palmer and John Dawson – the two leading American restitution scholars.[175] The findings of this chapter, however, suggest that impropriety of means is neither significant nor insignificant across the board. Instead, it becomes important only where relatively "weak" resources are at stake. That is, the type of the resource seems to be of primary importance, whereas the nature of the wrongful act plays only a secondary role.

Table 2 summarizes the conclusions of this chapter.

[175] See Laycock, *Modern American Remedies* at 534.

5 Talmudic civil law

Leaving the home court of American law in favor of Talmudic civil law and, in the next chapter, international law, entails some of the dangers of reporting as a tourist rather than a resident. This change in one's viewpoint seems especially venturesome regarding Talmudic civil law. The term Talmudic civil law refers to the legal – as distinguished from religious – part of the Jewish *Halakhah*, but the legal and the religious are inextricably woven together in the *Halakhah*, a fact which leads to numerous interpretive difficulties. Moreover, Talmudic civil law is the most ancient legal system which is still operative today. It is rooted in the Mosaic promulgation and has succeeded in maintaining uninterrupted development and continuity until and including this time.[1] And, finally, the abundance of various legal sources – not all of which are easily accessible to the modern non-orthodox lawyer – only adds to the caution with which I approach this chapter.[2]

None the less, I hope to demonstrate that – at least in so far as this book is concerned – the voyage is worthwhile: exploring the Jewish heritage and contrasting it with the American doctrine examined before demonstrates the accuracy of my retrodictions and hence supports the plausibility of my theory.

As may be recalled, I have concluded that – at least in comparison to American law – Judaic law is expected to frequently apply *sharing*. *Sharing* corresponds to Judaism's fundamental maxim of mutual responsibility. Moreover, the existence of a parallel social phenomenon of private

[1] See Aaron Kirschenbaum, *Equity in Jewish Law: Halakhaic Perspective in Law: Formalism and Flexibility in Jewish Civil Law* xxii–xxiv (1991).

[2] The methodological difficulties which derive from the properties of Talmudic civil law alluded to in the text are most critically introduced in Izhak Englard, "Research on Jewish Law: Its Nature and Function," 7 *Mishpatim* 34 (1976). No less forceful a reply is found in Menachem Elon, "More About Research into Jewish Law," 8 *Mishpatim* 99 (1977).

responsibility in the Jewish tradition, *tzedakah*, facilitated some specific conclusions regarding the circumstances in which *sharing* is expected to be at work. In particular, *tzedakah* suggests that *sharing* will apply if, and only if, (i) the defendant is in *need*; and (ii) the appropriation of the plaintiff's resource does not actually harm her (in the sense of diminishing the value of her estate or preventing her from capturing some expected gains she would have secured but for the invasion).

This chapter examines the specific rules of Talmudic civil law and demonstrates the accuracy of these retrodictions. But before embarking on this task, we need some preliminary remarks with respect to Talmudic civil law in general[3] and its doctrine of unjust enrichment in particular.

The fountain of authority and starting point of the entire *Halakhah* is the Bible, the basic norm for Judaism. Next to it, in chronology and authority, is the Talmud, the unquestioned premise of rabbinic jurisprudence, literally unchallenged by subsequent religious leaders and teachers. The Talmud collects studies and interpretations of scripture, traditions and innovations, discussions and debates of the great religious authorities of approximately 1,000 years (450 BCE to 550 CE). A Talmudic discussion opens with the recitation of a *Mishnah* and is followed by its *Gemara*. The *Mishnah* is a teaching of a *tanna* (teacher in Aramaic) or a debate between two *tannaim* (teachers) as recorded by the first compilation of the Oral Law (edited in 200 CE). The *Gemara* which follows is a study of the *Mishnah* by the scholars of the next 300 years who were called *amoraim*, expositors. It considers the authorship of the *Mishnah*, its scriptural underpinnings, its juridical basis, and its relationship to other similar *tannaic* statements.[4] Since there were schools of *amoraim* in Palestine and other schools in Babylonia, the products of their books are called Palestinian *Gemara* and Babylonian *Gemara*, and the generated Talmuds are the Palestinian Talmud and the Babylonian Talmud, respectively. The more authoritative of these two Talmuds is the Babylonian (hereinafter referred to simply as "the Talmud").

The post-Talmudic legal literature to this very day includes three genres: (i) commentaries or *novellae* (*hidushim*, creative commentaries) of older authoritative books, notably the Talmud;[5] (ii) codes, which are authoritative summations of the law; the definite code of the *Halakhah* to this very day is

[3] For a systematic description of the sources of the *Halakhah*, see Menachem Elon, *Jewish Law: History, Sources, Principles* (1994). The following materials are based on Kirschenbaum, *Equity in Jewish Law* at 289–304.

[4] The other *tannaic* statements with which the *Mishnah* is confronted are usually outside of the *Mishnah* collection and hence are termed *baraitot* (*baraita* meaning outside).

[5] The most authoritative commentary to the Talmud is that of Rashi (d. 1105).

the *Shulhan Arukh* by R. Joseph Caro of Sefad (d. 1575), an essentially Sepharadic code which gained universal acceptance when it was appended by glosses of R. Moses Isserles, Rema, of Poland (d. 1572);[6] and (iii) responsa, or *she'elot u-teshuvot* (queries and replies), which are rabbinic decisions in actual cases emanating from a great variety of countries and spanning well over 1,000 years.

The jurisprudence embodied in these sources is unique in many ways, but two characteristics are of major importance for this study: (i) Talmudic civil law is premised upon a certain set of values perceived as the divine attributes of justice and mercy which man is to imitate;[7] among such values, this book highlights the Judaic distributive scheme which is said to be at work in shaping the specific rules of the Talmudic doctrine of unjust enrichment; and (ii) Talmudic civil law is grasped as a medium for achieving changes in social norms, to educate the Jew to behave in accordance with the divine values. The law is thus perceived as a reformative institution, influencing character by regulating behavior, so that character, as it emerges, will regulate behavior in turn.[8] Thus, Talmudic civil law openly admits, and embraces, the formative function of law.

As this chapter demonstrates, our specific field of inquiry – the Judaic concept of unjust enrichment – posits no exception to these characteristics of Talmudic civil law. Based on a *Gemaraic sugya* (a discussion of the *amoraim*), the rabbis of Spain (*Sepharad*) and Franco-Germany (*Ashkenaz*) have articulated – primarily during the period of the *rishonim* (earlier authorities), i.e., 1000–1500 CE[9] – a full-blown doctrine. These teachings define practical rules[10] which are based on highly theoretical grounds and a

6 The other four major medieval codes are: *Sefer Halakhot* by R. Isaac Alfasi, Rif, of North Africa (d. 1103); *Mishneh Torah* (or *Yad Hahazakah*) by Maimonides, Rambam, of Spain–Egypt (d. 1204); *Piskei Ha-Rosh* (or *Hilkhot Ha-Rosh*) by R. Asher b. Yehiel, Rosh, of Germany and Spain (d. 1327); *Arba'ah Turim* by R. Jacob, the son of Rosh (known as the Tur) (d. 1340).

7 See Kirschenbaum, *Equity in Jewish Law* at 37, 48. See also, e.g., Ze'ev W. Falk, *Legal Values and Judaism: Towards a Philosophy of Halakha* 18, 26 (1980).

8 See, e.g., Lenn E. Goodman, *On Justice: An Essay in Jewish Philosophy* 35, 37 (1991); Boaz Cohen, "Law and Ethics in Light of the Jewish Tradition," in *Law and Tradition in Judaism* 182, 221 (1959).

9 See Kirschenbaum, *Equity in Jewish Law* at 231–32.

10 There are indeed many disputes and differing, sometimes conflicting, views regarding most of the rules of the doctrine. See, e.g. Berahyahu Lifshitz, "'One Derives a Benefit and the Other Sustains no Loss' – 'The Receipt of the Benefit did not Involve a Loss to the Benefactor'"? 37 *Hapraklit* 203, 204 (1986). None the less, as in a modern federative legal system, one can single out a dominant view, considering especially the weight of the advocates of each persuasion. *Cf.* Suzanne Last Stone, "In Pursuit of the Counter-Text: The Turn to the Jewish Legal Model in Contemporary American Legal Theory," 106 *Harvard Law Review* 813, 852–55, 860 (1993).

deliberate consideration of the purposes of each rule and the consequences of its adoption. Unlike its American counterpart, the Judaic theoretical discourse respecting our paradigm is intensive, and the doctrine has acquired a pivotal position in Judaic jurisprudence.[11] More importantly, the Judaic doctrine appears substantively different from its American counterpart.[12] Analyzed from the perspective of this book's theory, the specific rules of the doctrine correspond with what has been projected from the Judaic ethos. Similarly, the differences from American law are most easily explicable by reference to the differences between the Jewish and the American ethoses.

The first section of this chapter presents the *Gemaraic sugya* from which the doctrine of our paradigm emerges. It further alludes to some doctrinal premises suggested for the exemptive rule which governs our paradigm. The second section of this chapter adds some details and complexities of the doctrine, studying four important exceptions to the exemptive rule. The third section of this chapter returns to the thesis of this book. It shows the validity of the conclusions the theory generates. It also demonstrates how the Judaic cultural ideology gives coherence to the complex doctrine as a whole and explicates the important differences between it and its American counterpart.

The exemptive rule

The *Gemaraic sugya* starts by delineating the contours of the case under consideration:

R. Hisda said to Rami b. Hama: You were not yesterday with us in the House of Study where there were discussed some specially interesting matters. The other thereupon asked him: What were the specially interesting matters? He answered: [The discussion was whether] one who occupied his neighbor's premises unbeknown to him would have to pay rent [for the past] or not. But under what circumstances?

It could hardly be supposed that the premises were not for hire [and would in any case have remained vacant], and he [the one who occupied them] was similarly a man who was not in the habit of hiring any [as he had friends who were willing to accommodate him without any pay], for [what liability could there be attached to a case where] the defendant derived no benefit and the plaintiff sustained no loss? If on the other hand the premises were for hire and he was a man whose wont it

[11] *Cf.* Bernard S. Jackson, "Introduction to Symposium: Unjust Enrichment," 3 *Jewish Law Annual* 3, 6 (1980).

[12] See, e.g., Kirschenbaum, *Equity in Jewish Law* at 241, 252. But see Irwin H. Haut, "Abuse of Rights and Unjust Enrichment: A Proposed Restatement of Jewish Law," 2 *National Jewish Law Review* 31, 59–60 (1987).

was to hire premises, [why should no liability attach since] the defendant derived a benefit and the plaintiff sustained a loss?

No; the problem arises in a case where the premises were not for hire, but his wont was to hire premises. What therefore should be the law? Is the occupier entitled to plead [against the other party]: "What loss have I caused to you [since your premises were in any case not for hire]?" Or might the other party retort: "Since you have derived a benefit [as otherwise you would have had to hire premises], you must pay rent accordingly"?[13]

The Talmud narrows down the problem at hand to our paradigm. In passing, it assumes that if the defendant derived no benefit and the plaintiff sustained no loss, no liability attaches. The Talmudic passage similarly conceives as non-controversial the defendant's liability where he did derive a benefit and the plaintiff did sustain a loss.[14] But the "specially interesting" question, according to R. Hisda, arises in an extreme case of our paradigm: where the defendant derives a benefit and the plaintiff sustains no loss, for example where the premises of the plaintiff-landowner were not for hire (so that the *harm* was zero), and the defendant-squatter had no alternative accommodation.[15] Is the squatter liable to pay the owner the rental value of his residency in the premises for the period of his unauthorized sojourn there?

The rest of our *sugya* struggles with this difficult question, presenting a most extensive and hot debate between the participating *amoraim*.[16] Five

[13] *Babylonian Talmud, Baba Kamma* 20a–21a (I. Epstein ed. and E. W. Kirzner trans. 1977). Both the additions of the translator and those of his notes which seem helpful for this chapter appear in the text itself, bracketed.

[14] The discussion at pp. 115–17 below, however, considers the applicable measure of recovery where the defendant derived a benefit and the plaintiff sustained a loss. The fourth case, in which the defendant derived no benefit but the plaintiff sustained a loss, is not referred to by the *Gemara* and is beyond the scope of this chapter: this case is discussed in Norman Solomon, "Concepts of Zeh Neheneh . . . in the Analytic School," 3 *Jewish Law Annual* 49, 52–53 (1980).

[15] Towards the end of our *sugya* there is an additional passage which seems to suggest that the decisive factor for the exemptive rule is the benefit which the owner may derive from the squatting. This passage can thus imply that if the occupation does not benefit the owner, the squatter is liable. Although some authorities follow this conclusion, the majority view ignores it and regards the exemption as a function only of the circumstances to which the text above alludes. For documentation, see Kirschenbaum, *Equity in Jewish Law* at 204 and notes 70–71; Nahum Rakover, *Unjust Enrichment in Jewish Law* 34–35 (1987); Aharon Lichtenstein, "Towards an Understanding of 'Coercion over Sodom Qualities,'" in I *Hagut Ivrit Be'Amerika* 362, 370 note 36 (M. Zohori *et al.* eds. 1972).

[16] Talmudic Source Criticism scholars suggest that three different sources, of *amoraim* from different generations, are woven together in the composition of our *sugya*. See Haut, "Abuse of Rights and Unjust Enrichment" at 37 note 36.

tannaic statements are invoked as precedents for one view or another, and the fine points of each are discussed and ultimately rejected. The *Gemara* eventually concludes with no Talmudic resolution of the question, but with what appears to be a majority opinion in favor of exempting the squatter.[17] Latter codes – as authoritative as Maimonides' *Mishneh Torah*[18] and the *Shulhan Arukh*[19] – adopt this "exemptive rule" as the cornerstone of the unjust-enrichment doctrine of Talmudic civil law. The exemptive rule prescribes that where "the one derives a benefit and the other sustains no loss," no payment for the benefit need be made (*Zeh neheneh ve-zeh lo hasser patur*). Contemporary scholars follow this rule.[20]

The robust post-Talmudic literature occupied itself with two main tasks: defining the precise circumstances in which the exemptive rule applies and studying the doctrinal basis for its application. The former objective is of paramount importance for this book and will be studied in some detail in the following pages. In contrast, the latter goal is not very significant for a study which is generally uninterested in classifications. None the less, mentioning one of the suggested grounds for the exemptive rule – known as *Kofin* – can still help understand the thrust of our doctrine.[21]

The rule of *Kofin al Middat Sodom* (literally: coercing not to act in the manner of the Sodomite[22]) holds that if B has a legal right and the infringement upon such right by A generates no loss to B and at the same time affords A the opportunity to secure a benefit or avoid a loss, then the advantage-taking (free of charge) of B's right is (*ex ante*!) allowed, even coerced.[23] This rule springs from Judaism's condemnation of the practice of inordinary standing upon one's proprietary rights; it reflects the law's

[17] See, e.g., Kirschenbaum, *Equity in Jewish Law* at 195; Rakover, *Unjust Enrichment* at 20.

[18] See Maimonides, *Torts, Robbery and Lost Articles* 3:9.

[19] See *Shulhan Arukh, Hoshen Mishpat* 363:6.

[20] See, e.g., Isaac Herzog, "Quasi Contract," in II *The Main Institutions of Jewish Law: The Law of Obligations* 54 (2nd edn. 1967); Kirschenbaum, *Equity in Jewish Law* at 188, 190, 204; Zeh Neheneh Ve-zeh Lo Haser, in XII *Encyclopedia Talmudit* 1, 3 (1967).

[21] A strong supporter of the view that finds the doctrinal basis of the exemptive rule in *Kofin* is R. Jacob Joshua Falk (d. 1756). See his *Pnei Yehoshua to Baba Kamma* 20a. See also, e.g., Solomon, "Concepts of Zeh Neheneh" at 55–62 (discussing the same view as deliberated in the *Novellae of R. Hayyim of Telz to Baba Batra* 109). The other suggested grounds for exemption are implied waiver, lack of legal claim, and lack of standing. See respectively, e.g., R. Efrayim Navon, *Mahane Efrayim, Hilkhot Gezela*, 10; *Novellae of R. Shim'on Yehuda Ha-Kohen to Baba Kamma* 19:3; *Novellae of R. Hayyim of Telz to Baba Kamma* 39.

[22] In scripture, Sodom is the embodiment of evil, known for the cruelties perpetrated by its inhabitants. See, e.g., Kirschenbaum, *Equity in Jewish Law* at 188–89.

[23] For a detailed discussion of the *Kofin* doctrine see, e.g., Shmuel Shilo, "'Kofin Al Midat Sdom': Jewish Law's Concept of Abuse of Rights," 15 *Israel Law Review* 49 (1980).

regard of the denial of a benefit from one's fellow even though that benefit is of no cost to oneself as reprehensible and morally defective.[24]

The claim that the exemptive rule stems from *Kofin* was subject to some criticism. The critics who dispute this contention focus especially on the lack of cross-references between the Talmudic discussions of these two doctrines and the difference between the *ex post* perspective of the exemptive rule and the *ex ante* outlook of *Kofin*.[25] But this debate need not be resolved, or even addressed, here. For our purposes suffice it to acknowledge that both *Kofin* and the exemptive rule spring from the same ethical concerns; that they both reflect the Judaic underlying philosophy of mutual responsibility.[26]

This close connection between ethos and doctrine is not only manifested with regard to the exemptive rule itself, but also appears throughout our doctrine's details and specifics. The following section considers these details. It discusses the exceptions to the exemptive rule. Furthermore, it demonstrates the correspondence between the subtleties of the legal rules and the nuances of the mutual responsibility outlook.

Some exceptions

Some loss to the plaintiff

As formulated, the exemptive rule does not apply where the plaintiff sustains a loss, and our *sugya* even starts with the assumption that if such a loss is sustained, liability does attach. However, two main questions arise in understanding this exception. (i) What constitutes "loss" which triggers its applicability? Does it include, more particularly, the owner's lost opportunity to bargain with the squatter himself for the use of the premises? (ii) What measure of recovery applies in the circumstances of the exception? That is, would the squatter of our *sugya* be liable for the loss he inflicted upon the landowner, or would the latter be entitled to the benefit such a squatter captured even if such benefit exceeds the owner's loss? And, how does Talmudic civil law justify the applicable measure of recovery? These

[24] See, e.g., Kirschenbaum, *Equity in Jewish Law* at 185–86.

[25] See, e.g., Haut, "Abuse of Rights and Unjust Enrichment" at 37, 41–42; Rakover, *Unjust Enrichment* at 20–21. Other objections are interpretive. See Kirschenbaum, *Equity in Jewish Law* at 306; Haut, "Abuse of Rights and Unjust Enrichment" at 42, 44, 49; Solomon, "Concepts of Zeh Neheneh" at 53, 59.

[26] The common ethical foundations of the *Kofin* rule and the exemptive rule of our paradigm probably explain why the cases and opinions which consider these sister doctrines frequently converge. See Kirschenbaum, *Equity in Jewish Law* at 198; Lifshitz, "One Derives a Benefit" at 218.

questions, focal to the analysis of this study, are the subject of extensive deliberation in the post-Talmudic literature.

We will begin with the second of these questions: the applicable measure of recovery. Among the *rishonim* who shaped the contours of our doctrine, a clear majority opinion emerges. The majority holds that once the plaintiff establishes her[27] loss, minimal as it may be, the defendant must pay for the entire benefit, even if it indeed exceeds the plaintiff's loss.[28] This norm is said to have its roots in our Talmudic *sugya*. One of the *tannaic* statements cited by our *Gemara* as an apparent proof for the view that the squatter is liable is a dictum made by R. Judah. Respecting a complicated fact pattern, R. Judah opined that a dweller in newly built premises is liable to pay rent although the homeowner was uninterested in the use of his property and thus apparently sustained no loss. Interpreting this opinion, the *amoraim* conclude that it cannot support a parallel view regarding the case of the squatter. The reason for distinguishing R. Judah's opinion is that the dweller's liability in that case is based on "the blackening of the walls," i.e., on the loss to the owner of his walls' newness generated by the ordinary occupancy and use of the dweller. Hence, the *Gemara* implicitly states that if indeed the plaintiff sustains even a slight loss – the defendant is liable and his liability is measured on the basis of the full benefit derived (the rent in the case under consideration), rather than the loss inflicted.

Notwithstanding some opposition which preferred limiting the squatter's liability to the actual *harm* caused,[29] this stricter view, which prescribes gain-based remedy in cases of harmful invasions,[30] has been codified in the *Shulhan Arukh*,[31] and is undisputed by modern Talmudic civil law scholars.[32]

27 Although Talmudic civil law does not use the feminine pronoun, I continue my practice of referring to the plaintiff as a "she."

28 The relevant sources are listed in Jonathan Blass, *Jewish Law for Israel: Unjust Enrichment Law* 70 note 116 (1991).

29 See *ibid.* at 69.

30 The precise measure of recovery is not, however, very clear in Talmudic civil law since it is not easy to distinguish the cases in which the award is limited to *fair market value* from those in which it extends to *profits* (or any portion thereof). For an attempt to solve this puzzle see Blass, *Jewish Law for Israel* at 91–95.

31 See *Shulhan Arukh, Hoshen Mishpat* 363:7.

32 See Blass, *Jewish Law for Israel* at 69–70; Herzog, "Quasi-Contract" at 55; Kirschenbaum, *Equity in Jewish Law* 195, 213; Rakover, *Unjust Enrichment* at 31; Lifshitz, "One Derives a Benefit" at 207–08. For interesting attempts to reconcile the competing views alluded to in the text or to find an intermediate path between them, see R. Ezekiel Landau, II *Responsa Noda Bihudah, Hoshen Mishpat, responsum* 24 (implying that where the loss is substantial, a gain-based recovery would be appropriate even according to the minority view); R. Abraham Samuel of Raseiniai, *Responsa Amudei Esh* 67b–67c (interpreting the minority view as intended to apply where the owner would waive

Prescribing a gain-based recovery in the "loss-inflicting squatter" case may seem, at first sight, somewhat surprising given the fundamental exemptive rule that governs our paradigm. None the less, as proponents of the view tying the exemptive rule with *Kofin* happily explain, this exception is compatible with the philosophy of *Kofin*: once a loss has been inflicted – no matter how small – insisting on one's proprietary rights can no longer be considered reprehensible (*Middat Sodom*).[33]

But notice that the loss inflicted on the owner does not only negate the justification for exemption. This objective could have been achieved, to be sure, by still limiting recovery to the actual *harm* inflicted. Prescribing a gain-based recovery does more than that, actually deterring a potential squatter from committing such harmful invasions.[34] But why does the law make this dramatic change, and why is it not contented with the mere reversal of the inflicted *harm*? Put differently, what is the reason for choosing the point of "actual-loss-inflicting" as the watershed for discarding the *sharing* rationale in favor of its dichotomous alternatives, be it *well-being* or *control*, both of which are mostly concerned with the plaintiff's interests rather than those of the defendant?

I believe that this choice derives from the doctrine's attempt to delineate carefully the delicate line between *sharing* and *sacrifice*. Where the invasion threatens actually to diminish the value of the plaintiff's estate, it amounts to imposed *sacrifice* and not only imposed *sharing*. At that point, the limited communitarian impulse of Judaism reaches its limits and the law reintroduces the importance of the owner's interests, giving clear priority to the self over the other. One possible way of preventing the apparent slippery slope between *sharing* and *sacrifice* and of vindicating the concern for the legitimate interests of the owner is to prescribe a gain-based recovery which is aimed at deterring any such harmful invasions.

the benefit if only he will be compensated for his loss); R. Isaac Arieli, *Eynayim La-Mishpat, Baba Batra* 4b (at 8b) as analyzed in Blass, *Jewish Law for Israel* at 69 (explaining that the majority view applies in cases where we do not find any reason to justify the defendant's gain from his wrongdoing).

33 See R. Jacob Joshua Falk, *Pnei Yehoshua to Baba Kamma* 20a. Similarly, the plaintiff's implied waiver – which is presumed to apply where no loss is inflicted – is justifiably reversed where the squatter does harm the landowner, and a (presumed) protest comes in its place. See, e.g., R. Abraham Samuel of Raseiniai, *Responsa Amudei Esh* 67c. For an attempt to accommodate the other two suggested premises for the exemptive rule (lack of legal claim and lack of standing) with the rule which prescribes gain-based recovery in cases of harmful invasions, see Blass, *Jewish Law for Israel* at 70. But see Meyer Minkowitch, "Zeh Neheneh Ve-Zeh Lo Hasser," in *Studies in Talmudic Law* 107, 113–14 (1956).

34 See R. Isaac Arieli, *Eynayim La-Mishpat, Baba Batra* 4b (at 8b).

The analysis suggested above is reinforced by examining the doctrinal definition of "loss." "Loss" in the context of our paradigm is carefully specified by Talmudic civil law to include all the components of *harm* as defined in this book.[35] It includes, of course, any actual reduction of the value of the resource invaded, such as the blackening of the walls discussed by the *Gemara*. It also includes "lost profits"; that is, any diversion of expected gains the owner would have secured in his dealings with third parties but for the invasion. The lost-profits alternative is already evident from our *sugya* which assumes that a case in which the squatter did not have alternative accommodation and the premises were for hire – so that a profitable transaction with third parties would have been possible – is non-problematic, since where one derives a benefit and the other sustains a loss liability does attach.[36]

However, in order to establish the lost-profits alternative, Talmudic civil law insists upon the *plaintiff's* showing that at the time the invasion took place she was indeed able and willing to extract profits from the invaded resource. Thus, R. Moses Isserles (the Rema) prescribes that the status of the invaded premises – "for rent" (so that the invasion presumably results in lost profits) or not – is defined according to the specific circumstances of the case. The pertinent question, he explains, is whether the particular owner offered such premises for rent at the particular time the invasion took place, and was moreover in fact present – in person or by an agent – in town, so that he was also able to let the property at that relevant time.[37]

An apparent anomaly is a prescription made by R. Eliezer b. Natan (the Ra'avan) (d. 1170) regarding the "rentability" of houses, as distinct from other types of real property. The Ra'avan declares that "[i]n our times, houses are normally considered as if they were up for rent (this holds true even for those houses that have never been leased before), for everyone who, having his own home, does not use his house for himself rents it to others."[38] Contemporary scholars emphasize, however, the factual premise

[35] There is one proviso to the equation between the "loss" dealt with by Talmudic civil law and harm, i.e., the exclusion of depriving the plaintiff of the enjoyment of his own resource from being a loss for the purposes of triggering the exception to the exemption rule. This proviso seems peculiar and is incoherent particularly given the plaintiff's protest exception to the exemptive rule discussed at pp. 120–21 below. See Blass, *Jewish Law for Israel* at 62–63, 68.

[36] See pp. 112–13 above. See, similarly, R. Ezekiel Landau, II *Responsa Noda Bihudah, Hoshen Mishpat, responsum* 24; R. Abraham Samuel of Raseiniai, *Responsa Amudei Esh* 67b–67c; R. Malkiel Zvi Tennenbaum, *Responsa Divrei Malkiel* 3:157. See also Rakover, *Unjust Enrichment* at 27, 32–34; Blass, *Jewish Law for Israel* at 61, 67–68.

[37] See glosses of the Rema in *Shulhan Arukh, Hoshen Mishpat* 363:6, 10. See also R. Izhak Flakser, "Yishuv Piskei Ha-Rema," 13 *No'am* 51, 59–60 (1970).

[38] See *Sefer Ra'avan, Baba Kamma* 21a (the translation is from Kirschenbaum, *Equity in*

underlying this presumption, suggesting that where houses do not ordinarily stand for rent – the rule may be reversed.[39] This observation seems to limit the conclusiveness of the Ra'avan's presumption to the circumstances of its time of promulgation; it is also insistent that, although the practical result of this presumption is indeed far reaching, its effect is merely evidentiary, and it is not meant to circumvent or frustrate the substantive aspect of the doctrine, i.e., the exemptive rule.

Indeed, lost profits – which are deemed part of the owner's loss – are carefully distinguished by Talmudic civil law from the hypothetical harm of losing the opportunity to bargain with the defendant. Unlike "loss," hypothetical harm does not trigger the application of our exception to the exemptive rule. The law accepts the defendant's claim that, had he known that the owner would charge him for the benefit, he would have deprived himself of such benefit rather than pay what is being charged.[40] Hence, as long as there is any possibility that the defendant could have foregone the benefit – be it by self-deprivation or due to the generosity of other members of the community – the plaintiff's lost opportunity to bargain with the defendant cannot in itself justify the reversal of the exemptive rule, and the defendant is, accordingly, absolved.[41]

In sum, as long as no actual *harm* is being inflicted – be it the diminution of the value of the plaintiff's estate or the diversion of her prospective gains

Jewish Law at 210). This presumption has been codified by the Rema in his gloss to the *Shulhan Arukh, Hoshen Mishpat* 363:6.

[39] See Rakover, *Unjust Enrichment* at 28; Blass, *Jewish Law for Israel* at 61 note 56.

[40] The presumption of unwillingness to pay is problematic in the context of public law: allowing one to enjoy the profit of projects for which he refused to pay the expenses encourages him to freeride the efforts of others. Such difficulties of collective action may, in turn, undermine the community's cohesion which is supposed to be promoted, rather than frustrated, by the mutual-responsibility philosophy which underlies both the exemptive rule and the *Kofin* doctrine. Talmudic civil law is indeed sensitive to this challenge. Thus, one *responsum* issued by R. Yair Hayyim Bachrach of Germany (d. 1701) discusses the acceptability of a stipulation in a contract between some members of a community and an expert of *shofar* blowing, according to which the ritual service is to be performed only in the name of the paying members of the community. In his *responsum*, R. Bachrach is fully aware of the apparent classification of the circumstance as a "one benefits and the other sustains no loss." But he is also attentive to the detrimental incentive effects of applying the *Kofin* rule to the public realm. The result seems unavoidable: the contracting members are allowed to restrict the group of beneficiaries of their enterprise to themselves only. See R. Hayyim Yair Bachrach, *Responsa Havat Yair, responsum* 186. See also R. Meir b. Baruch, IV *Responsa Maharam of Rotenberg, responsum* 39.

[41] For some documentation see Blass, *Jewish Law for Israel* at 12–13 and notes 51–54. For the parallel discourse regarding the definition of "loss" for the purposes of *Kofin* – the sister doctrine of the exemptive rule – see Kirschenbaum, *Equity in Jewish Law* at 199–202, 207–11, 232, 249–50; Lichtenstein, "Towards an Understanding" at 368–70; Shilo, "'Kofin Al Midat Sdom'" at 54–64.

– the applicable rationale is *sharing*. Since, however, in such circumstances there is no actual *harm* to compensate for, the result of a *sharing* rule – which limits recovery to *harm* – is exemption; hence the exemptive rule of our doctrine. On the other hand, where the defendant actually harms the plaintiff, i.e., at the point where real sacrifice is being imposed, the communitarian impulse of Judaism ceases to be operative and the concern for the individual takes its place. This concern is strong enough not only to reverse the *harm* inflicted, but also to seek vindication of the wrongfulness of the invasion. To achieve this latter purpose it dictates a gain-based recovery which discourages the occurrence of such harmful invasions.

The plaintiff's protest

A second exception to the exemptive rule provides that, once the owner has protested the invasion, the squatter is liable for full rent.[42] This rule applies whether the premises are for rent or not, that is whether the owner sustains a loss or simply insists on her proprietary prerogative.[43]

On its face, the applicability of this exception in the "no loss" scenario seems difficult to reconcile with the notion of mutual responsibility which is said to be the underlying thrust of our doctrine. And indeed, at least one rabbi vehemently contests this exception, arguing that, where no loss has been incurred, there is no justification to require the squatter to pay rent even if the owner did protest his sojourn.[44]

The latter view may well be more in line with the communitarian impulse of the Judaic ethos than its antecedent. But notice its startling implications in so far as the owner's independence and control are concerned.[45] The minority view allows others to ignore the wishes of the resource-holder regarding his own property and thus virtually voids his control over it.[46] The Judaic ethos, however, attempts to accommodate personal indepen-

[42] See *Shulhan Arukh, Hoshen Mishpat* 363:6. The protest exception is also said to be derived from our *sugya*. See Rakover, *Unjust Enrichment* at 23 and the sources there.

[43] See *Sefer Me'irat Eynayim to the Shulhan Arukh*, 363:14. *Cf.* the Rema's gloss to the *Shulhan Arukh, Hoshen Mishpat* 363:6 (limiting to a considerable extent the possibility of an *ex ante* curtailment of the owner's entitlement, i.e., the availability of the *Kofin* rule to the squatter case).

[44] See R. David Tevel, *Nahalat David to Baba Kamma* 21a. *Cf.* Kirschenbaum, *Equity in Jewish Law* at 197–98, 204 and note 66, 225–26, 232, 249 (surveying and analyzing a parallel [minority] objection regarding the inapplicability of the *Kofin* rule in the squatter case).

[45] *Cf.* Kirschenbaum, *Equity in Jewish Law* at 203; Lifshitz, "One Derives a Benefit" at 217.

[46] Moreover, the minority ignores the practical ability of the protesting owner to convert the case to a "one derived a benefit and the other sustained a loss." She can simply use the premises in person or put them up for rent.

dence and communal responsibility. It is, therefore, no surprise that it rejects the extreme communitarian rule advanced by the minority.

Instead, in order to allow the owner to keep some measure of control over the resources at her disposal, the doctrine sets an escape option in the form of the protest exception. This option is none the less formulated only as a departure from the general rule. Setting an exception to the exemptive rule which enables the subject of the rule to reverse totally the results prescribed by the rule may seem strange from a contemporary Western point of view. But a legal system – like Talmudic civil law – which openly aspires to educate its constituents to abide themselves by the maxim of mutual responsibility does not hesitate to set such an exception. It respects each resource-holder's ability to be informed by the rule-exception structure of the legal doctrine,[47] and to strike the appropriate balance under the relevant circumstances between herself and her fellow.

Positive enrichment

It is a well-accepted prerequisite for the applicability of the exemptive rule that the defendant does not extract any "positive" gain from the invasion of the plaintiff's resource. This exception delineates the important distinction between mere enjoyment of another's property and generating actual profits from such property. The former case, of the "passive, non-defined benefit,"[48] is represented in the Talmudic discussion by the case of the squatter. This is the case on which the unjust-enrichment doctrine of Talmudic civil law focuses and with regard to which it sets the exemptive rule. This subsection discusses the latter case, of positive enrichment, in which the defendant is generally liable.

Nowhere in the Talmud or the Codes is the exception of positive enrichment discussed as such. None the less, there seems to be unanimity of opinion among both the later medieval authorities and contemporary commentators regarding its validity. Thus, it has been held that the exemptive rule is applicable only to simple acts of enjoyment of another's property – like the squatter's sojourn – where the benefit has been assimilated into one's assets, unidentifiable and unrecognizable as such. But where one uses his fellow's property as a profit-making enterprise to generate an actual, specific gain – i.e., a positive increase in his own wealth

[47] But see Frederick Schauer, *Playing by the Rules: A Philosophical Examination of Rule-Based Decision-Making in Law and in Life* 45 note 7 (1991).

[48] Kirschenbaum, *Equity in Jewish Law* at 238.

– then he must pay for such gain, even if the other has sustained no loss.[49]

The latter rule generalizes a cluster of specific sub-rules. These sub-rules can be divided into two categories.[50] The first deals with cases of transacting business with another's property. It emanates from the following *Mishnah*:

> If a man hires a cow from his neighbor, lends it to another, and it dies a natural death, the hirer must swear that it died naturally, and the borrower must pay the hirer. [A hirer is free from liability in the case of natural death, but not a borrower.] Said R. Jose: How shall one do business with his neighbor's cow? [Surely it is inequitable that the hirer shall be paid for an animal that never belonged to him!] Hence the [value of the] cow must be returned to its owner.[51]

Subsequently, in the post-Talmudic era, R. Jose's position was extended to analogous cases,[52] such as the unauthorized subletting of premises[53] or the case of a converter who rents the converted chattel to a third party.[54] R. Jose's rule was also adopted as law by both Maimonides' *Mishneh Torah*[55] and the *Shulhan Arukh*.[56] Furthermore, the phrase he coined – "How shall one do business with his neighbor's cow?" – has become shorthand for the rule

[49] See R. Hanoch H. Agus, I *Marheshet* 35:2b; Israel Z. Gustman, *Kuntresei Shiurim to Baba Kamma* 12; *Novellae of R. Shim'on Yehuda Ha-Kohen to Baba Kamma* 19:6; R. Joab Joshua Weingarten, *Responsa Helkat Yoav, Hoshen Mishpat* 9; Blass, *Jewish Law for Israel* at 10–13, 53–54; Kirschenbaum, *Equity in Jewish Law* at 198–99, 232, 238; Rakover, *Unjust Enrichment* at 43; Haut, "Abuse of Rights and Unjust Enrichment" at 55–56 and note 158; Lifshitz, "One Derives a Benefit" at 216.

[50] The classification follows Blass, *Jewish Law for Israel* 10–12.

[51] *Mishnah, Baba Mezia* 3:2; *Babylonian Talmud, Baba Mezia* 35b (I. Epstein ed. and H. Freedman trans. 1962). Both the additions of the translator and those of his notes which seem helpful for this chapter appear in the text itself, bracketed.

[52] See also R. Solomon b. Abraham Aderet, *Hidushe Ha-Rashba to Baba Kamma* 21a, who discusses a case in which a squatter – who is not liable for rent according to the exemptive rule – none the less pays such rent to Reuben, whom he mistakenly thinks to be Simeon, the owner of the premises. Although the Rashba hesitates whether the money should be paid to the owner or remitted to the squatter, he has no doubt whatsoever that Reuben is not to be allowed to keep the payment, i.e., that R. Jose's rule governs the Reuben–Simeon relationships.

[53] See R. Joseph Habiba, *Nimmukei Yoseph* 9a who relies on R. Jose's rule to hold that the owner of premises is entitled to the proceeds of an unauthorized subletting of his premises by his tenant, in so far as such proceeds exceed the rent upon which he agreed with the tenant. This holding has been later codified in a gloss of the Rema to the *Shulhan Arukh*. See *Shulhan Arukh, Hoshen Mishpat* 363:10.

[54] See R. Jacob b. Asher, *Tur, Hoshen Mishpat* 363:5; R. Moses Isserles (the Rema), *Darkei Mosheh to the Tur, Hoshen Mishpat* 363:2; and the Rema's gloss to the *Shulhan Arukh, Hoshen Mishpat* 363:5. It should be noted that while R. Joseph Caro challenged the Tur's original view – see his *Bet Yosef to the Tur, Hoshen Mishpat* 363:5 – he did not express this opinion in his *Shulhan Arukh*.

[55] See Maimonides, *Hilkhot Skhirut* 1:6.

[56] See *Shulhan Arukh, Hoshen Mishpat* 307:5.

which nullifies any advantages from the unauthorized use of another's property for one's positive enrichment.[57]

Alongside R. Jose's rule, a second category of cases has been identified, representing a somewhat more subtle species of profitable appropriations. It does not deal with "simple gains" generated from a profitable transaction effectuated by means of another's property. Instead, it concentrates on cases of avoiding inescapable expense or loss due to the unauthorized use of such property. Having its roots in the Talmud,[58] this category – known as *mishtarshei* – includes any case in which the unavoidability of the expenses avoided through the use of the plaintiff's entitlement renders such expenses tantamount to positive enrichment and hence subject to the exception of this subsection.[59]

Few attempts have been made to unearth the theoretical underpinnings of the exception of positive enrichment or of any one of its branches.[60] But given my perspective on the law, such a task does not seem especially burdensome. Recall the maxim of mutual responsibility which underlies the exemptive rule. The social program embedded in this maxim emphasizes providing relief for the needy; but at the same time it neither refutes the legitimacy of private property nor calls for an equal distribution of society's wealth.

Hence, the application to our paradigm of the communitarian imperative prescribed by the mutual-responsibility maxim has to be limited to cases – like the squatter case – in which the defendant's *genuine need* of the plaintiff's resource is at stake. But capturing a positive enrichment through the infringement of another's entitlement amounts to persuasive (albeit circumstantial) evidence that no such specific need is involved. Where the defendant positively increases his own wealth through the forced transfer, it appears plausible that he can afford sharing the extra wealth he achieves

[57] See Blass, *Jewish Law for Israel* at 11, 21. Rakover explains that the first view expressed in the Mishnah can also be reconciled with the rule under consideration. The dispute is, says Rakover, only regarding the question whether the legal right to the damages paid by the borrower lies with the hirer or the owner. See Rakover, *Unjust Enrichment* at 45 note 11. This observation seems to me valid. It diverts the debate to the issue of choosing the proper default rule in the chattel-rental contract, and suggests unanimity of opinion regarding the problem of positive enrichment from another's property. In fact, this seems to be the way in which the issue was codified in the *Shulhan Arukh*, which provides a rule of liability subject to a possibility of an opt-out arrangement in the owner–hirer contract.

[58] See Blass, *Jewish Law for Israel* at 11–12.

[59] See R. Meir Simhah of Dvinsk, *Ohr Sameah on Mishneh Torah, Hilkhot Nizkei Mamon* 3:2; Blass, *Jewish Law for Israel* at 12.

[60] See Blass, *Jewish Law for Israel* at 21–22, 53; Solomon, "Concepts of Zeh Neheneh" at 61; Rakover, *Unjust Enrichment* at 46–49.

thereby with the owner of the resource (compare this case to the squatter case, which is characterized by a presumption of the defendant's no choice but to forego the benefit had it been known to be for rent). These considerations, to be sure, do not directly address the issue of neediness. None the less, they seem to approximate this concern well enough to establish reasonable proxies enabling decision-makers to refrain from bluntly checking the parties' social status in a private-law dispute.[61]

This explication, however, can hardly stand for the *mishtarshei* prong of our exception. The inescapability of expense which characterizes *mishtarshei* cases does not tell us a great deal about the defendant's need or the absence thereof. It therefore appears that, although R. Jose's rule and the *mishtarshei* exception seem doctrinally connected, their theoretical underpinnings diverge. The appropriate focus in extricating the justification for the *mishtarshei* exception appears to be on the plaintiff rather than on the defendant. In *mishtarshei* cases the defendant has no choice but to incur the expense. Hence, allowing him to appropriate the invaded interest free of charge amounts to the loss of a real (and not merely hypothetical) opportunity from the plaintiff's viewpoint. Indeed, the unavoidability factor – which distinguishes the *mishtarshei* category – transforms the hypothetical opportunity of transacting business with the defendant to actual lost profits; it reverses the presumption that the defendant would have foregone the benefit had it been known to be for hire. Thus, it necessitates the conclusion that absolving the defendant would be tantamount to an actual reduction of the owner's estate, i.e., to *sacrifice*. And, as is already clear by now, Talmudic civil law does not allow its communitarian impulse to reach that far.

The defendant's readiness to pay

If one derives a benefit while the other sustains no loss indicates that he is ready to pay for the benefit, his exemption is reversed and he is liable for rent.[62] The squatter's willingness to pay can obviously be deduced from express words. It can also be inferred from actions, but only if the squatter is one who would otherwise rent premises.[63]

[61] The need to substitute the relevant considerations of a legal rule with factors which are cruder but less likely to be mistakenly applied, or simply abused, is discussed in Schauer, *Playing by the Rules* § 8.3.

[62] Liability for rent in cases of readiness to pay is prescribed in the *Shulhan Arukh, Hoshen Mishpat* 363:8. For a discussion of the Talmudic underpinnings of the rule and the opposition thereto, see Blass, *Jewish Law for Israel* at 58–59; Rakover, *Unjust Enrichment* at 24.

[63] See *Arukh Ha-Shulhan, Hoshen Mishpat* 363:19.

Two instructive explanations have been suggested for this exception to the exemptive rule.[64] First, it has been argued that, since the exemption is founded on an assumption of the premises not being for rent, the squatter's readiness to pay transforms the premises to rentable ones, and thus constitutes a loss to the owner. This loss, in turn, reverses the exemptive rule according to the exception discussed in the first subsection above,[65] and justifies the squatter's liability.[66] That is, this explanation highlights the reasoning for excluding the lost opportunity to bargain with the defendant from the definition of the plaintiff's loss. Such exclusion is based on a presumption that the defendant would have foregone the benefit had he known that the owner would charge him for it. But once the defendant himself indicates that he is willing to pay, the presumption is reversed and the plaintiff's *actual* loss is established. Allowing the defendant in such circumstances to appropriate without paying would be tantamount to the imposition of *sacrifice*.

The second explanation focuses on the squatter rather than the owner, building upon the third exception, that of positive enrichment. Once the squatter appears to have been willing to pay – and is actually not paying – for the benefit, so the argument goes, the situation is no longer of mere enjoyment of the owner's resource, but of positive enrichment.[67] But, as we saw in the third subsection above,[68] positive enrichment does not justify exemption since it does not represent genuine need on the part of the benefactor. In other words, knowing that the squatter would not have foregone the benefit had he had to pay for it, indicates that his financial difficulties are not hard enough to override the owner's proprietary interest. Where no genuine need of one's fellow is at stake, the balance between oneself and one's fellow tilts in favor of the self.[69]

But how much will a defendant who indicates a willingness to pay be liable for? R. Ezekiel Landau, one of the greatest Ashkenazic authorities of the eighteenth century, held that such a defendant cannot be liable for

64 Both explanations for the exception at hand are of R. Shim'on Yehuda Shkop of Grondo. For other explanations see R. Malkiel Zvi Tennenbaum, *Responsa Divrei Malkiel* 3:157 (implied partnership); Blass, *Jewish Law for Israel* at 59 (implied contract).

65 See pp. 115–20 above.

66 See *Novellae of R. Shim'on Yehuda Ha-Kohen to Baba Kamma* 19:5.

67 See *Novellae of R. Shim'on Yehuda Ha-Kohen to Baba Kamma* 19:6, 20:2. See also R. Joab Joshua Weingarten, *Responsa Helkat Yoav, Hoshen Mishpat* 9 (same).

68 See pp. 121–24 above.

69 The needs explanation corresponds to the rule which allows the inference of a willingness to pay from actions only where the squatter is one who would otherwise rent premises.

more than the actual amount which he indicated he is willing to pay for the benefit.[70] A contemporary commentator opines that such a rule conforms only with the latter explanation for the willingness to pay exception (the one I analyzed as "no-need"), and not with the former rationale for this exception (of "actual-loss").[71] This is because once a loss has been established, the exception discussed in the first subsection above is triggered, and this exception prescribes full liability irrespective of the extent of the loss involved.[72] But is this really the case? I submit that if the explanations are examined in view of their underlying justifications, a different result emerges.

Consider first the "no-need" justification, derived from the positive-enrichment explanation. Here, the outcome of applying the doctrinal explanation and that of the underlying justification clearly coincide. The amount the defendant was ready to pay represents his positive enrichment, which is to be reversed according to the applicable exception. By the same token, if the defendant could have paid only so much (X) for the benefit, and any extra charge would have caused him to forego the transfer, then such an extra charge also approximates his *need*. The extra charge is thus tantamount to the value of the entire benefit in the "pure" case of our *sugya* in which the defendant is presumed to have foregone the transfer had he had to pay *anything* for it. Hence, the extra charge – but only the extra charge – fully falls within the ambit of the exemptive rule. On the other hand, since Talmudic civil law does not legitimize appropriations which are not needs-based, it is plausible that it fixes the defendant's liability at X.

Consider now the "actual-loss" justification. As indicated above, the result of a direct application of the doctrinal explanation indeed entails a full-liability outcome. However, recall the justification I suggested for the doctrinal rule of "loss to the plaintiff entails full liability," that Talmudic civil law deters invasions which result in actual diminution of the value of the plaintiff's estate. But the circumstances of our case are by definition of "no-*harm*," meaning that there is no other demand – apart from the defendant's – for the invaded resource. Therefore, deterrence considerations – which guide the law in prescribing gain-based recovery with respect to harmful invasions – are moot, and its only remaining objective is to compensate the plaintiff for her loss. Where the defendant – the only potential transferee of the invaded interest – indicates that he is willing to

[70] R. Ezekiel Landau, II *Responsa Noda Bihudah, Hoshen Mishpat, responsum* 24.
[71] See Blass, *Jewish Law for Israel* at 59.
[72] See pp. 115–17 above.

pay X for the benefit, this indeed establishes a loss of X once such a payment is not effectuated; but it cannot indicate a larger loss, of the "objective value" of the benefit. X, and not any larger amount, represents the prospected revenues denied from the plaintiff as a result of the defendant's invasion.

To summarize, the exception of willingness to pay is premised on reasons which match the underlying ethos of mutual responsibility. It emphasizes both the "need-based" justification of infringing the owner's entitlement, and the "no-loss" limit of this communitarian impulse. Once this dual justification is uncovered, the appended holding – which limits recovery to the amount the defendant has indicated he is actually willing to pay – is also comfortably explicated.[73]

The integrating ideology

Contemporary scholars of Talmudic civil law have discussed the correlation between the exemptive rule (and its *Kofin* counterpart) and the social, economic, and cultural characteristics of Judaism.

Thus, it has been pointed out that our area of law underscores the underlying concept of property,[74] setting as a leitmotif the qualification of the institution of private property as a domain of full self-control.[75] This qualification, in turn, is said to eradicate the destructive effects of an inordinate obsession with one's private preserve which weakens the concern for others and creates excessive legal and psychological barriers between people.[76] Hence, the rabbis attempt to inculcate into the hearts and the minds of the laity the duty of freely acceding to someone else's

[73] However, none of the explications mentioned by the text holds for a peculiar proviso to the willingness-to-pay exception. This proviso holds that willingness to pay in a "no-*harm*" scenario reverses the exemptive rule only if it is directed to the owner, and does not change the squatter's exemption if it is directed to a third party whom the squatter mistakenly thought to be the owner. See *Shulhan Arukh, Hoshen Mishpat*, 363:9. Some have tried to explain this proviso. See details in Blass, *Jewish Law for Israel* at 58 note 35; Rakover, *Unjust Enrichment* at 27 and note 66. Unfortunately, none of these excuses seems very convincing, especially given the justifications elaborated by the text. And, indeed, contemporary Talmudic civil law scholars who discuss the willingness-to-pay exception tend either to ignore this proviso or to dispute it. See Kirschenbaum, *Equity in Jewish Law* at 212–13; Rakover, *ibid.*; Lifshitz, "One Derives a Benefit" at 209.

[74] See Jackson, "Introduction to Symposium: Unjust Enrichment" at 3.

[75] See Lichtenstein, "Towards an Understanding" at 379–82; *cf.* Kirschenbaum, *Equity in Jewish Law* at 231.

[76] See Kirschenbaum, *Equity in Jewish Law* at 189. *Cf.* Falk, *Legal Values and Judaism* at 92–93; Aaron Levine, *Economics and Jewish Law* 110 (1987).

advantage;[77] this attempt strives to achieve a desirable degree of social cohesion, concern for others, and mutual responsibility.

But, at the same time, as these commentators observe, Talmudic civil law is attentive to the dangers of too strongly restricting individual freedom of action and of obviating the need to secure consent prior to a transfer of an interest in her resource. Hence, the great caution with which the underlying objectives of the doctrine are applied.[78]

Finally, this dualistic attitude which shapes our doctrine is in itself meant to achieve a double – albeit inseparable – goal: it is both an instrument to help the needy and a means for the spiritual betterment of property owners.[79]

This chapter concurs with these observations. Furthermore, it is aimed at both making these observations somewhat more concrete and setting them within the analytical framework of this book. Thus, it demonstrates how the unique Judaic social ethos of mutual responsibility is translated into a set of complex, yet coherent, doctrinal rules. The baseline of the doctrine – the exemptive rule – seems highly communitarian. But studying the exceptions to the rule in detail reveals the rabbis' great sensitivity to the exact balance between oneself and one's fellow which the Judaic ethos strikes.

These exceptions insist on keeping the doctrine within the realm of a *sharing* rationale and protecting against slippage into actual *sacrifice*. Hence, no *harm* to the plaintiff is tolerated. Once the invasion results in a direct devaluation of her interest or a loss of profits she could have otherwise reaped, the exemptive rule is reversed, and a deterring gain-based recovery takes its place. Lost profits – which trigger the reversal of the exemptive rule – are by and large meant to indicate the possibility of transactions with third parties. But the exemptive rule is reversed also where the facts of the case positively indicate that profits could have been secured from the defendant himself, such as where he indicated a willingness to pay or where he had no choice but to incur the expenses involved with the use of the invaded resource.

Moreover, the care for the individual and the cautious approach to overriding her interests are demonstrated not only in guarding against the diminution of her well-being. They are also operative in allowing her to recapture the control over the resource; a control of which the exemptive rule deprives her. Hence, we find the existence of the protest exception

[77] See Kirschenbaum, *Equity in Jewish Law* at 252.

[78] See *ibid.* at 216, 233, 235, 248; *cf.* Shilo, "'Kofin Al Midat Sdom'" at 77.

[79] See Lichtenstein, "Towards an Understanding" at 377–78; *cf.* Kirschenbaum, *Equity in Jewish Law* at 252.

which gives an owner latitude in striking the appropriate balance between the needs of others and those of her own.

Finally, the underlying social platform is aimed not at an equal distribution of wealth, but only at providing relief for the needy. Accordingly, the doctrine insists that the exemptive rule will apply only where the defendant is indeed in need to use the invaded property. The communitarian impulse prescribes, to be sure, a presumption of neediness, that is, the presumption that had the use of the resource been known to be charged for, the defendant would have foregone his invasion of it. However, this is not a conclusive presumption, but a rebuttable one. If, in the circumstances of the case, it appears that the defendant captured a positive enrichment, or was willing – and thus supposedly able – to pay for an even undefinable benefit, the presumption of neediness is refuted and liability attaches.

This complicated and artfully tailored web of doctrinal details stands in sharp dissonance to the American doctrine. The vast majority of chapter 4 which studied that doctrine designates which resources are to be protected by a *control* rationale and which by a *well-being* one, and is hence preoccupied with the choice between the concomitant measures of recovery of *profits* and *fair market value*. In contrast, this chapter does not mention such considerations. It focuses instead on a baseline rule of *sharing*, and manifests the efforts of Talmudic civil law to prevent it from shifting further to the communitarian pole of *sacrifice*. Such a dramatic change of outlook should not be surprising. Once we accept the connection between social ethos and doctrinal rules (as the third section of chapter 2 does[80]), observing diametrically opposing doctrines for diametrically opposing ethoses seems expected, if not obvious.

[80] See pp. 34–40 above.

6 International law

Our consideration of the third, and last, legal system must begin with some measure of surprise. How can a theory which is primarily designed to explain domestic legal systems and speaks in terms of the personhood of human agents and their interaction with one another, account for what seems *a priori* the most "non-human" legal system of them all, whose constituents are – at least traditionally – only states?[1] Can we speak seriously of a cultural and social ethos, or of the intrinsic connectedness of resources to actors, where the parallel to the municipal society is the planet as a whole, and the analogue to a person is a state? Is it not absurd to speak of ethical preconceptions of all nations, and does it not undermine the whole premise of a theory which emphasizes so much multiculturalism and its effects?

These seem weighty questions, deserving of some attention at the outset. Thus, this introduction offers initial justifications (to be substantiated below) for selecting international law as the third legal system discussed herein. The following pages demonstrate the limitations of applying the theory to international law and suggest the unique contribution this chapter offers to the book as a whole.

For my purposes, international law serves as more than an anecdotal situation to show the reach of the explanatory power of the theory. Rather, like its predecessor, this chapter focuses on the importance of cultural ideology,[2] and illuminates some important points heretofore over-

[1] According to the Statute of the International Court of Justice, TS No. 993 (at 25) § 34-1 (1945) "[o]nly states may be parties in cases before [that] Court." The espousal of a private party's grievance against another state depends upon the discretion of the relevant decision-maker of her own state. See generally, e.g., I F. V. Garcia-Amador, *The Changing Law of International Claims* 76–86 (1984).

[2] International law can also provide some support for the other prong of my theory: the claim of the importance of the resource itself in shaping the doctrinal rules. Thus, respecting a case which deviates from the contours of our paradigm (a case of specific

shadowed with regard to this aspect of the thesis. In order to point out these themes, a brief description of the scenario in which our paradigm manifests itself in international law is first required.

Note that, just as in the context of American law, I do not attempt to cover all the cases which invoke the principle against unjust enrichment. Moreover, I do not necessarily discuss cases that make use of this principle which – as may be recalled – I do not find very helpful in resolving the questions our paradigm raises.[3] Rather, I focus on the international law analogue to our paradigmatic case, hoping to gain some insights to my theory of the relations between measures of recovery and normative ethos.

B, who remains the plaintiff as she has been throughout this study, is now the owner of a certain profit-making asset in state A (the "host country"). This asset is, in the typical case, a natural resource, such as land or, even more typically, concessionary rights to copper or oil properties in A. B, however, usually a corporation, is not a national of A, which is a developing country, but is instead a national of C, a developed country. At the crucial moment of the events, there is neither a treaty between A and C (B's "home state") respecting the treatment of C's nationals in A, nor is there any consensual obligation made by A to B to cover the contingency of a future taking of B's asset by A.[4]

restitution), one can observe a distinctive treatment accorded to one category of resources, that of cultural property. Cultural property is becoming a special category subject to unique legal rules. The fundamental principle of this emerging regime is that states which have been substantively deprived of their own cultural heritage are entitled to retrieve an adequate collection of it, and that holding states and their institutions should cooperate to that end notwithstanding the financial costs involved. This principle is largely premised on the significance of the cultural property to the requesting state's cultural identity: its being an internalization of the pertinent people's common history; a part of its self-realization. This argument may explain why the return of cultural property is not limited to cases of illicit appropriation, but also extends to cases in which transactions were apparently legal. See, e.g., Lyndel V. Prott and P. J. O'Keefe, *Law and the Cultural Heritage*, vol. 3: *Movement* 802–923, 928 (1989).

3 For the conflicting uses of the principle against unjust enrichment in the context of our paradigm see p. 155 below.

4 The purpose of the qualifications of the text is to exclude cases of any kind of preexisting relationships between the parties involved. This seems obvious given our paradigm's insistence of the parties being strangers contractually. However, in order to tighten the correspondence of our case to the paradigm of this book and to fully exclude the considerations typically taken into account in cases involving contractual interactions, one further assumption seems to be required: that no prospective contractual relationships between the parties is anticipated. Moreover, one can assume that even if the parties themselves do not expect to be repeat players, the mere expectation of the host country that it may desire to seek future contractual relationships with other potential investors may inject certain reputational

But this very unhappy occasion, from B's standpoint, does occur. A new regime reaches power in the host country and it immediately initiates a large-scale reform.[5] The plan seeks an overall socio-economic reorganization of A and a redistribution of its wealth. An important component of the plan announced by the new government is the expropriation, or nationalization,[6] of all the country's natural resources, notably – but by no means only – of B's interests. B, supported by her home state, seeks compensation.

Since our hypothetical case involves a general and impersonal nationalization in the pursuit of development policies and socio-political objectives, there is no doubt that it complies with the two classic requirements international law prescribes for the legality of expropriation, i.e., public purpose and non-discrimination.[7] Thus, the only remaining question is the focal question of this book, i.e., what is the applicable measure of recovery to which B is entitled due to the appropriation of her resource.

The traditional doctrine, elaborated in the first section of this chapter, calls for the tripartite formula of "prompt, adequate, and effective" compensation. This doctrine has been challenged by the developing countries in the framework of their call for a New International Economic Order to be premised, among other things, on a more equitable distribution of the world's resources and on a different balance between the sanctity of

considerations which are inoperative in our paradigm. Assuming that no such contingency is contemplated by the host state may seem unrealistic. But at the same time one should not overstate the incentive effects of the future need for more investments. As David Leebron observes, there are many circumstances in which, the reputational costs notwithstanding, the incentive to expropriate is expected to prevail. See David W. Leebron, "A Game Theoretic Approach to the Regulation of Foreign Direct Investment and the Multinational Corporation," 60 *University of Cincinnati Law Review* 305, 323–27 (1991). This theoretical observation is supported empirically by the fact that expropriation is (or at least was) in fact a prevalent phenomenon in certain regions of the world, especially with respect of certain industry groups. See, e.g., Alan C. Shapiro, *Multinational Financial Management* exhibits 19.1–19.3 (3rd edn. 1989).

5 The announcement of a formal taking relieves our discussion from considering the gray area of "creeping expropriation," i.e., the *de facto* diminution of the value of B's asset by gradual obstructions – by regulation or otherwise – to the effective enjoyment of B from the asset.

6 I use the terms "expropriation" and "nationalization" interchangeably. Although such a use is imprecise is some respects, it does not intend to import any overtones but merely to echo the terminology used by most of the sources mentioned and cited herein. For the terminology's nuances see Ignaz Seidl-Hohenveldern, "Semantics of Wealth Deprivation and Their Legal Significance," in *Foreign Investment in the Present and a New International Economic Order* 218 (Detlev Chr. Dicke ed. 1987).

7 Parenthetically, one should recall that the requirements of public purpose and non-discrimination turn out to be somewhat insignificant even in so far as the developed states are concerned. See, e.g., *Restatement (Third) of the Foreign Relations Law* § 712 comments e and f (1987).

property rights and the state's sovereign right to promote the general welfare. Hence, the second section of this chapter considers the perspective of the Third World and summarizes the claims of these countries for a different legal regime.

The direct resort to distributive considerations in the discussion of those rules of international law that govern our paradigm provides the first reason for including a chapter on international law in this book: this unique attribute of international law[8] supports my claim of a close – although generally covert – relationship between the doctrinal rules of our paradigm and the larger prevailing distributive scheme.

The question of whether the traditional doctrine of compensation has been modified is highly controversial among international lawyers.[9] This chapter endeavors to take sides in this truly complicated question by indicating – albeit in a tentative and inconclusive fashion – the existence of *some* change. Although the third section of this chapter does not purport to supply the salvaging formula which represents the current state of the law, it concludes that the evidence does indicate some softening of the traditional norms.

Fortunately, characterizing these conclusions as tentative and inconclusive does not compromise the purposes of this chapter. For this study, it is vitally important to underscore the *possibility* of a *dynamic* dimension in the aspect of the theory connected to cultural ideology. Such a possibility may have been dwarfed to some extent by the two preceding chapters which describe two different social ethoses and their manifestations in the doctrinal rules. With consideration of international law, we have the opportunity to capture its existence and thereby enrich the theory's inter-cultural aspect by demonstrating a parallel possibility of an *inter-temporal* dimension. All of which suggests two more reasons for the importance of this chapter.

The first advantage in demonstrating the inter-temporal dimension of our paradigm is that it enables me to show how the development of the doctrinal rules both affects and is affected by the parallel evolution of the distributive perceptions of the constituents of the relevant community. Thus, the dynamic dimension highlights the "interwovenness" of the

8 See, e.g., Charles Lipson, *Standing Guard: Protecting Foreign Capital in the Nineteenth and Twentieth Centuries* 56 (1985).

9 Compare, e.g., Patrick M. Norton, "A Law of the Future or a Law of the Past? Modern Tribunals and the International Law of Expropriation," 85 *American Journal of International Law* 474 (1991) with M. Sornarajah, *The Pursuit of Nationalized Property* (1986).

doctrine of our paradigm and the governing distributive scheme, demonstrating the maxim – which is only abstractly introduced in chapter 2[10] – that the law both reflects and shapes distributive preferences.[11]

The second reason for emphasizing the dynamic dimension is to demystify my frequent reference to social ethos. This chapter insists that demonstrating the correlation between doctrinal rules and a social ethos does not entail, and is not based upon, any presupposition as to the reasons for the prevalence of any specific social ethos.[12] In other words, while the redistributive thrust of the change of the traditional doctrine falls fully within the thesis of this book, it appears that whatever success the revisionist movement has achieved is attributable – at least in part – to a change in the power relationships between the developed and the developing countries, and not – or at least not only – to a change of heart, an ethical revolution instigated by the persuasive force of the developing countries' arguments.[13] The relative influence of the benign and the less benign considerations in the crystallization of the distributive scheme of the international community – or, for that matter, of any domestic regime – deserves separate consideration. For our purposes, suffice it to say that it is likely that the less benign factors are of some importance. This possibility in itself illustrates the indifference of this book to the origins of the ethos and its focus on the doctrinal consequences of the ethos only.

Given all these expectations, let us turn now to the description of the actual development of the doctrine and of the changes it reflects (and shapes) in the thin, but none the less existent, common ethical presuppositions of the world's community.

The traditional formula

Had B's grievance arisen prior to World War II, there seems little doubt that she was entitled – according to the doctrine of international law prevailing in that era – to "prompt, adequate, and effective" compensation. This

[10] See pp. 37–39 above.

[11] *Cf.* Nathaniel Berman, "Modernism, Nationalism, and the Rhetoric of Reconstruction," in *After Identity: A Reader in Law and Culture* 229, 230 (Dan Danielsen and Karen Engle eds. 1995).

[12] In other words, I do not deny that an ethos conservation or an ethos change can be brought about through the influence of those who are most likely to gain from it. See, e.g., Duncan Kennedy, "Form and Substance in Private Law Adjudication," 89 *Harvard Law Review* 1,685, 1,721 (1976).

[13] See Lipson, *Standing Guard* at chapter 5; Kenneth A. Rodman, *Sanctity Versus Sovereignty: The United States and the Nationalization of Natural Resource Investments* 1–16, chapters 2 and 3 (1988).

tripartite formula was coined by US Secretary of State Hull in the diplomatic correspondence concerning a dispute over the compensation owed due to the Mexican expropriations of agrarian and oil properties owned by United States citizens.[14] The "Hull formula," as it has come to be known, was well settled at the pre-war era.

This section focuses on the middle prong of the Hull formula which calls for the payment of adequate – understood to mean *full* – compensation. It explores the cases which established, unfolded, and defended this norm, and further studies the socio-economic presuppositions underlying the rationale of a full compensation rule. This focus should not, however, be understood as an attempt to downplay the practical significance of the promptness and effectiveness prongs of the Hull formula.[15] The time over which payment is spread and the way in which it is paid are of course determinative of the amount received by the claimant. None the less, since the positions of the parties involved regarding these two requirements and the development of these two prongs of the Hull formula mirror the positions and trend respecting the primary issue of adequacy,[16] no further discussion of these parasitic components of the traditional doctrine is provided.

The *locus classicus* for the pre-war doctrine is the holding of the Permanent Court of International Justice in the *Chorzow Factory* case.[17] Most of this complicated opinion deviates from the contours of our hypothetical case, since the expropriation there was characterized by the court as unlawful, being contrary to the 1922 Geneva Convention, whereas in our hypothetical case it is deemed lawful. None the less, the court's opinion is correctly considered as an endorsement of the full-compensation standard. Given the premise of illegality, the *Chorzow Factory* court insisted on not placing the claimant's interests "in a situation more unfavorable than that in which . . . these interests would have been if Poland had respected the said Convention." This can be achieved, says the court, by removing the limitation to recovery applicable to cases of lawful expropriation, i.e., its being measured

[14] For excerpts of this diplomatic exchange and some commentary see Henry J. Steiner *et al.*, *Transnational Legal Problems: Materials and Text* 455–60 (4th edn. 1994).

[15] These requirements call for the payment of compensation "at the time of the taking, or within a reasonable time thereafter with interest from the date of taking, and in a form economically usable by the foreign national." See *Restatement (Third) of the Foreign Relations Law* § 712 and comment d (1987).

[16] See, e.g., Maarten H. Muller, "Compensation for Nationalization: A North–South Dialogue," 19 *Columbia Journal of Transnational Law* 35, 46–49 (1981); Wil D. Verwey and Nico J. Schrijver, "The Taking of Foreign Property under International Law: A New Legal Perspective?" 15 *Netherlands Yearbook of International Law* 3, 17–19 (1984).

[17] *Factory at Chorzow* case (*Germany* v. *Poland*), 1928 PCIJ (ser. A) No. 17 (Indem.) (Merits) (13 September).

as the "value of the undertaking at the moment of dispossession plus interest to the day of payment." Instead, where *un*lawful expropriation is involved, pecuniary remedy can exceed this measure of *fair market value*, and be "a sum corresponding to the value which a restitution in kind would bear," i.e. the *profits* actually reaped by the expropriating state.[18] As National Judge Rabel observed, this alternative seems to be an option to the claimant.[19] Hence, the resulting measure of recovery prescribed by the *Chorzow Factory* case for cases of *un*lawful expropriation is the deterring measure of the greater of *fair market value* and *profits*.

But what is more important for our purposes is that, as we see, the *Chorzow Factory* court considered payment of the full value of the asset at the time of its expropriation to be the international minimum standard for *lawful* expropriations of alien-owned property.[20] Other international tribunals in the same period have also decided unequivocally that the only "fair" and "just" measure of recovery is the "full" value of the expropriated asset.[21] Given the dominance of judge-made law regarding expropriation at that time,[22] and the unanimity presented by the holdings of the cases, it does not seem surprising that most contemporary scholars – from whatever current persuasion – agree that the concept of full compensation properly characterizes the pre-war doctrine.[23]

The pre-war international jurisprudence also explains the economic meaning of such full compensation. Thus, the cases clearly establish that the host country must pay not only the value of the physical properties (*damnum emergens*), but also – and in most cases more significantly – the

[18] *Ibid.* at 47–50. [19] *Ibid.* at 66.

[20] For further support in the court's opinion for its support of this standard see M. H. Mendelson, "Agora: What Price Expropriation?: Compensation for Expropriation: The Case Law," 79 *American Journal of International Law* 414, 415–16 (1985).

[21] See, e.g., *Delgoa Bay Railway* case, translated in III Marjorie M. Whiteman, *Damages in International Law* 1,694, 1,698 (1943) (Blaesi, Heusler and Soldan arbitrators 1900) (hereinafter *Delgoa Bay*). Other cases are collected in Mendelson, "Agora: What Price Expropriation?" at 415–18.

[22] See Richard B. Lillich and Burns H. Weston, *International Claims: Their Settlement by Lump Sum Agreements* 20–30 (1975).

[23] See, e.g., Norton, "A Law of the Future" at 475 (a proponent of the traditional rules); Rudolf Dozler, "New Foundations of the Law of Expropriation of Alien Property," 75 *American Journal of International Law* 553, 557–59 (1981) (a proponent of change). Oscar Schachter claims, however, that full compensation has never been established as customary international law. See Oscar Schachter, "Compensation for Expropriation," 78 *American Journal of International Law* 121 (1984). In so far as this assertion concerns the pre-war era, it is convincingly disproved in Mendelson, "Agora: What Price Expropriation?" at 414–18. Schachter's response does not face this challenge. See Oscar Schachter, "Agora: What Price Expropriation?: Compensation Cases – Leading and Misleading," 79 *American Journal of International Law* 420 (1985).

expected profits that would have been captured by the claimant had the expropriation not taken place (*lucrum cessans*).[24] Such profits were, to be sure, appropriately discounted to their present value to account for the time value of money and for relevant risks.[25]

The cases fully acknowledge that the computation of lost profits is purely theoretical and cannot be absolutely accurate,[26] but they nevertheless insist on the inclusion of this component. The line of argument supporting this position can be summarized by the following propositions:

1. The purpose of the chosen measure of recovery is to make the claimant whole, i.e., to place her in as good an economic position as she had been before the expropriation occurred by compensating her for the complete level of welfare of which she has been deprived due to the expropriation.[27]
2. This level of welfare would have been best captured by reference to the *fair market value* of the asset expropriated at the time of the taking had the expropriation not taken place, i.e., as a going concern.[28] However, in order to be able to properly value an asset, the pertinent market must meet some rather stringent prerequisites such as the free entry of buyers and sellers. Unfortunately, rare are the cases of expropriation in which there exists such an active and free market for the expropriated asset, which in most cases, as in our hypothetical case, is a "unique good" like land or a natural resource.[29]

24 See *Norwegian Shipowners' Claims* (*Norway* v. *US*), 1 RIAA 307, 338 (Perm. Ct. Arb. 1922); *May* case (*US* v. *Guatamala*), 15 RIAA 47, 71–75 (Jenner arbitrator 1900); *Greek Tel. Co.* case, described in J. Gillis Wetter and Stephen M. Schwebel, "Some Little Known Cases on Concessions," 40 *British Yearbook of International Law* 183, 216 (1964) (Streit, Anagnostopoulos and Papaligauras arbitrators 1935); *Delgoa Bay* at 1,697. See also *Palestine Railway* case, described in Wetter and Schwebel, *ibid.* at 222 (Beichmann, Mance and Mayer arbitrators 1922); *Shufedt* case (*US* v. *Guatamala*), 2 RIAA 1,079, 1,099 (Sisnett arbitrator 1930). The inclusion of lost profits in the appropriate remedy for expropriation (lawful and unlawful) is also supported by the *Chorzow Factory* case, as convincingly analyzed in William C. Lieblich, "Determinations by International Tribunals of the Economic Value of Expropriated Enterprises," 7 *Journal of International Arbitration* 37, 45–46 (1990). More cases are collected in Brice M. Clagett, "Just Compensation in International Law: The Issues Before the Iran–United States Claims Tribunal," in IV *The Valuation of Nationalized Property in International Law* 31, 62 note 124 (Richard B. Lillich ed. 1987).

25 See *Delgoa Bay* at 1,699; *Lena Goldfields Ltd* v. *USSR*, excerpted in 36 *Cornell Law Quarterly* 42, 51–52 (1950) (Stutzer and Scott arbitrators 1930) (hereinafter *Lena Goldfields*).

26 See *Delgoa Bay* at 1,699.

27 See *Norwegian Shipowners' Claims* (*Norway* v. *US*), 1 RIAA 307, 338 (Perm. Ct. Arb. 1922).

28 See *Lena Goldfields* at 52.

29 See, e.g., Norman Mintz, "Economic Observations on Lump Sum Settlements," in Lillich and Weston, *International Claims: Their Settlement by Lump Sum Agreements* at Appendix A, 264, 265–66.

3. Hence, the tribunal needs to simulate the calculations which would have been made by a hypothetical transferee in a consensual transfer of the profit-making asset. Such an imaginary transferee would have considered, no doubt, the potential profits the asset is expected to generate. Therefore, the tribunal must also resort to this consideration, utilizing the accumulated experience of valuation in parallel consensual transactions. Only in this way can it ascertain the fair purchase price of the asset as a going concern, which is the best approximation of the wealth deprived from the claimant by the state's act of expropriation.[30]

In principle, contemporary theory of economics approves this approach to the question of valuation. It perceives value as a forward-looking concept, and thus recognizes the primary importance of an asset's productiveness, that is its capacity to generate future revenues. However, there is one qualification that a modern economist would insist upon before endorsing the pre-war international jurisprudence. In calculating the present value of an expropriated asset or enterprise, the cases apparently employed the accrual accounting concept of "income," whereas the focus of modern valuation methodology is the expected net cash flows.[31] Hence, given today's knowledge of economic theory, the appropriate analogue for the pre-war concept of "discounted profits" is the discounted-cash-flow method of valuation.[32]

All this seems non-problematic. If these truisms had to be reiterated here at such length it is only because of the apparent recent debate as to the "correct" method of valuation of expropriated property. Thus, one can find in the post-war jurisprudence and literature suggestions of alternative methods of valuation which are based on some backward-looking measures of cost, notably the book value of the enterprise.[33] But in so far as the "correct" method of valuation means an economically correct valuation of the asset taken, it would seem that these suggestions are manifestly wrong.[34] The obvious imprecision of calculating the discounted cash flow to

[30] See *Lena Goldfields* at 52; *Delgoa Bay* at 1,699.

[31] See, e.g., Lieblich, "Determinations by International Tribunals" at 37–42.

[32] See, e.g., Richard A. Brealey and Stewart C. Myers, *Principles of Corporate Finance* 73, 96 (4th ed. 1991).

[33] See, e.g., Norman Girvan, "Expropriating the Expropriators: Compensation Criteria from a Third World Viewpoint," in III Lillich, *The Valuation of Nationalized Property* at 149, 166–68 (1975).

[34] See, e.g., Joseph S. McCosker, "Book Values in Nationalization Settlements," in II Lillich, *The Valuation of Nationalized Property* at 36, 51; Haliburton Fales, "A Comparison of Compensation for Nationalization of Alien Property with Standards of Compensation Under United States Domestic Law," in IV Lillich, *The Valuation of Nationalized Property* at 173, 195 (1987). The imperfection of cost-based methods of valuation was already observed in the *Factory at Chorzow* case (*Germany* v. *Poland*), 1928

which contemporary commentators point is not unique to the nationalization cases, and thus cannot warrant the abandonment of this method in that context. The attack on the method of valuation is but a subterfuge for a much less technical charge against the norm of full compensation.[35]

To be sure, an economically correct estimate of the full value of the expropriated asset does not, in and of itself, render the discounted-cash-flow method of valuation the "natural," "neutral," "just," or "desirable" method of valuation,[36] as sometimes claimed by advocates of the traditional doctrine.[37] In the final analysis, the choice of a valuation method, which is a derivative of the choice of a measure of recovery, depends on deliberate policy choices.[38] A long list of economic, sociological, and political factors has to be considered in order to arrive at the normatively "right solution."[39] Such an enterprise is beyond the scope of this chapter.

Fully within our interest, however, is the correspondence between the traditional rule of full compensation – and the ensuing discounted-cash-flow method of valuation – on the one hand, and the prevailing ethical preconceptions within the international community at the period under consideration, on the other hand. Traditional international law, and in particular the doctrine discussed herein, was developed in an homogeneous Western environment.[40] As one Indian commentator puts a well-known theme:

> The industrially advanced nations of Western Europe had a common faith in *laissez faire* economics, and identical values, interests and institutions. They also had a common goal, *viz.*, safety of foreign investments made by them in the colonies and underdeveloped territories. This made it necessary to spread European standards of civilization which eventually gave birth to international law of "civilized nations."[41]

PCIJ (ser. A) No. 17, at 50 (Indem.) (Merits) (13 September).

35 *Cf.* Elihu Lauterpacht, *Aspects of the Administration of International Justice* 130–36 (1991).

36 See, e.g., Adeoyea A. Akinsanya, *The Expropriation of Multinational Property in the Third World* 235 (1980); Wolfgang Friedmann, "Social Conflict and the Protection of Foreign Investment," 57 *Proceedings of the American Society of International Law* 126, 128 (1963).

37 See, e.g., Clagett, "Just Compensation in International Law" at 59, 60; Fales, "A Comparison of Compensation" at 176.

38 See, e.g., Muller, "Compensation for Nationalization" at 38–39.

39 See, e.g., Dale W. Weigel and Burns H. Weston, "Valuation upon the Deprivation of Foreign Enterprise: A Policy Oriented Approach to the Problem of Compensation under International Law," in I Lillich, *The Valuation of Nationalized Property* at 3, 38–39 (1972).

40 See Lipson, *Standing Guard* at 31.

41 Subhash C. Jain, *Nationalization of Foreign Property: A Study in North–South Dialogue* 13 (1983). See also, e.g., James W. Weller, "International Parties, Breach of Contract, and the Recovery of Future Profits," 15 *Hofstra Law Review* 323, 331–32 and notes 60–61 (1987); Lipson, *Standing Guard* at 11–12.

Indeed, the standards prescribed by the Hull formula presuppose "a liberal regime of private property, in particular the inviolability of private property and sanctity of contract."[42] One can account for the predominance of the requirement of full compensation, only given the dominance of these presuppositions among the shapers of international law in the pre-war era.[43]

But does this traditional rule of full compensation still represent the current state of the law? Before we address this complex question, we must analyze the intellectual attack on the traditional norms.

The challenge

Without delving into the details of the historical development – a task aptly performed elsewhere[44] – suffice it to observe that the attack on the traditional rules, with its roots in regional – notably Latin American – pre-war challenges, has been dramatically intensified in the post-war era with the emergence of the Third World. Few subjects of international law in general, and the so-called "North–South dialogue" in particular, have engendered as much passion, bitterness, and polarization as this battle over the compensation due for the nationalization of foreign-owned property.[45] Culminating in a series of UN resolutions during the 1960s and 1970s, the process targeted the Western pre-war doctrine, and attempted to modify international law to accommodate certain values (and interests, to be sure) which this section seeks to identify.

The call for change has taken two distinct forms, both of which perceive the rules of our paradigm as central to the distributive scheme of the world community. One form – call it "extreme revisionism" – maintains that in

[42] See Samuel K. B. Asante, "International Law and Foreign Investment: A Reappraisal," 37 *International and Comparative Law Quarterly* 588, 595 (1988).

[43] See Kenneth L. Karst, "Land Reform in International Law," in *Essays on Expropriation* 41, 42, 70 (Richard S. Miller and Ronald J. Stanger eds. 1967). See also, e.g., Girvan, "Expropriating the Expropriators" at 149–50; Lipson, *Standing Guard* at 12 note *, 38; Lillich and Weston, *International Claims: Their Settlement by Lump Sum Agreements* at 29. Not surprisingly, the United States, which may be considered the flag-bearer of the liberal regime of private property, has been a long-standing and continuing supporter of the full-compensation regime. See, e.g., Richard J. Smith, "The United States Government Perspective on Expropriation and Investment in Developing Countries," 9 *Vanderbilt Journal of Transnational Law* 517 (1976); Davis R. Robinson, "Expropriation in the Restatement (Revised)," 78 *American Journal of International Law* 176 (1984). For the thin exception to the full-compensation rule recognized by the United States see *Restatement (Third) of the Foreign Relations Law* § 712 comment d (1987).

[44] See Lipson, *Standing Guard* at Part 1.

[45] See, e.g., Muller, "Compensation for Nationalization" at 35.

cases of expropriation sovereignty entails the predominance of national law to the total exclusion of any international minimum standard. The second, more moderate, revisionist persuasion acknowledges the relevance of international standards in nationalization contexts but none the less seeks to adapt the traditional doctrine to the New International Economic Order which the Third World seeks to promote. The following pages demonstrate that both extreme and moderate revisionism challenge the distributive scheme reflected in, and shaped by, the traditional doctrine. Each of these revisionist positions advocates a change which is intended to create, via the change of the doctrinal rules, a new and more equitable distributive scheme.

Consider first the more revolutionary idea of "national treatment" known as the Calvo doctrine.[46] In the context of nationalization cases, this doctrine asserts that a foreigner doing business in a country is entitled only to non-discriminatory treatment, i.e., to the rights and privileges – or, more specifically, the amount of compensation, if any – prescribed by the pertinent national law of the host country. Additionally, the doctrine maintains that the exclusive jurisdiction of the host state over its territory entails exclusive jurisdiction of its domestic courts (or authorized administrative bodies) over the dispute following the expropriation. Hence, the deprived alien in our hypothetical case can only turn – as per Calvo – to the host state's domestic authorities in seeking redress for her grievances. Correspondingly, the doctrine proscribes any intervention, diplomatic or other, of a state to enforce its citizens' claims in a foreign country.[47]

These rules, advocated by extreme revisionists, are premised on a two-fold equality-based thesis: (i) equality between sovereign and independent states dictates that each should enjoy the complete freedom from interference of any sort by any other state; while (ii) equality between person and person prescribes that aliens should be entitled to the same measure of protection as nationals, but does not entail, and in fact even proscribes, any preferential treatment afforded to aliens only.[48]

This appeal to equality has been attacked vigorously: Allowing each state to fix the standard of treatment it is bound to accord aliens, say the critics, makes each state the judge of its own responsibility. Hence, the Calvo

46 The Calvo doctrine is named after the Argentinean jurist Carlos Calvo.

47 See, e.g., Asante, "International Law and Foreign Investment" at 592; Dozler, "New Foundations" at 560 note 28. For a detailed and documented description of the Calvo doctrine and its legacy see I Garcia-Amador, *The Changing Law* at 52–67.

48 See Donald R. Shea, *The Calvo Clause: A Problem of Inter-American and International Law and Diplomacy* 17–20 (1955).

regime constitutes a scheme of *non*-responsibility which practically immunizes all states from the claims of the international legal order.[49] It does not promote equality in any meaningful sense; it merely legitimizes anarchy. Moreover, the equality which extreme revisionism preaches appears superficial since there are *a priori* good grounds for drawing a distinction between nationals and non-nationals in so far as compensation is concerned: the latter are generally non-participants in the local political process and are thus more vulnerable to domestic legislative action; and, even more importantly, the justifications for requiring them to bear a certain burden in the public interest are different from (some say lesser than) the relevant justifications which apply regarding nationals.[50]

This criticism is not applicable, however, to the more moderate revisionist persuasion. While the traditional doctrine calls for full compensation and extreme revisionism calls for no internationally prescribed compensation, moderate revisionists advocate a new international norm of *partial* compensation. In support of this new regime, they advance some interrelated arguments. These arguments can be divided into three prongs: inability to pay; different social meanings of property; and vindication of past wrongs.

The first argument, of inability to pay full compensation, starts from the premise of sovereignty, which was also the foundation of the Calvo doctrine. But instead of claiming absolute sovereignty as the latter doctrine seems to maintain, it advocates a much more subtle conception of sovereignty. According to this conception, for a developing country in its decolonization process sovereignty entails the state's right to restructure its political and economic order; attain control over vital and strategic industries; and safeguard its economic independence. Such large-scale economic and social reform may require (or be perceived by the state to require) the nationalization of foreign-owned property. But encumbering a developing state's socio-economic reform with the exacting requirements of the Hull formula – "prompt, adequate, and effective" compensation – may inhibit or even frustrate altogether such nationalization, and thus the reform plan itself. It may jeopardize the state's social and economic progress, and at times even be tantamount to an exercise of an (unacceptable) veto power over a basic and legitimate component of the developing state's sovereignty. Therefore, moderate revisionists insist that in such

[49] See, e.g, Richard B. Lillich, "The Current Status of the Law of State Responsibility for Injuries to Aliens," in *International Law of State Responsibility for Injuries to Aliens* 1, 5 (Richard B. Lillich ed. 1983).

[50] See, e.g., *Lithgow* v. *UK*, 102 *European Court of Human Rights* (Ser. A.) at 48–49 (1986).

circumstances the traditional doctrine must yield to a standard that considers the host country's inability to pay full compensation.[51]

The payment of less than full compensation in cases of nationalization for socio-economic reform is of course a redistributive measure, which, just like a special tax, transfers wealth from the alien to the host country.[52] But "a redistributive measure" is still a general term, and this book attempts to correlate specific doctrinal rules with not-less-specific distributive schemes. In this case, the distributive scheme seems clear enough. Recall the two factors which trigger the applicability of the moderate revisionist rule, i.e., the "sovereign right to development" and the "unfortunate poverty" which brings about the inability to pay. The latter component appears to help identify the applicable distributive criterion. It is an overt appeal to the criterion of needs, similar to the one we took such great pains to uncover in chapter 5. This criterion seems to respond to the emerging political demands for more equitable distribution of the world's resources and the reorganization of the economic relations between rich and poor countries.[53]

Furthermore, the concept of minimal needs is defined in this context by the first triggering factor which warrants the payment of partial rather than full compensation. Put differently, a reform that could not have been made but for the redistribution is considered a basic need of the host country which should be secured due to its "right to development."[54] This newly emerging right[55] is conceived as the prerequisite for meaningful freedom and independence; it is hence the international counterpart of the

[51] See Asante, "International Law and Foreign Investment" at 594, 598, 600. See also, e.g., I Hersch O. Lauterpacht, *Oppenheim on International Law* 352 (8th edn. 1955); Akinsanya, *The Expropriation of Multinational Property* at 235–37, 244; S. Friedman, *Expropriation in International Law* 207 (Ivor C. Jackson trans. 1953); I Garcia-Amador, *The Changing Law* at 330–33; Frank G. Dawson and Burns H. Weston, "'Prompt, Adequate and Effective': A Universal Standard of Compensation?" 30 *Fordham Law Review* 727, 735–36, 738 (1962); Friedmann, "Social Conflict" at 133; Greta Gainer, "Nationalization: The Dichotomy Between Western and Third World Perspectives in International Law," 26 *Howard Law Journal* 1,547, 1,555–56 and note 30, 1,558–59 (1983).

[52] See Karl M. Meessen, "Domestic Law Concepts in International Expropriation Law," in IV Lillich, *The Valuation of Nationalized Property* at 157, 169–71 (1987). *Cf.* C. F. Amerasinghe, "The Quantum of Compensation for Nationalized Property," in III Lillich, *The Valuation of Nationalized Property* at 91, 91 (1975).

[53] See Oscar Schachter, *Sharing the World's Resources* 6–8 (1977); Burns H. Weston, "The New International Economic Order and the Deprivation of Foreign Proprietary Wealth: Some Reflections upon the Contemporary International Law Debate," in Lillich, *International Law of State Responsibility for Injuries to Aliens* at 89, 90–92.

[54] See Verwey and Schrijver, "The Taking of Foreign Property" at 20.

[55] See generally F. V. Garcia-Amador, *The Emerging International Law of Development: A New Dimension of International Economic Law* (1990).

notion of providing the necessary conditions for the exercise of liberty which was described in the second section of chapter 2[56] as one premise of (weak) needs-based distribution schemes.

It should also be mentioned that the developing state's need alone does not justify the redistribution; the alien's real or perceived affluence is also frequently mentioned as a cumulative reason for acknowledging the inability-to-pay theory. Stereotyped – rightly or wrongly – as a thriving transnational corporation, the foreigner is said to be generally better suited to bear the costs of nationalization than the developed country.[57]

Along with, and related to, this main distributive claim, moderate revisionists make two complementary assertions. The first regards the moderates' alternative conception of private property. As we have seen, the traditional norm tacitly assumes an international community of shared fundamental values and thus correlates with the liberal conception of property. But the assumption of a common perspective on the role of private property in international law, say the developing countries, is incorrect. Their competing conceptions of property are more in line with pre-colonial cultures and support the case for partial compensation.[58] In particular, they refer to the Western imposition of individual ownership regimes in lieu of their traditional collective forms of ownership and shared-use rights.[59] In addition, they refer to twentieth-century modifications in the municipal legal orders of the West, which are said to counteract the strong individualistic emphasis of the nineteenth-century conceptions of property,[60] and to (what seemed to be at the time) the innovative and challenging communist conception of property.[61]

Since property is a social artifact, embedded in the social, political, and cultural community in which it is established,[62] there is no justification, so the argument goes, to sustain the historically contingent and culturally specific Western conception of property in our current multicultural *inter*national community.[63] Hence, the claim for importing a social or public

56 See pp. 29–30 above.

57 See, e.g. Weston, "The New International Economic Order" at 117–18.

58 See, e.g., Girvan, "Expropriating the Expropriators" at 149–50.

59 See, e.g., Lipson, *Standing Guard* at 20–21; Gainer, "Nationalization" at 1,554 note 28, 1,566.

60 See, e.g., Sornarajah, *The Pursuit of Nationalized Property* at 26–27; Dozler, "New Foundations" at 568–69.

61 See, e.g., Lipson, *Standing Guard* at 67–68; Asante, "International Law and Foreign Investment" at 592, 598–99.

62 See, e.g., Joseph William Singer and Jack M. Beermann, "The Social Origins of Property," 6 *Canadian Journal of Law and Jurisprudence* 217, 228–30 (1993).

63 See I Garcia-Amador, *The Changing Law* at 13, 17; Lipson, *Standing Guard* at 3–4, 32. *Cf.*

dimension to the international conception of property. But once this step has been taken, one can no longer dismiss out of hand the further, more practical, assertion of the developing countries, i.e., that a developing state's sovereign right to promote the general welfare takes precedence over the sanctity of property rights acquired by foreign investors.[64] One result of the balance of interests prescribed by a more community-oriented conception of property may be a new norm of partial compensation with regard to all of these circumstances.[65]

One of the most often mentioned circumstances is the painful past. This brings us to the third argument claimed by moderate revisionists. This argument takes two forms: a plea for a general vindication and an appeal for the reversal of past excess profits. The first part of this argument has been most forcefully articulated by Norman Girvan, who contends that claims for compensation for nationalization should be counteracted by parallel claims for compensation of the nationalizing countries. These counter-claims are premised, says Girvan, on the assertion that "the immiserizing poverty and demoralizing economic impotence of the Third World peoples today in most cases can be traced back to the destructive effects of the European impact and to the characteristics of the systems erected to the service of the European interest." Compensation is therefore required in order to reverse these alleged past wrongs, which are responsible, in large measure, for "the present affluence of the developed world."[66]

These are serious accusations that cannot be fully examined here.[67] For our purposes, suffice it to note that these assertions carry mixed messages of corrective and retributive justice,[68] and that this far-reaching contention is actually more significant in terms of the atmosphere of the discussion[69] than in terms of its content.[70]

A less ambitious branch of the vindication argument did attain some

Thomas F. Bergin, "The Compensation Rule: An Imaginary Debate," in II Lillich, *The Valuation of Nationalized Property* at 3, 17 (1973).

64 See, e.g., Rodman, *Sanctity Versus Sovereignty* at 14.

65 See, e.g., Sornarajah, *The Pursuit of Nationalized Property* at 28; Asante, "International Law and Foreign Investment" at 600–01.

66 Girvan, "Expropriating the Expropriators" at 150, 152. See also Akinsanya, *The Expropriation of Multinational Property* at 240–41.

67 For some of the difficulties in rectifying past wrongs see, e.g., Robert Nozick, *Anarchy, State, and Utopia* 152 (1974).

68 *Cf.* Sornarajah, *The Pursuit of Nationalized Property* at 25.

69 See, e.g., Dale B. Furnish, "Days of Revindication and National Dignity: Petroleum Expropriations in Peru and Bolivia," in II Lillich, *The Valuation of Nationalized Property* at 55, 83 (1973).

70 See Dozler, "New Foundations" at 573.

consideration. This branch advances a more specific claim for the set-off of excess profits which are said to have been made by the pertinent foreign concessionaire under conditions of political and economic domination.[71] Such claims raise, of course, thorny problems of defining international criteria for excess profits, or for a "just price,"[72] and invoke – albeit indirectly – whatever distributive components need be taken into account by contract law.[73] Needless to say, neither the concept of just price, nor the distributive characteristics of contract law, can be properly discussed herein.

To summarize, it emerges that while the extreme revisionist claim is founded on a somewhat superficial conception of equality, all the three main contentions of moderate revisionism are embedded – directly or indirectly – in a vision of what is said to be a more just international community. Such a vision, like any other social vision, encompasses a corresponding conception of property. More specifically, all three lines of argument contain distributive aspirations. The intellectual impetus which stimulates the cry for an international redistribution focuses both on the vindication of past wrongs or the reversal of excess profits, and – perhaps primarily – on the present need of the expropriating country to realize its sovereign right to development and the ability of the alien to bear the resulting costs.

In fact, the preceding pages have demonstrated a movement to change the rules governing our paradigm in the context of international law; a movement which is premised upon an almost overt appeal to claims of distributive justice,[74] and is moreover motivated by a desire to reshape the world community's distributive outlook. Thus, they highlight the distributive underpinnings of our paradigm and underscore the reciprocal relation of ethos and law.

[71] See, e.g., Friedmann, "Social Conflict" at 133. For some accounts of the historic circumstances in which claims of excess profits were aroused and the controversies involved, see, e.g., Akinsanya, *The Expropriation of Multinational Property* at 241–43; Muller, "Compensation for Nationalization" at 51–54.

[72] See, e.g., Schachter, *Sharing the World's Resources* at 129; Roger C. Wesley, "A Compensation Framework for Expropriated Property in the Developing Countries," in III Lillich, *The Valuation of Nationalized Property* at 3, 25–40 (1975). But see Dozler, "New Foundations" at 583–84.

[73] See generally Anthony T. Kronman, "Contract Law and Distributive Justice," 89 *Yale Law Journal* 472 (1980).

[74] Notice that the two alternatives to the traditional doctrine considered above – that of no compensation and of partial compensation – are classified in my terminology as a *sacrifice* rationale since both call for the actual diminution of the deprived party's estate.

Indeed, once the connection of our doctrine and the underlying distributive scheme has been shown (in the conspicuous fashion which is typical only of international law), and the dynamics of changing these "symbiotic twins," law and ethos, have been fully acknowledged, the question of whether the traditional doctrine has in fact been modified seems almost redundant for our purposes. None the less, in order not to leave the story incomplete, the next section provides its (current) finale.

An emerging consensus?

The difficulty

Diplomats, international lawyers, and commentators alike are vigorously debating the current content of the international norms governing our paradigm. Evaluating the evidence advanced by the disputants regarding the present state of the law is a complex task. The sources are confusingly inconsistent, at times simply contradictory. Moreover, the issue is doubly complicated since the incompatibility of the various sources is compounded by a jurisprudential debate over the relative normative importance of the sources themselves. Since the attitudes of the disputing parties to this debate also seem to be determined to a large extent by the ensuing results regarding the doctrinal rules, chaos seems almost inevitable.

Still, I believe that something can be said regarding the state of the law today; in any case, both an international lawyer and an international adjudicator are bound to give advice or resolve a dispute, respectively, notwithstanding any murkiness.[75] None the less, the account offered below is quite modest. It does not suggest any formulation of the state of the law, but instead contents itself with the exclusion of two opposite alternatives. That is, while I conclude that the traditional doctrine has been so degraded that it can no longer be considered good law and that extreme revisionism has never been accepted as its replacement, the evidence does not lend affirmative support to any specific intermediate stance. The (indeterminate) norm of "less than full" compensation seems, on balance, to reflect better the emerging law than any of the alternatives, but the specific contours of the new doctrine are yet to be clarified and cannot be equated at this stage with moderate revisionism.[76]

[75] See generally Hersch O. Lauterpacht, "Some Observations on the Prohibition of 'Non-Liquet' and the Completeness of Law," in II *Collected Papers* 213 (1975).

[76] *Cf.* Norton, "A Law of the Future" at 491.

Article 38(1) of the Statute of the International Court of Justice[77] can be our methodological starting point. Although challenged, it is still commonly considered an authoritative statement of the sources of international law.[78] It designates as primary sources:

a. international conventions, whether general or particular, establishing rules expressly recognized by the contesting states;
b. international custom, as evidence of a general practice accepted as law;
c. the general principles of law recognized by civilized nations;

In addition, article 38 mentions two "subsidiary means for the determinations of rules of law": (i) "judicial decisions," which are, as per article 59, of "no binding force except between the parties and in respect to the particular case"; and (ii) "the teachings of the most qualified publicists of the various nations."

Since no general convention covers the doctrine under consideration,[79] since our hypothetical case excludes the existence of any relevant specific convention between the host and the home states, and since, finally, the teachings of international law scholars are as diverse as the range of the possible solutions to our hypothetical case, the following subsections survey the pertinent evidence regarding the other three sources: custom (or state practice), general principles, and cases. The first source is further divided into three sub-categories all of which are frequently analyzed as purported evidence for state practice: (i) lump-sum settlement agreements; (ii) bilateral investment treaties; and (iii) a series of the United Nations General Assembly resolutions. With respect to each of these groups of data, the following pages specify not only the substantive rule indicated by it (if any), but also the intricacy of its normative status. The findings are summarized in table 3.[80]

Lump-sum settlement agreements

Consider first the lump-sum settlement agreements concluded between host (nationalizing) states and home states. Richard Lillich and Burns Weston have conducted an empirical study of the norms emanating from

[77] Statute of the International Court of Justice, TS No. 993 (at 25) (1945).
[78] See, e.g., Norton, "A Law of the Future" at 497 and sources therein.
[79] The law of international claims – of which our subject matter is a part – was subject to numerous efforts of codification, none of which has been accorded general acceptance. For an annotated collection see II Garcia-Amador, *The Changing Law* at 765–891.
[80] See p. 166 below.

168 post-war agreements.[81] The results of this painstaking analysis are unambiguous. Partial compensation has become the predominant pattern of behavior. It has been established as such over many years in many settlement agreements concluded by many states; it is, in short, more the norm than the exception.[82] As some other commentators maintain, these agreements are also indicative of at least some significance of the host state's capacity to pay.[83]

While no serious attempts have been advanced to challenge the substantive outcomes of that study, its jurisprudential significance has been denigrated.[84] Thus, judges, arbitrators, and champions of both the Hull formula and extreme revisionism alike have treated lump-sum settlement agreements as but voluntary concessions to socio-economic and political expediency. As such, the argument goes, they are of no more legal significance than are out-of-court compromises in any domestic context.

Lillich, Weston, and their supporters still insist on the evidentiary power of international settlement agreements as expressions of state practice or international custom. To their adversaries' thesis they reply primarily by emphasizing that unlike its municipal counterpart, there is no compulsory adjudication mechanism in the international arena, and that in fact, during the post-war era, settlements – rather than judicial decisions – have

[81] Lillich and Weston's two-volume treatise covers 139 agreements concluded between World War II and 1975. See Lillich and Weston, *International Claims: Their Settlement by Lump Sum Agreements*. In a subsequent article, these authors indicate that an initial assessment of 29 more recent agreements generally reinforces their previous conclusions. Regarding the adequacy of the compensation agreed, they say that it appears that the less lump-sum settlements involve war-time or immediate post-war nationalizations, the more compensation they provide. Thus, the finding of partial compensation becomes less sharpened, but none the less still existent. See Richard B. Lillich and Burns H. Weston, "Lump Sum Agreements: Their Continuing Contribution to the Law of International Claims," 82 *American Journal of International Law* 69, 70, 78 (1988).

[82] Lillich and Weston, *International Claims: Their Settlement by Lump Sum Agreements* at 218, 239, 251. See also Asante, "International Law and Foreign Investment" at 605–06.

[83] See I Garcia-Amador, *The Changing Law* at 131; Dozler, "New Foundations" at 582–83; and Verwey and Schrijver, "The Taking of Foreign Property" at 20, 22. It should be mentioned, however, that Lillich and Weston themselves maintain that lump-sum settlement agreements do not prescribe normative guidelines concerning the quantum of compensation to be awarded. See Lillich and Weston, *International Claims: Their Settlement by Lump Sum Agreements* at 252–53.

[84] The recent sources of the debate regarding the normative significance of settlement agreements are collected in Lillich and Weston, "Lump Sum Agreements: Their Continuing Contribution." These authors' contentions are detailed in Lillich and Weston, *International Claims: Their Settlement by Lump Sum Agreements* at chapter 1 and at 262–63.

become the major mechanism for resolving nationalization cases.[85] As such, settlement agreements create community-wide expectations, and therefore their role of generating and clarifying norms cannot be ignored. Hence, any commonalities or general trends emerging from lump-sum settlement agreements must be considered as "a general practice" within the meaning of article 38(1)(b).

Bilateral investment treaties

Not less complicated is the legal significance of bilateral investment treaties. Unlike lump-sum agreements, this purported evidence to international custom does not reflect an erosion of the traditional doctrine. On the contrary, Wil Verwey and Nico Schrijver's analysis of 195 bilateral (and one multilateral) investment-protection treaties[86] leads to the opposite conclusion. These treaties generally reinforce the Hull formula. In particular, their research demonstrates that both treaties concluded between developed and developing countries, and treaties concluded between developing countries *inter se*, refer predominantly to a standard of full compensation (or an equivalent thereof). Interestingly enough, this phenomenon has become sharpened since 1962, considered to be the year in which the attack on the traditional doctrine has been "officially" launched.[87]

Here again the data seems undisputable, but its significance highly debatable.[88] Thus, on the one hand, it has been maintained that the widespread and consistent use of the traditional compensation standard in

[85] The arbitration cases discussed at pp. 156–64 below are perceived as the exception which proves the general proposition of the relative rarity of international arbitration or adjudication.

[86] See Verwey and Schrijver, "The Taking of Foreign Property" at 60–75.

[87] The general conclusions of Verwey and Schrijver correspond, in particular, to the treaty practice of the United States with developed and developing states alike, especially in recent years. See K. Scott Gudgeon, "Valuation of Nationalized Property under United States and other Bilateral Investment Treaties," in IV Lillich, *The Valuation of Nationalized Property* at 101 (1987). Notice, in this context, Mexico's recent submission to the Hull formula (albeit in different words) within the framework of the North American Free Trade Agreement (NAFTA), which seems especially satisfying, in American eyes, given the context in which this formula was announced (see pp. 134–35 above). See Tali Levi, " NAFTA's Provision for Compensation in the Event of Expropriation: A Reassessment of the 'Prompt, Adequate and Effective' Standard," 31 *Stanford Journal of International Law* 423 (1995); But *cf.* Justine Dali, "Has Mexico Crossed the Border on State Responsibility for Economic Injury to Aliens? Foreign Investment and the Calvo Clause in Mexico After the NAFTA," 25 *St. Mary Law Journal* 1,147, Part VI (1994) (who believes that Mexico's apparent abandonment of the Calvo doctrine in NAFTA is rather insignificant).

[88] For a good survey of the pertinent views see Verwey and Schrijver, "The Taking of Foreign Property" at 84–88.

a large number of recent bilateral treaties constitutes an important element of state practice, and thus valuable evidence to customary international law.[89] On the other hand, it has been argued that the inclusion of traditional compensation clauses in *bi*lateral treaties can suggest an opposite result respecting customary international law, namely that but for such an explicit clause the rule under consideration was not applicable. Thus perceived, the Hull formula enunciated by specific treaties is but a part of the developing country's *quid pro quo* induced by a proper consideration.[90]

United Nations General Assembly resolutions

The third alleged evidence of state practice, which is also considered the most important attack on the traditional doctrine, are the resolutions of the General Assembly of the United Nations. The first resolution pertaining to this chapter – No. 1,803 – was passed in 1962 declaring that:

> Nationalization, expropriation or requisitioning shall be based on grounds or reasons of public utility, security or the national interest which are recognized as overriding purely individual or private interest, both domestic and foreign. In such cases, the owner shall be paid *appropriate compensation*, in accordance with the rules in force in the State taking such measures in the exercise of its sovereignty and *in accordance with international law*.[91]

Two points seem clear from the wording of Resolution No. 1,803:[92] (i) extreme revisionism was clearly rejected as the resolution acknowledges

[89] See *Kalamazoo Spice Extraction Co.* v. *Provisional Military Goverment of Socialist Ethiopia*, 729 F 2d 422, 427 (6th Cir. 1984); Clagett, "Just Compensation in International Law" at 76–77; Gudgeon, "Valuation of Nationalized Property" at 121.

[90] See Asante, "International Law and Foreign Investment" at 601–02, 607–08; Dozler, "New Foundations" at 566–67; Schachter, *Sharing the World's Resources* at 126–27. See also *SEDCO Inc.* v. *National Iranian Oil Co.*, 10 Iran–US CTR 180, 185 (1986). The argument against the significance of bilateral treaties as evidence of state practice holds also with respect to municipal foreign-investment laws. See Dozler, *ibid.* at 567 note 53.

[91] Permanent Sovereignty over Natural Resources, GA Res. 1,803, UN GAOR, 17th Session, Supplement No. 17, at 15, UN Doc. A/5217, art. 4 (1962), reprinted in 2 ILM 223 (1963). The emphases are mine.

[92] See, e.g., *Banco Nacional De Cuba* v. *Chase Manhattan Bank*, 658 F 2d 875, 889–91 (2nd Cir. 1980); Lipson, *Standing Guard* at 88; Jerzy Makarczyk, *Principles of a New International Economic Order* 229–30 (1988); Allahyar Mouri, *The International Law of Expropriation as Reflected in the Work of the Iran–US Claims Tribunal* 363–65 (1994); Subrata Roy Chowdhury, "Permanent Sovereignty and its Impact on Stabilization Clauses and Patterns of Development Co-Operation," in *Permanent Sovereignty Over Natural Resources in International Law: Principles and Practice* 42, 61 (Kamal Hossain and Subrata Roy Chowdhury eds. 1984); Verwey and Schrijver, "The Taking of Foreign Property" at 41, 53.

the relevance of international law to the issue of compensation;[93] and (ii) the term "appropriate" which quantifies the standard of compensation seems intentionally vague, and was indeed inserted in order to facilitate a compromise which will enable the broad acceptance accorded to this resolution.[94] Although the precise meaning of "appropriate" has remained unclear, it seems safe to say that it was intended to mean neither "no compensation" nor "full compensation."

To be sure, champions of the traditional doctrine – mainly US diplomats and lawyers – vigorously attempt to advance the theory of equating appropriate compensation with the Hull formula. They advocate this position notwithstanding the failure of a US amendment that defined "appropriate" as "prompt, adequate, and effective," basing their theory on the general acquiescence to the US delegate's expression of confidence that the term will be interpreted this way.[95] There are obvious difficulties in according legal significance to such a statement which did not succeed in entering the record through the main door of the resolution's wording.[96] But even if this obstacle is overcome, and the interpreter opens the record of discussions to be utilized in her interpretive task, there is no compelling reason to prefer the US statement over the statements of other delegates. Once the whole record is examined, no clear answer emerges. Various interpretations were stated, none of which was directly opposed or contradicted in debate, from Hungary's statement to the effect that the question of appropriateness is to be determined by the host state, through Ceylon's assertion that "appropriate" leaves room for the consideration of the taking state's capacity to pay, to the US statement mentioned above.[97]

A decade later the challenge of Resolution No. 1,803. to the traditional doctrine came to seem gentle. As more voting power shifted toward the developing countries, and as they pushed to a more radical agenda, they were no longer content with a compromise and sponsored instead three confrontational resolutions which clearly reject any notion of international regulatory norm. The most vivid and strident of these resolutions is the

[93] An amendment to Resolution No. 1,803 that had the effect of endorsing extreme revisionism was in fact defeated.

[94] The vote was eighty-seven in favor to two opposed (France and South Africa) and twelve abstentions (mainly the Soviet bloc countries). See Stephen M. Schwebel, "The Story of the UN's Declaration on Permanent Sovereignty Over Natural Resources," 49 *American Bar Association Journal* 463, 463 (1963).

[95] See, e.g., Fales, "A Comparison of Compensation" at 182–83 and authorities therein.

[96] See, e.g., William N. Eskridge, Jr., "The New Textualism," 37 *UCLA Law Review* 621, 649–50 (1990).

[97] See Verwey and Schrijver, "The Taking of Foreign Property" at 56.

1974 Charter of Economic Rights and Duties of States ("the Charter").[98] Its pertinent part – article 2(2)(c) – reads as follows:

> Each state has the right to nationalize, expropriate or transfer ownership of foreign property in which case appropriate compensation should be paid by the State adopting such measures, taking into account its relevant laws and regulations and all the circumstances that the State considers pertinent. In any case where the question of compensation gives rise to a controversy, it shall be settled under the domestic law of the nationalizing State and by its tribunals, unless [it otherwise] is freely and mutually agreed by all States concerned.[99]

There can be no doubt that this resolution domesticates the issue of compensation and calls for a total repudiation of the traditional doctrine. It is an attempt to "liberate" nationalizing states from any international limitations whatsoever; a pure expression of extreme revisionism. No wonder that, unlike the 1962 resolution, the Charter is highly controversial and most developed countries either dissented or abstained.[100]

Obviously, resolutions of the General Assembly of the United Nations do not have the force of law.[101] But even conservative writers agree that where a resolution expresses *opinio juris communis*, it "may legitimize conduct which, when it develops (by acts and acquiescence in combination) into *usus communis*, eventually becomes legalized by the emergence of new customary international law."[102]

[98] See Lipson, *Standing Guard* at 19 note * and 88; Verwey and Schrijver, "The Taking of Foreign Property" at 55; Weston, "The New International Economic Order" at 93.

[99] Charter of Economic Rights and Duties of States, GA Res. 3,281, UN GAOR, 29th Session, Supplement No. 31, at 50, UN Doc. A/9631, art. 2(2)(c) (1974), reprinted in 14 ILM 251 (1975).

[100] See II Garcia-Amador, *The Changing Law* at 690–705; Makarczyk, *Principles* at 235–39; Lillich, "The Current Status of the Law" at 15–16; Verwey and Schrijver, "The Taking of Foreign Property" at 43–45, 54–55; Weston, "The New International Economic Order" at 93. *Contra*, e.g., Sidney Dell, *The United Nations and International Business* 49 (1990). As the text above indicates, extreme revisionism was already manifested in two earlier resolutions. See Permanent Sovereignty over Natural Resources, GA Res. 3,171, UN GAOR, 28th Session, Supplement No. 30, at 52, UN Doc. A/9030, paragraph 3 (1973), reprinted in 13 ILM 238 (1974); Declaration on the Establishment of a New International Economic Order, GA Res. 3,201, UN GAOR, 6th Special Session, Supplement No. 1, at 3, UN Doc. A/9559, paragraphs 4(e), 4(f) (1974), reprinted in 13 ILM 715 (1974).

[101] See UN Charter art. 10. For an account of the minimizing school respecting the force of UN resolutions, see Stephen M. Schwebel, "The Legal Effect of Resolutions and Cases of Conduct of the United Nations," 7 *Forum Internationale* 1, 3–13 (1985). Other secondary sources are collected in Clagett, "Just Compensation in International Law" at 44–45 and notes 69–70.

[102] Verwey and Schrijver, "The Taking of Foreign Property" at 77. See also, e.g., *SEDCO Inc.* v. *National Iranian Oil Co.*, 10 Iran–US CTR 180, 199 (1986) (separate opinion of arbitrator Brower).

Applying this premise to article 2(2)(c) of the Charter deprives it of any legal significance since, as Weston demonstrates,[103] "it was not expected to have binding legal effect,[104] because large segments of the international economic community opposed its adoption, and because it has not been confirmed in postadoption practice."

The 1962 resolution, and in particular its novel concept of "appropriate compensation," seems importantly different: there is a considerable unanimity in international arbitral practice and scholarly opinion that this resolution "at least reflects, if it does not evidence, current international law."[105]

Some commentators reply to this proposition by emphasizing that the ambivalence of the language of Resolution No. 1,803 entails the curious result that each persuasion clings to the "appropriate compensation" language with its own predetermined (often opposing) precepts. In such a case, the argument goes, there is no sense in according legal significance to a resolution which says everything, and therefore nothing.[106] But this contention goes one step too far. Although it cannot be disputed that no clear positive content springs from the "appropriate compensation" language, one should not disregard the negative implications of the 1962 resolution, that is the rejection of both extreme revisionism and the Hull formula. In this respect, one should also keep in mind that, even if the Charter has no legal power, it at least accentuates the derogatory impact of the UN resolutions upon the traditional doctrine.[107]

Accordingly, I believe that Charles Lipson is correct in observing that the UN resolutions "expose the cumulative shift in international values" from the values of capital-exporting states which put clear limits on expropriation and endorse full compensation, to the current prevailing interna-

103 Weston, "The New International Economic Order" at 124. See also, e.g., *Texaco Overseas Petroleum Co.* v. *Libyan Arabic Republic*, 53 ILR 389, 486–95 (Dupuy sole arbitrator 1977); Oscar Schachter, *International Law in Theory and Practice* 321–22 (1991).

104 *Contra*, e.g., Dozler, "New Foundations" at 563.

105 *SEDCO Inc.* v. *National Iranian Oil Co.*, 10 Iran–US CTR 180, 186 (1986) and authorities therein. It should be mentioned that the language of Resolution No. 1,803 is echoed in paragraph 5.5 of the Declaration on the Progressive Development of the Principle of Public International Law relating to the NIEO made by the International Law Association in its 1986 Seoul conference. This declaration acknowledges the right of a state to nationalize property within its territory subject to "appropriate compensation as required by international law." See generally Makarczyk, *Principles* at 246–54.

106 See, e.g., Verwey and Schrijver, "The Taking of Foreign Property" at 80–81.

107 See Dozler, "New Foundations" at 564.

tional values which corrode the ability of major capitalist states to assure investment security.[108]

General principles

A second primary source of international law which may inform our discussion is called "general principles of law." Two principles are repeatedly mentioned as candidates: the principle of "acquired" or "vested" property rights[109] and the principle against unjust enrichment.[110] Unfortunately, none of these principles sheds any specific light over the standard (or valuation) of compensation in cases of nationalization. The reason for this should be obvious by now: as social artifacts both principles are open to conflicting interpretations, and in a multicultural world community are bound to be subjected to such opposite views.

This disappointing lack of definite content has already been demonstrated regarding the notion of property. It is, of course, not less conspicuous respecting the principle against unjust enrichment, which is analyzed throughout this book as an essentially contested concept.[111] This basic claim is reinforced by the diametrically opposed uses made by the notion of unjust enrichment in the context of this chapter's hypothetical case. Thus, on the one hand, the principle of unjust enrichment is said to provide a basis for the claim of full compensation by highlighting the unjustness of the plaintiff's wealth deprivation. But on the other hand, moderate revisionists underscore the equitable foundations of the notion of unjust enrichment and advocate accordingly a rule of less than full compensation which takes account of all the basic equities of the situation.[112]

Indeed, just as the jurisprudence of American law and of Talmudic civil law cannot be explained by reference to the abstract principle against unjust enrichment, so the debate over standards of compensation for nationalization has not been conducted – and certainly cannot be resolved – in these terms. The principle against unjust enrichment is a framework which absorbs and manifests divergent social (in particular distributive)

108 See Lipson, *Standing Guard* at 89–90. See also Steiner *et al.*, *Transnational Legal Problems* at 483–84; Schachter, *Sharing the World's Resources* at 3–4, 28–29.

109 See, e.g., "Note, General Principles of Law in International Commercial Arbitration," 101 *Harvard Law Review* 1,816, 1,829–33 (1988).

110 See Wayne Mapp, *The Iran–United States Claims Tribunal: The First Ten Years 1981–1991* 210–16 (1993).

111 See W. B. Gallie, "Essentially Contested Concepts," 56 *Proceedings of the Aristotelian Society* 167 (New Ser. 1956).

112 See, e.g., Detlev Chr. Dicke, "Unjust Enrichment and Compensation," in Dicke, *Foreign Investment* at 268, passim; Dozler, "New Foundations" at 580–81; Meessen, "Domestic Law Concepts" at 161–65 and sources therein.

values. Hence, without direct reference to these (conflicting) values it is of no justificatory or explanatory force.

Another way to deduce a relevant "general principle of law" might have been by direct reference to national laws of expropriating (i.e., developing) countries. But since those authors who conducted such an analysis reached the (unsurprising) conclusion of great diversity and variation, this path is also of no assistance for our purposes.[113]

Judicial decisions

This brings us to the last relevant source of international law: the pertinent case law. Before outlining the diverse case law, one should put this source itself – which is so central to common law legal regimes – in proper perspective. Three preliminary remarks may clarify the unique status of the cases as means for ascertaining the current state of the international doctrine of nationalization. First, in surveying the cases we should be attentive to the nature or identity of the pertinent decision-maker, which becomes crucial in the international arena where there is no compulsory adjudication mechanism. Thus, it is important to mention that *not one* of the post-war cases which discuss the issue of the proper standard of compensation comes from the International Court of Justice. This apparently bizarre phenomenon derives from the reluctance of home states to submit their expropriation claims to a court which in recent years has been composed largely of judges from socialist and Third World countries.[114]

The cases reported below come from myriad other fora. Most of them are the results of arbitrations, both *ad hoc* and administered; one is a celebrated case of the US Second Circuit, another is a *dictum* of the European Court of Human Rights. Drawing a systematic account from such sources is a delicate matter as the cases are frequently contradictory. A telling example is the three Libyan nationalization arbitrations which arose out of very similar facts and involved virtually identical issues of law but were none the less resolved quite differently.[115] Moreover, with no institutional priority

[113] See, e.g., Amerasinghe, "The Quantum of Compensation" at 97–107; Verwey and Schrijver, "The Taking of Foreign Property" at 83.

[114] See Brice N. Clagett, "Present State of the International Law of Compensation for Expropriated Property and Repudiated State Contracts," in *Private Investors Abroad – Problems and Solutions in International Business in 1989* 12-1, 12–13 (Carol J. Holgren ed. 1989). See also Sornarajah, *The Pursuit of Nationalized Property* at 195. *Cf.* F. A. Mann, "Foreign Investment and the International Court of Justice: The ELSI case," 86 *American Journal of International Law* 92, 100 (1992).

[115] See Robert B. von Mehren and P. Nicholas Kourides, "International Arbitration Between States and Foreign Private Parties: The Libyan Nationalization Cases," 75 *American Journal of International Law* 476 (1981).

amongst the different fora, one may be tempted to concentrate on the most recent forum – the Iran–US Claims Tribunal – the opinions of which regarding our hypothetical case outnumber the opinions of the rest of the fora combined. But this would be an unfortunate mistake since this distinguished tribunal is but one forum (with specific characterizations, to be sure) among many fora. More specifically, one should bear in mind Rahmatullah Khan's suggestion that the relatively traditionalist jurisprudence of this forum derives from the mere fact that the neutral arbitrator of each of this tribunal's chambers is appointed by the President of the Constitutional Court of Netherlands, and is hence usually Western-educated.[116]

Our second caveat concerns the difficulty of extricating legal rules from the cases. Many cases are not clearly and exclusively based on international law,[117] as our hypothetical case presumes. The most conspicuous reason for this is the existence in many cases – notably the ones decided by the Iran–US Claims Tribunal – of a treaty clause which governs the question of compensation. Such clause is said to supersede customary international law and the cases are decided on the premise of its being a *lex specialis*,[118] making it especially difficult to speculate how the pertinent jurisprudence will be perceived by future international decision-makers.[119]

This complexity only intensifies the hostility with which international law conventionally approaches judge-made law, as distinct from state-made law (that is, custom). But this traditional subsidiary status of case law in international law, which introduces our third caveat, has been challenged by Patrick Norton. In discussing the doctrine of our hypothetical case, Norton attempts to blur the distinction between cases and state practice by arguing that:

> The decisions have their authority because states have agreed to submit the dispute in question to judicial or arbitral resolution and have generally abided by the results. Indeed, by expressly agreeing to have these disputes determined by law, states have arguably shown a much greater *opinio juris* than in most forms of state practice.[120]

This observation appears valid, but it necessarily evokes an especially urgent need for a realist analysis of the cases. Indeed, where the authority of

[116] See Rahmatullah Khan, *The Iran–United States Claims Tribunal: Controversies, Cases, and Contribution* 259–60 (1990). *Cf.* Meessen, "Domestic Law Concepts" at 158.

[117] See, e.g., Meessen, "Domestic Law Concepts" at 157–58.

[118] See, e.g., Khan, *The Iran–United States Claims Tribunal* at 203–13.

[119] *Cf. Case Concerning the Barcelona Traction, Light and Power Company, Limited (New Application: 1962) (Belguim* v. *Spain)* 1970 ICJ 3, 40 (5 February).

[120] Norton, "A Law of the Future" at 504.

the cases derives only from their acceptance by the parties, the need to examine what a tribunal has done, and not only what it has said, is especially acute. This is because the practical result, and not the reasoning, is the part to which states reveal their abidance. Not surprisingly, such a realist analysis uncovers an even more emphatic erosion of the traditional doctrine than the opinions reveal. Norton also is aware of the frequently unpersuasive arguments given – and the even more frequent habit of not providing an argument – for reducing the amount of the award. None the less, he claims that this phenomenon should concern only practitioners, and that it has no bearing on legal theory.[121] This maneuver may serve Norton's purposes, being a champion of the traditional doctrine, but this chapter avoids the strategy of "having it both ways." It indeed treats the cases as an important source of law, but it also emphasizes the unavoidable realist perspective this premise entails.

All these caveats considered, I believe that the following propositions properly summarize the case law pertinent to our hypothetical case. In cases of mixed tribunals, I refer primarily to the neutral arbitrator's opinion.

1. There is virtually no case which repudiates the notion of an international minimum standard altogether. Moreover, even cases which openly acknowledge the erosion of the traditional doctrine, unequivocally reject extreme revisionism.[122]

2. Some cases adhere to the traditional norm of "full compensation." This category is composed of virtually all of the handful of arbitration awards which addressed the international law of expropriation prior to the initiation of the UN ideological debate.[123] It also includes more recent awards given by the International Centre for Settlement of Investment Disputes ("ICSID"), the *Texaco* arbitration, and several cases of the Iran–US Claims Tribunal.[124] Cases in this category – such as the *Amco* case, issued by

[121] See *ibid.* at 495.

[122] See *Libyan American Oil Co. (Liamco)* v. *Libyan Arab Republic*, 62 ILR 140, 200–02 (Mahmassani sole arbitrator 1977). See also, e.g., *Banco Nacional De Cuba* v. *Chase Manhattan Bank*, 658 F 2d 875, 891 (2nd Cir. 1980); John A. Westberg, *International Transactions and Claims Involving Private Parties* 212–13 (1991).

[123] See Norton, "A Law of the Future" at 477–78 and authorities therein.

[124] In addition to the cases considered below, there are four other cases which are mentioned at times as belonging to the full-compensation category of cases, but seem to me of a limited relevance:

1. In *BP Exploration Co. (Libya)* v. *Libyan Arab Republic*, 53 ILR 297, 347 (Lagergren sole arbitrator 1973) the arbitrator mentioned – as one of his arguments for denying the remedy of *restitutio in integrum* – the fact that this concept "has been employed merely as a vehicle for establishing the amount of damages."

ICSID – hold explicitly that international law prescribes the award of "the full compensation of prejudice," i.e., both the *damnum emergens* and the *lucrum cessans.*[125] Alternatively, their fidelity to the Hull formula can be inferred by implication. This conclusion seems appropriate with regard to the *AIG* case of the Iran–US Claims Tribunal, where it was held that the value of the property taken, to which its former owner is normally entitled, is best calculated as a "going concern," taking into account not only the "net book value of the assets, but also such elements as good will and likely future profitability had the company been allowed to continue its business under its former management."[126] Similarly, it seems fair to claim that the *Texaco* award, in which the arbitrator acknowledged the claimant's entitlement to the remedy of *restitutio in integrum*,[127] also lends support to the traditional norms, since it seems plausible that if specific restitution is

Pamela B. Gann, in "Compensation Standard for Expropriation," 23 *Columbia Journal of Transnational Law* 615, 627 note 46, theorizes that this sentence demonstrates the arbitrator's endorsement of the full-compensation standard. This seems to be a dubious theory, the weakness of which is amplified once one reads the more recent – and directly relevant and comprehensive – opinion of arbitrator Lagergren in the *INA* case discussed at p. 161 below.

2. In *AGIP Co.* v. *Popular Republic of Congo*, 21 ILM 726 (ICSID arbitration 1979) the tribunal recognized, primarily on the basis of Congolese law, the claimant's right to lost profits, and awarded the claimant – as it requested for this element of damages – three francs.
3. In *Benvenuti et Bonfant* v. *People's Republic of Congo*, 21 ILM 740 (ICSID arbitration 1980) the tribunal, determining the amount of damages *ex aequo et bono*, was willing to grant the claimant the cost of its (recent) investment, but since the claimant limited its petition to its value (calculated according to the discounted-cash-flow method), which was a smaller amount than the cost, it awarded accordingly.
4. In *SEDCO Inc.* v. *National Iranian Oil Co.*, 10 Iran–US CTR 180 (1986) the tribunal held that the claimant is entitled to the full value of its expropriated interest, explicitly emphasizing that it considers that case as a case of a discrete expropriation, as distinguished from large-scale nationalization like our hypothetical case, and that the remedy sought is the *damnum emergens*, and not the disputed lost-profits component: *ibid.* at 187–88. Hence, while Judge Brower's insistence in his separate opinion that this case does not prescribe a deviation from the traditional doctrine (*ibid.* at 203 note 36) is valid, his opening declaration that this case "abundantly reconfirms" the traditional rules (*ibid.* at 189) is an overstatement. See M. Pellonpaa and M. Fitzmaurice, "Taking of Property in the Practice of the Iran–United Stated Claims Tribunal," 19 *Netherlands Yearbook of International Law* 53, 117–18 (1988).

[125] *Amco Asia Corp.* v. *Indonesia*, 24 ILM 1,022, 1,036–37 (1985), annulled on other grounds, 25 ILM 1,441 (ICSID arbitration 1986). See also *Tippets, Abbett, McCarthy, Stratton* v. *TAMS-AFFA Consulting Engineers of Iran*, 6 Iran–US CTR 219, 225 (1984).

[126] *American International Group Inc.* v. *Islamic Republic of Iran*, 4 Iran–US CTR 96, 105, 109 (1983).

[127] *Texaco Overseas Petroleum Co.* v. *Libyan Arabic Republic*, 53 ILR 389 (Dupuy sole arbitrator 1977).

allowed a pecuniary recovery of full compensation would have been granted had the claimant sought such a remedy.[128]

Some of the cases in this category also endorse the discounted-cash-flow method of valuation, which they consider as the most appropriate method for calculating a full compensation award.[129] Another subset includes cases which describe this standard of compensation as the correct interpretation of the "appropriate compensation" language of Resolution No. 1,803 which is – they accept – the current prevailing norm.[130]

3. Several other cases take the impact of the post-war sources described above more seriously. They typically include extensive discussions of these sources and an endorsement of "appropriate compensation" as current international law. They point to the difficulty of ascribing a definite meaning to this elusive term.[131] Nevertheless, they acknowledge its being a compromise solution which indicates the possibility of a standard of less than full compensation.

A good example for this category can be found in the *Liamco* case, where the arbitrator emphasized the gradual evolution of the concept of property and the erosion of its sacredness, and accorded considerable significance to the UN resolutions and to lump-sum settlements as evidence of the recent dominant trend of international opinion.[132] Thus, he concluded that the traditional doctrine has undergone such an evolution which justifies the adoption of a new norm – "equitable compensation" he called it – the calculation of which is guided, and the amount of which is capped, by the traditional norm of full compensation.[133]

[128] See Gann, "Compensation Standard for Expropriation" at 627–28.

[129] See *Amco Asia Corp.* v. *Indonesia*, 24 ILM 1,022, 1,037 (1985), annulled on other grounds, 25 ILM 1,441 (ICSID arbitration 1986); *Starrett Hous. Corp.* v. *Islamic Republic of Iran*, 16 Iran–US CTR 112, 201 (1987). *Cf. Phillips Petroleum Co. Iran* v. *Islamic Republic of Iran*, 21 Iran–US CTR 79, 122–23 (1989) (while not expressing any view as to the alleged erosion of the traditional doctrine, founding its opinion on the pertinent treaty clause as a *lex specialis*, the tribunal followed the logic of the discounted-cash-flow method of valuation as the approximation of the fair market value in the absence of an active and free market for comparable assets at the date of taking).

[130] See *Sola Tiles Inc.* v. *Islamic Republic of Iran*, 14 Iran–US CTR 223, 235–37 (1987) (holding that the drafters of Resolution No. 1,803 "used the word 'appropriate' in the sense of 'adequate'"); *Texaco Overseas Petroleum Co.* v. *Libyan Arabic Republic*, 53 ILR 389 (Dupuy sole arbitrator 1977) (endorsing the "appropriate compensation" standard while acknowledging the claimant's right to *restitutio in integrum*).

[131] See, e.g., *Banco Nacional De Cuba* v. *Chase Manhattan Bank*, 658 F 2d 875, 891 (2nd Cir. 1980).

[132] On the other hand, the arbitrator discounted the importance of the pre-war jurisprudence.

Similar conclusions can be drawn from cases of other fora, be it the US Second Circuit,[134] the *Aminoil* arbitration,[135] or a *dictum* from the European Court of Human Rights.[136] Even the Iran–US Claims Tribunal has acknowledged in several cases that the doctrine has been changed. Thus, in the *INA* case the tribunal held that in cases of large-scale nationalizations of commercial enterprises in a state undergoing a process of radical economic restructuring, international law has undergone a gradual reappraisal which undermined the doctrinal value of any full compensation standard. The principle of appropriate compensation, "which normally require[s] the 'fair market value' standard to be discounted in taking account of 'all circumstances,'" now appears to be regarded, according to the *INA* case, as the current legal standard for these cases.[137]

133 See *Libyan American Oil Co. (Liamco)* v. *Libyan Arab Republic*, 62 ILR 140, 183–89, 204–10, 218 (Mahmassani sole arbitrator 1977).

134 See *Banco Nacional De Cuba* v. *Chase Manhattan Bank*, 658 F 2d 875 (2nd Cir. 1980) (holding that "it may well be the consensus of nations that full compensation need not be paid 'in all circumstances' . . . and that requiring an expropriating state to pay 'appropriate compensation' – even considering the lack of precise definition of the term – would come closer to reflecting what international law requires": *ibid.* at 892. The court ascribes a flexible content to this emerging standard, so that it means neither partial compensation nor full compensation in all cases, but is subject to considerable judicial discretion. In the particular case, the court claimed that its award is both appropriate and full, insisting that this is one of those cases in which the standards converge: *ibid.* at 892–93. A realist analysis of this case may differ. See note 149 below.

135 *Kuwait* v. *American Independent Oil Co. (Aminoil)*, 21 ILM 976, 1,032–33 (Reuter, Sultan and Fitzmaurice arbitrators 1982) (after describing Resolution No. 1,803 as being the "most general formulation of the rules applicable for lawful nationalization," the tribunal added that both extreme interpretations thereof – as prescribing symbolic compensation, and as assimilating the compensation due for a legitimate takeover to that due in respect of an illegitimate one – were "in mutual opposition in the United Nations" and do not reach the level of "unanimous acceptance" as does the appropriate compensation standard).

136 See *Lithgow* v. *UK*, 102 *European Court of Human Rights* (Ser. A) at 82–84 (1986) (Pettiti J., dissenting) (holding that the pertinent rules of international law "have been somewhat altered under the pressure of the Third World," so that we are now "far from the definition of the *Chorzow* judgement," as "arbitral tribunals tend to be less demanding with regard to nationalizations carried out by Third World States"; the majority disputed the relevance of international law and hence did not address our issue).

137 *INA Corp.* v. *Islamic Republic of Iran*, 8 Iran–US CTR 373, 378, 388, 390 (1985). See also *Amoco International Finance Corp.* v. *Islamic Republic of Iran*, 15 Iran–US CTR 189, 222–24 (1985) (same). Recently, the tribunal held again that "customary international law favors [the] 'appropriate' compensation standard" over the Hull formula. This prevailing standard permits, according to the tribunal, flexibility and "must not be construed either to always require partial compensation or to always exclude full compensation." See *Ebrahimi* v. *Islamic Republic of Iran*, No. 560-44/46/47-3, slip op.

4. Some of the cases in category 3 above attempt to delineate the contours of the new standard by differentiating types of damages or by refuting their economically correct method of calculation. Thus, the *Liamco* award raises a doubt whether *lucrum cessans* (lost profits) is recoverable in nationalization cases,[138] while the *Amoco* case of the Iran–US Claims Tribunal attempts to distinguish between "lost profits" which are not recoverable, and "future prospects" which are said to be a part of the asset's current value and hence recoverable. *Amoco* also raises doubts respecting the propriety of the discounted-cash-flow method of valuation.[139] Finally, some other cases – for example, the *Phillips* case of the Iran–US Claims Tribunal – endorse the discounted-cash-flow method, but do so in a qualified fashion, adding reservations such as the need to consider all the relevant circumstances or the need of the "second opinion" of another valuation method.[140] As I emphasized in the first section of this chapter, all these suggestions seem to have no economic validity[141] and can hence be explained only as attempts to draw some line (ill-founded as it may be) between the recoverable and the irrecoverable.

5. Another trend within category 3 above speaks of limiting the recoverable profits to what may be considered within the *legitimate expectations* of the claimant, a notion which boils down to an *ex post* assessment of the *reasonable* rate of return (as per the arbitrator, of course).[142] This intermediary concept was first introduced in the *Aminoil* award[143] which is considered an important case due to the unanimity with which it was decided by a

38–41 (Iran–US Claims Tribunal, 12 October 1994). The analysis of this case by one reporter concludes that it actually applies a standard of partial compensation. See Merritt R. Blakeslee, "Standard of Compensation: Prompt, Adequate and Effective versus Appropriate Compensation," 89 *American Journal of International Law* 385, 389 (1995).

138 See *Libyan American Oil Co. (Liamco)* v. *Libyan Arab Republic*, 62 ILR 140, 204–10 (Mahmassani sole arbitrator 1977). See also Derek W. Bowett, "Claims Between States and Private Entities: The Twilight Zone of International Law," 35 *Catholic University Law Review* 929, 939–41 (1986).

139 See *Amoco International Finance Corp.* v. *Islamic Republic of Iran*, 15 Iran–US CTR 189, 246–51, 255–71 (1985).

140 *Phillips Petroleum Co. Iran* v. *Islamic Republic of Iran*, 21 Iran–US CTR 79, 123–24 (1989).

141 See also Lieblich, "Determinations by International Tribunals" at 47–49, 58-65, 70–71, 73–74.

142 An *ex post* assessment of the reasonable rate of return may be perceived as a moderate version of the "excess profits" theme of moderate revisionism. See Muller, "Compensation for Nationalization" at 70.

143 *Kuwait* v. *American Independent Oil Co. (Aminoil)*, 21 ILM 976, 1,033–35, 1,037–38 (Reuter, Sultan and Fitzmaurice arbitrators 1982).

tribunal that included two Western and one Third World arbitrators.[144] The *Aminoil* tribunal held that "appropriate compensation" should be determined "by means of an enquiry into all the circumstances relevant to the particular concrete case, [rather] than through abstract theoretical discussion." Hence, it rejected the claimant's contention that the value of its expropriated enterprise is represented by either the discounted cash flow or the sum of the discounted profits and the value of the physical assets, and introduced in their stead the notion of legitimate expectations.

It seems clear from the *Aminoil* award that this novel concept implies an *ex post* imposition of a reasonable rate of return. Thus, the award ascribed to the claimant – in a somewhat artificial fashion – a consent to a proposal of the host state for readjustment of its return, and a further overriding consent for a "moderate estimate" of a "reasonable rate of return," as distinguished from "speculative profits." Moreover, *Aminoil* further reduces such rate of return so as to exclude the profit margin needed for preserving incentives and keeping proper allowance for risks, explaining that once the asset has been nationalized, the risk "has *ex hypothesi* vanished."[145]

Aminoil's theory is echoed (although not specifically mentioned) in the *SPP* award of the International Chambers of Commerce Court of Arbitration ("ICC"). In this case, the tribunal rejected the claimants' discounted-cash-flow quantification of the profits they would have earned if the Pyramids Project had been allowed to reach completion. In doing so it pointed out, among others, to the "disparity between the amount of the investment made by the claimants [i.e., the original cost] and its supposed value at the material date." Hence, the tribunal concluded that it is "more appropriate to take the amount of the claimant's actual investment and add to that an incremental factor representing the increase in the value of the investment over its actual cost." Accordingly, it awarded a sum which was about 2.5 times the cost, but only about 30 percent of the value.[146]

144 See Meessen, "Domestic Law Concepts" at 158.

145 In addition, the *Aminoil* tribunal suggested a distinction between host states which "intend to do away with foreign investment entirely," and host states which "welcome foreign investment." Since Kuwait undoubtedly belongs to the latter category, it was expected to compensate expropriated investors in a way that would not "render foreign investment useless, economically." This qualification led the tribunal to the legitimate-expectations theme discussed above, leaving the reader of the opinion speculating what even more reduced standard applies regarding host states of the former category.

146 See *SPP (Middle East) Ltd.* v. *Arab Republic of Egypt*, 22 ILM 752, 782–83 (ICC arbitration 1983).

6. Finally, at least a few cases, which on the rhetorical level clearly belong to category 2 (of the "full compensation" standard) may be shifted to category 3 (of the "less than full" recovery) upon a realist analysis. These are cases which seem to pay mere lip-service to the Hull doctrine. Several such cases – notably from the Iran–US Claims Tribunal – include an explicit endorsement of the traditional norms followed by an unreasoned dismissal of the claimant's approximation of the value of the expropriated asset, and a purely discretionary determination of the amount due at a figure which is considerably lower than its value according to the discounted-cash-flow method.[147] In other cases, the rejection of the claimant's valuation and the reduction of the amount awarded is established through a factual manipulation of some sort. A frequent – but not the only[148] – example for such a manipulation is the attribution of a large portion of the loss sustained to the political happenings for which there is no international responsibility. Thus, for example, in the *Phillips* case, the Iran–US Claims Tribunal held that the valuation of an expropriated asset should take into account, among others, "the risk of reduced future production as a result of national policy changes flowing from the Iranian Revolution."[149]

Summary

The complications which emerge from the survey of the preceding section need not be surprising. Once the distributive underpinnings of our paradigm are exposed – as they are in the context of international law – it is

[147] See, e.g., *Phillips Petroleum Co. Iran* v. *Islamic Republic of Iran*, 21 Iran–US CTR 79 (1989). For a realist analysis of previous cases of this tribunal see Khan, *The Iran–United States Claims Tribunal* at 217–49. For a critical attitude see Lauterpacht, *Aspects of the Administration of International Justice* at 130–136.

[148] Recall that the *Aminoil* award, which belongs to category 3, also appears – on fair analysis – to employ some dubious attributions of consent in order to reduce the amount awarded.

[149] *Phillips Petroleum Co. Iran* v. *Islamic Republic of Iran*, 21 Iran–US CTR 79, 123 (1989). For other cases of this tribunal which use a similar strategy see Pellonpaa and Fitzmaurice, "Taking of Property" at 147, 166. For similar cases in other fora see *Banco Nacional De Cuba* v. *Chase Manhattan Bank*, 658 F 2d 875, 893–94 (2nd Cir. 1980) (holding that the claimant is not to be allowed to recover lost profits which are part of its asset's going-concern value since in the post-revolution economic situation of Cuba a potential consensual buyer would not have paid a premium in anticipation of future earnings; for a critique of this aspect of the case see Monroe Leigh, "Decision," 76 *American Journal of International Law* 847 (1982)); *SPP (Middle East) Ltd.* v. *Arab Republic of Egypt*, 22 ILM 752, 782–83 (ICC arbitration 1983) (suggesting that the unfavorable political and economic climate is one justification for forsaking the discounted-cash-flow method of valuation).

clear that prescribing specific rules is not a mechanical task. It requires a clarification of the social ethos and necessitates some degree of consensus respecting the distributive scheme the pertinent society aspires to achieve. This is a manageable (although by no means trivial) task on the domestic level. It is an extremely demanding duty in a multicultural world community.[150]

None the less, it is fair to conclude that some minimal consensus has emerged, namely, that a nationalizing state in the circumstances of our paradigm is liable to pay compensation for foreign-owned property it expropriates and that the compensation need not be the full economic value of such property.[151] The intermediate (and vague) standard of appropriate compensation, which "permits the absorption of competing claims into an overall compensation framework,"[152] seems to have prevailed. This consensus is indeed far from being robust, let alone definite. Still, it seems doubtful that any more precision of the legal norm's formulation has any chance of widespread recognition in the current conditions of a multicultural and conflicting world community.[153] Moreover, the appropriate standard of compensation seems to be the dominant norm in the relevant sources of international law as emerges from Table 3.

Whatever the current state of the law, what is crucial for this book is the demonstration of the possibility of evolution in the underlying distributive scheme and its derivative doctrinal norms. By showing the possibility of such an inter-temporal dimension, this chapter achieves its three goals: (i) the covert appeal of the international law doctrine to distributive considerations reinforces the thesis of close connection between the rules of our

150 *Cf. Banco Nacional De Cuba* v. *Sabbatino*, 376 US 398, 429–30 (1964).

151 The conclusion of an erosion of the traditional doctrine is shared by the two leading political scientists who have recently studied our field. See Lipson, *Standing Guard* at 24; and Rodman, *Sanctity Versus Sovereignty* at 2–3, 16. It is also admitted – albeit only respecting "comprehensive non-discriminatory nationalizations effected in the process of large-scale social reforms under exceptional circumstances of revolution, war and similar exigencies" – by the World Bank Group, *Guidelines on the Treatment of Foreign Direct Investment* § 10, 31 ILM 1,366, 1,383 (1992).

152 Richard B. Lillich, "The Valuation of Nationalized Property in International Law: Toward a Consensus or More Rich Chaos," in III Lillich, *The Valuation of Nationalized Property* at 183, 196 (1975). See also, e.g., Chowdhury, "Taking of Property" at 71; Mouri, *The International Law of Expropriation* at 365. *Cf.* C. F. Amersinghe, "Issues of Compensation for the Taking of Alien Property in The Light of Recent Cases and Practice," 41 *International and Comparative Law Quarterly* 22, 47–50, 61–65 (1992).

153 See, e.g., Friedmann, "Social Conflict" at 132; Francisco Orrego Vicuna, "The International Regulation of Valuation Standards and Processes: A Reexamination of Third World Perspectives," in III Lillich, *The Valuation of Nationalized Property* at 130, 134 (1975).

Table 3 *Measure of compensation for the nationalization of foreign-owned property in various sources of international law*

<table>
<tr><th colspan="2">The sources</th><th>Normative status</th><th>Substantive content</th></tr>
<tr><td colspan="2">Lump-sum settlement agreements</td><td>debated</td><td>partial compensation</td></tr>
<tr><td colspan="2">Bilateral investment treaties</td><td>debated</td><td>full compensation</td></tr>
<tr><td rowspan="2">United Nations General Assembly resolutions</td><td>No. 1803</td><td>widely acknowledged</td><td>"appropriate" (i.e., less than full) compensation</td></tr>
<tr><td>the Charter of Economic Duties and Rights of States</td><td>dubious</td><td>extreme revisionism</td></tr>
<tr><td colspan="2">General principles</td><td>primary</td><td>indeterminate</td></tr>
<tr><td colspan="2">Arbitral awards</td><td>subsidiary; but, if a realist analysis is taken into account, case law can also be considered as evidence to custom, which is in turn a primary source</td><td>a jurisprudence divided between adherence to the traditional doctrine and the development of a new norm of less than full compensation; it seems, however, fair to conclude that there is some tilt toward the latter alternative</td></tr>
</table>

paradigm and an underlying distributive scheme; (ii) the parallel evolution of doctrine and claims of distributive justice, and the reciprocal influence the distributive preferences and the doctrinal rules had on one another, confirms the contention of the dualistic function of unjust enrichment law as reflecting and shaping the prevailing distributive scheme; and, finally, (iii) the clear emphasis on power and interest as the sources of change helps demystify the key concept of social ethos.

7 Epilogue

While this book was seemingly limited to one core paradigm governed by the law of unjust enrichment, the paradigm also served, as the book unfolded, to illuminate the intricate relation of law and ethos. This paradigmatic case turned out to help unveil the way in which ethos informs the technical details of a legal doctrine. It may also end up offering some preliminary account of the reciprocity of ethos and law.

I contended that the spectrum of alternative measures of recovery represents a deeper continuum of underlying rationales: the *control–sharing* continuum. This continuum of primary social goods corresponds, in its turn, to a yet more fundamental spectrum which describes the possible attitudes people may have towards one another: the particular position each of us holds on this "self-regarding/other-regarding" spectrum is the key to the choice we make among the available primary goods (or rationales). But our dispositions do not merely shape the rules under which we choose to live; they are also, to some extent, the outcome of these very rules; we are all partly encumbered by the communities we inhabit. Therefore, as long as societies differ in their moral cultures, the typical selves of such societies will be differently motivated, and will thus produce a diversity of political programs and a corresponding diversity of legal doctrines.

This component of socio-economic ethos is the primary factor which shapes our doctrine, but it is not the only one. The normative ethos applies to the "average" resource, but the resources regulated by the doctrine are diverse, and this diversity is mirrored in the degree of protection available to the holding in each particular resource. I suggested that the variability of protected interests is rooted in the differing degrees to which actors are attached to the various resources they hold, which turn upon the different degrees to which the relevant resources reflect their holders' identity. I further argued that the resulting spectrum of resources is neither universal nor is it subjective. Rather, it is primarily a social construction. Hence, the significance of the particular social meanings of the protected resources.

Accordingly, if one wishes to reconstruct the specific rules of our paradigm – or to provide an explanation thereof – a particularistic investigation is mandated. Such an investigation must probe into the specific socio-economic ethos – the way the members of the pertinent legal community perceive their relationships with one another; it also needs to examine the "social meaning," in terms of reflection-and-attachment, accorded to the various regulated resources. Only with these data, as analyzed by the translation formulae developed herein, can we account for the inter-cultural and the intra-cultural diversity of measures of recovery demonstrated by the final three chapters of this book.

Indeed, in attempting to come up with a transcultural positive theory – structurally valid for various communities, though substantially different for each – this study highlights the crucial impact of the specific cultural properties of the legal community. It emphasizes the thickness of the human disposition and its rootedness in its socio-cultural environment.[1] It further recognizes the divergence of such environments and the variability in people's outlooks. It thus acknowledges the engendered diversity of legal doctrines.

And yet, thin as it may be, there is also a universal component to my story. The problems the doctrine faces, if not its particular solutions, are the same all over. More importantly, the values underlying the variety of possible configurations of our doctrine – although conflicting and controversial – all address the same question faced by people everywhere; they are all possible (and probably tentative) solutions to our constant search for an equilibrium along the self-regarding/other-regarding spectrum. Indeed, "[f]orms of life differ. Ends, moral principles, are many. But not infinitely many: they must be within the human horizon."[2]

[1] *Cf.* Clifford Geertz, "Thick Description: Toward an Interpretive Theory of Culture," in *The Interpretation of Cultures: Selected Essays* 3 (1973).

[2] Isaiah Berlin, "The Pursuit of the Ideal," in *The Crooked Timber of Humanity: Chapters in the History of Ideas* 1, 11 (Henry Hardy ed. 1991).

Bibliography

Primary sources

Statutes

Copyright Act of 1976, 15 USC § 504
Patent Act of 1952, 35 USC § 284
Small Business Act of 1978, 15 USC § 631
Trademark Act of 1946, 15 USC § 1,117
Uniform Probate Code § 2-803, 8 ULA 172 (1983 and Supplement 1996)
Uniform Trade Secrets Act, 14 ULA 437 (1990 and Supplement 1993)

Cases

United States

Ablah *v.* Eyman, 365 P 2d 181 (Kansas 1961)
American Air Filter Co. *v.* Michael J. McNichol & John F. Scanlan Inc., 527 F 2d 1,297 (3rd Cir. 1975)
Aro Manufacturing *v.* Convertible Top Replacement Co., 377 US 476 (1964)
Automatic Laundry Serv. Inc. *v.* Demas, 141 A 2d 497 (Maryland 1958)
Banco Nacional De Cuba *v.* Chase Manhattan Bank, 658 F 2d 875 (2nd Cir. 1980)
Banco Nacional De Cuba *v.* Sabbatino, 376 US 398 (1964)
Bell *v.* Smith, 32 So. 2d 829 (Florida 1947)
Blackman *v.* Hustler Magazine Inc., 800 F 2d 1,160 (DC Cir. 1986)
Blue Bell Co. *v.* Frontier Refining Co., 213 F 2d 354 (10th Cir. 1954)
Bowen *v.* Detroit United Railway, 180 NW 495 (Michigan 1920)
Burbridge *v.* Bradley Lumber Co., 239 SW 2d 285 (Arkansas 1951)
Business Trends Analysts Inc. *v.* Freedonia Group Inc., 887 F 2d 399 (2nd Cir. 1989)
Cablevision of Breckenridge Inc. *v.* Tannhauser Condominium Assn., 649 P 2d 1,093 (Colorado 1982)

Carter Products Inc. *v.* Colgate-Palmolive Co., 214 F Supp. 383 (D Maryland 1963)

Caskie *v.* Philadelphia Rapid Transit Co., 184 A 17 (Pennsylvania 1936)

Cason *v.* Baskin, 20 So. 2d 243 (Florida 1944)

Certified Lab. of Texas Inc. *v.* Rubinson, 303 F Supp. 1,014 (ED Pennsylvania 1969)

Champion Spark Plug Co. *v.* Sanders, 331 US 125 (1947)

Colorado Interstate Gas Co. *v.* Natural Gas Pipeline Co. of American, 885 F 2d 683 (10th Cir. 1989)

Cream Records Inc. *v.* Joseph Schlitz Brewing Co., 864 F 2d 668 (9th Cir. 1989)

Crofoot Lumber Inc. *v.* Ford, 191 Cal. App. 2d 238 (Ct. App. 1961)

D. B. Frampton and Co. *v.* Saulsberry, 268 SW 2d 25 (Kentucky Ct. App. 1954)

Deltak Inc. *v.* Advanced Systems Inc., 767 F 2d 357 (7th Cir. 1985)

Developers Three, A Partnership *v.* Nationwide Ins. Co., 582 NE 2d 1,130 (Ohio App. 1990)

Don *v.* Trojan Construction Co., 2 Cal. Rptr. 626 (1960)

Dorsett Carpet Mills Inc. *v.* Whitt Tile and Marble Distributing Co., 734 SW 2d 322 (Tennessee 1987)

Douglass *v.* Hustler Magazine Inc., 769 F 2d 1,128 (7th Cir. 1985), cert. denied, 475 US 1,094 (1986)

E. I. duPont Nemours and Co. *v.* Christopher, 431 F 2d 1,012 (1970), cert. denied, 400 US 1,024 (1971)

Eales *v.* Environmental Lifestyles Inc., 958 F 2d 876 (9th Cir. 1992)

Edwards *v.* Lee, 96 SW 2d 1,028 (Kentucky 1936)

Electro-Craft Corp. *v.* Controlled Motion Inc., 332 NW 2d 890 (Minnesota 1983)

Evans *v.* City of Johnstown, 410 NYS 2d 199 (Supreme Court 1978), reversed on other grounds, 470 NYS 2d 451 (App. Div. 1983)

F. W. Woolworth Co. *v.* Contemporary Arts Inc., 344 US 228 (1952)

Factors Etc. Inc. *v.* Pro Arts Inc., 496 F Supp. 1,090 (SDNY 1980), reversed on other grounds, 652 F 2d 278 (2nd Cir. 1981)

Federal Sugar Refining Co. *v.* US Sugar Equalization, 268 F 575 (SDNY 1920)

Felder *v.* Reeth, 34 F 2d 744 (9th Cir. 1929)

Fleer Corp. *v.* Topps Chewing Gum Inc., 539 A 2d 1,060 (Delaware 1988)

Fordice Construction Co. *v.* Central States Dredging Co., 631 F Supp. 1,536 (SD Mississippi 1986)

Foster *v.* American Mach. and Foundry Co., 492 F 2d 1,317 (2nd Cir. 1974), cert. denied, 419 US 833 (1974)

Frank Music Corp. *v.* Metro Goldwyn Mayer Inc., 772 F 2d 505 (9th Cir. 1985)

Frank Music Corp. *v.* Metro Goldwyn Mayer Inc., 886 F 2d 1,545 (9th Cir. 1989)

Fuller Prods. Co. *v.* Fuller Brush Co., 299 F 2d 772 (7th Cir. 1962), cert. denied, 370 US 923 (1962)
George Basch Co. Inc. *v.* Blue Coral Inc., 968 F 2d 1,532 (2nd Cir. 1992)
Georgia-Pac. Corp. *v.* US Plywood Corp., 243 F Supp. 500 (SDNY 1965)
Gonzales *v.* Kentucky Derby Co., 189 NYS 783 (App. Div. 1921), affirmed, 135 NE 938 (1922)
Granchelli *v.* Walters S. Johnson Building Co., 446 NYS 2d 755 (App. Div. 1981)
Haelen Laboratories Inc. *v.* Topps Chewing Gum Inc., 202 F 2d 866 (1953), cert. denied, 346 US 816 (1953)
Hamilton-Brown Shoe Co. *v.* Wolf Bros. and Co., 240 US 251 (1916)
Hart *v.* E. P. Dutton and Co., 93 NYS 2d 871 (Supreme Court 1949), affirmed, 98 NYS 2d 773 (App. Div. 1950), appeal denied, 301 NY 814 (1950)
Hogan *v.* A. S. Barnes and Co., 114 *United States Patents Quarterly* 314, 321 (Pennsylvania Trial Ct. 1957)
Iconco, A Corp. *v.* Jensen Construction Co., 622 F 2d 1,291 (8th Cir. 1980)
Integrity Management International Inc. *v.* Tombs and Sons Inc., No. 83-4231-0, 1988 US Dist. LEXIS 7,162 (D. Kansas 20 June 1988)
International News Service *v.* Associated Press, 248 US 215 (1918)
John A. Artukovich and Sons *v.* Reliance Truck Co., 614 P 2d 327 (Arizona 1980)
Kalamazoo Spice Extraction Co. *v.* Provisional Military Government of Socialist Ethiopia, 729 F 2d 422 (6th Cir. 1984)
Kewanee Oil Co. *v.* Bicron Corp., 416 US 470 (1974)
King County *v.* Odman, 111 P 2d 228 (Washington 1941)
Kori Corp. *v.* Wilco Marsh Buggies and Draglines Inc., 761 F 2d 649 (Fed. Cir. 1985), cert. denied, 474 US 902 (1985)
Lottie Joplin Thomas Trust *v.* Crown Publishers Inc., 592 F 2d 651 (2nd Cir. 1978)
Lugosi *v.* Universal Pictures, 603 P 2d 425 (California 1979)
McRoberts Protective Agency Inc. *v.* Lansdell Protective Agency Inc., 403 NYS 2d 511 (App. Div. 1978)
Maier Brewing Co. *v.* Fleischmann Distilling Corp., 390 F 2d 117 (9th Cir. 1968)
Marcus, Stowell and Beye Government Sec. Inc. *v.* Jefferson Inv. Corp., 797 F 2d 227 (5th Cir. 1986)
Masonite Corp. *v.* Tate, 404 So. 2d 565 (Mississippi 1981)
Mederacke *v.* Becker, 205 NE 2d 519 (Illinois App. Ct. 1965)
Mishawaka Rubber and Woolen Manufacturing Co. *v.* S. S. Kresge Co., 316 US 203 (1942)
Monarch Accounting Supplies Inc. *v.* Prezioso, 368 A 2d 6 (Connecticut 1976)
Moore *v.* Regents of the University of California, 793 P 2d 479 (1990)
Nalpac Ltd. *v.* Corning Glass Works, 784 F 2d 752 (6th Cir. 1986)

National Merchandising Corp. *v.* Leyden, 348 NE 2d 771 (Massachusetts 1976)
Nationwide Roofing and Sheet Metal Inc. *v.* Trotwood Heating Inc., 520 NE 2d 602 (Ohio Ct. App. 1987)
Nickson Industries Inc. *v.* Rol Manufacturing Co., 847 F 2d 795 (Fed. Cir. 1988)
Olwell *v.* Nye and Nissen Co., 173 P 2d 652 (Washington 1947)
Orgel *v.* Clark Boardman Co., 301 F 2d 119 (2nd Cir. 1962), cert. denied, 371 US 817 (1962)
Panduit Corp. *v.* Stahlin Bros. Fibre Works Inc., 575 F 2d 1,152 (6th Cir. 1978)
Pearce *v.* G. R. Kirk Co., 602 P 2d 357 (Washington 1979)
Phillips Chemical Co. *v.* Morgan, 440 So. 2d 1,292 (Florida App. 1983)
Phillips Petroleum Co. *v.* Cowden, 241 F 2d 586 (5th Cir. 1957)
Playboy Enterprises Inc. *v.* Baccarat Clothing Co., 692 F 2d 1,272 (9th Cir. 1982)
Price *v.* Hal Roach Studios Inc., 400 F Supp. 836 (SDNY 1975)
Quality Excelsior Coal Co. *v.* Reeves, 177 SW 2d 728 (Arkansas 1944)
Ramona Manor Convalescent Hospitals *v.* Care Enterprises, 225 Cal. Rptr. 120 (Ct. App. 1986)
Raven Red Ash Coal Co. *v.* Ball, 39 SE 2d 231 (Virginia 1946)
Raxton Corp. *v.* Anania Associates Inc., 668 F 2d 622 (1st Cir. 1982)
Rite-Hite Corp. *v.* Kelley Co., 774 F Supp. 1,514 (ED Wisconsin 1991)
Rogers *v.* Koons, 960 F 2d 301 (2nd Cir. 1992)
Sandare Chem. *v.* Wako International Co., 820 SW 2d 21 (Texas App. 1991)
Sands, Taylor and Wood Co. *v.* Quaker Oats Co., 978 F 2d 947 (1992)
Schechter *v.* Friedman, 57 A 2d 251 (New Jersey 1948)
Schroeder *v.* William Morrow and Co., 566 F 2d 3 (7th Cir. 1977)
Second National Bank of Toledo *v.* M. Samuel and Sons Inc., 12 F 2d 963 (1926), cert. denied, 273 US 720 (1926)
Sheets *v.* Yamaha Motors Corp., 849 F 2d 179 (5th Cir. 1988)
Sheldon *v.* Metro-Goldwyn Pictures Corp., 106 F 2d 45 (1939), affirmed, 309 US 390 (1940)
Sheldon *v.* Metro-Goldwyn Pictures Corp., 309 US 390 (1940)
Sygma Photo News Inc. *v.* High Society Magazine Inc., 778 F 2d 89 (2nd Cir. 1985)
Taylor *v.* Meirick, 712 F 2d 1,112 (7th Cir. 1983)
USM Corp. *v.* Marson Fastener Corp. 467 NE 2d 1,271 (Massachusetts 1984)
Utah Foam Products Inc. *v.* Polytec Inc., 584 So.2d 1,345 (Alabama 1991)
Van Ruymbeke *v.* Patapsco Industrial Park, 276 A 2d 61 (Maryland 1971)
Vincent *v.* Lake Erie Transp. Co., 124 NW 221 (Minnesota 1910)
W. B. Bassett Co. *v.* Revlon Inc., 435 F 2d 656 (2nd Cir. 1970)
Waits *v.* Frito-Lay Inc., 978 F 2d 1,093 (9th Cir. 1992), cert. denied, 113 S.Ct. 1,047 (1993)
Walker *v.* Forbes Inc., 28 F 3d 409 (4th Cir. 1994)

Winston Research Corp. *v.* Minnesota Mining and Manufacturing Co., 350 F 2d 134 (9th Cir. 1965)
WSM Inc. *v.* Tennessee Sales Co., 709 F 2d 1,084 (6th Cir. 1983)
Young *v.* That Was The Week That Was, 312 F Supp. 1,337 (ND Ohio 1969)
Zacchini *v.* Scripps-Howard Broadcasting Co., 433 US 562 (1977)
Zegers *v.* Zegers Inc., 458 F 2d 726 (7th Cir. 1972), cert. denied, 409 US 878 (1972)
Zippertubing Co. *v.* Teleflex Inc., 757 F 2d 1,401 (3rd Cir. 1985)

Other Anglo-American jurisdictions
Athans *v.* Canadian Adventure Camps Ltd., 17 OR 2d 425 (HC 1977) (Canada)
Carr-Saunders *v.* Dick McNeil Associates, [1986] 1 WLR 922 (Chancery) (England)
Cassell and Co *v.* Broome, [1972] App. Cas. 1,027 (House of Lords) (England)
Daniel *v.* O'Leary, 14 NBR 2d 564 (Queen's Bench 1976) (Canada)
English *v.* Dedham Vale Properties Ltd., [1978] 1 WLR 93 (Chancery) (England)
Kirk *v.* Todd, 21 Ch. 484 (Court of Appeal 1882) (England)
Lamine *v.* Dorrell, 92 Eng. Rep. 303 (King's Bench 1705) (England)
Lightly *v.* Clouston, 127 Eng. Rep. 774 (CP 1808) (England)
Livingstone *v.* Rawyards Coal Co., 5 App. Cas. 25 (House of Lords 1880) (appeal taken from Scotland)
Morris *v.* Tarrant, [1971] 2 QB 143 (England)
Phillips *v.* Homfray, 24 Ch. 439 (Court of Appeal 1883) (England)
Stoke-on-Trent City Council *v.* W. and J. Wass Ltd., [1988] 1 WLR 1,406 (Court of Appeal) (England)
Strand Electric and Engineering Co. *v.* Brisford Entertainments Ltd., [1952] 2 QB 246 (Court of Appeal) (England)
Swordheath Properties Ltd. *v.* Tabet [1979] 1 WLR 285 (Court of Appeal) (England)
Whitwham *v.* Westminster Brymbo Coal and Coke Co., [1896] 2 Ch. 538 (Court of Appeal) (England)
Wrotham Park Estate Co. *v.* Parkside Homes Ltd., [1974] 1 WLR 798 (Chancery) (England)

International fora
AGIP Co. *v.* Popular Republic of Congo, 21 ILM 726 (ICSID arbitration 1979)
Amco Asia Corp. *v.* Indonesia, 24 ILM 1,022 (1985), annulled on other grounds, 25 ILM 1,441 (ICSID arbitration 1986)
American International Group Inc. *v.* Islamic Republic of Iran, 4 Iran–US CTR 96 (1983)
Amoco International Finance Corp. *v.* Islamic Republic of Iran, 15 Iran–US CTR 189 (1985)

Benvenuti et Bonfant *v.* People's Republic of Congo, 21 ILM 740 (ICSID arbitration 1980)

BP Exploration Co. (Libya) *v.* Libyan Arab Republic, 53 ILR 297 (Lagergren sole arbitrator 1973)

Case Concerning the Barcelona Traction, Light and Power Company Ltd. (New Application: 1962) (Belgium *v.* Spain) 1970 ICJ 3 (5 February)

Delgoa Bay Railway Case, translated in III Marjorie M. Whiteman, *Damages in International Law* 1,694 (1943) (Blaesi, Heusler and Soldan arbitrators 1900)

Ebrahimi *v.* Islamic Republic of Iran, No. 560-44/46/47-3 (Iran–US Claims Tribunal, 12 October 1994)

Factory at Chorzow Case (Germany *v.* Poland), 1928 PCIJ (Ser. A) No. 17 (Indem.) (Merits) (13 September)

Greek Tel. Co. Case, described in J. Gillis Wetter and Stephen M. Schwebel, "Some Little Known Cases On Concessions," 40 *British Yearbook of International Law* 183, 216 (1964) (Streit, Anagnostopoulos and Papaligauras arbitrators 1935)

INA Corp. *v.* Islamic Republic of Iran, 8 Iran–US CTR 373 (1985)

Kuwait *v.* American Independent Oil Co. (Aminoil), 21 ILM 976 (Reuter, Sultan and Fitzmaurice arbitrators 1982)

Lena Goldfields Ltd. *v.* USSR, excerpted in 36 *Cornell Law Quarterly* 42 (1950) (Stutzer and Scott arbitrators 1930)

Libyan American Oil Co. (Liamco) *v.* Libyan Arab Republic, 62 ILR 140 (Mahmassani sole arbitrator 1977)

Lithgow *v.* UK, 102 European Court of Human Rights (Ser. A) (1986)

May Case (US *v.* Guatemala), 15 RIAA 47 (Jenner arbitrator 1900)

Norwegian Shipowners' Claims (Norway *v.* US), 1 RIAA 307 (Perm. Ct. Arb. 1922)

Palestine Railway Case, described in J. Gillis Wetter and Stephen M. Schwebel, "Some Little Known Cases on Concessions," 40 *British Yearbook of International Law* 183, 222 (1964) (Beichmann, Mance and Mayer arbitrators 1922)

Phillips Petroleum Co. Iran *v.* Islamic Republic of Iran, 21 Iran–US CTR 79 (1989)

SEDCO Inc. *v.* National Iranian Oil Co., 10 Iran–US CTR 180 (1986)

Shufedt Case (US *v.* Guatemala), 2 RIAA 1,079 (Sisnett arbitrator 1930)

Sola Tiles Inc. *v.* Islamic Republic of Iran, 14 Iran–US CTR 223 (1987)

SPP (Middle East) Ltd. *v.* Arab Republic of Egypt, 22 ILM 752 (ICC arbitration 1983)

Starrett Hous. Corp. *v.* Islamic Republic of Iran, 16 Iran–US CTR 112 (1987)

Texaco Overseas Petroleum Co. *v.* Libyan Arabic Republic, 53 ILR 389 (Dupuy sole arbitrator 1977)

Tippets, Abbett, McCarthy, Stratton *v.* TAMS-AFFA Consulting Engineers of Iran, 6 Iran–US CTR 219 (1984)

Treaty sources

Statute of the International Court of Justice, TS No. 993 (at 25) (1945)
UN Charter art. 10

United Nations resolutions

Charter of Economic Rights and Duties of States, GA Res. 3,281, UN GAOR, 29th Session, Supplement No. 31, at 50, UN Doc. A/9631 (1974), reprinted in 14 ILM 251 (1975)
Declaration on the Establishment of a New International Economic Order, GA Res. 3,201, UN GAOR, 6th Special Session, Supplement No. 1, at 3, UN Doc. A/9559 (1974), reprinted in 13 ILM 715 (1974)
Permanent Sovereignty over Natural Resources, GA Res. 1,803, UN GAOR, 17th Session, Supplement No. 17, at 15, UN Doc. A/5217 (1962), reprinted in 2 ILM 223 (1963)
Permanent Sovereignty over Natural Resources, GA Res. 3,171, UN GAOR, 28th Session, Supplement No. 30, at 52, UN Doc. A/9030 (1973), reprinted in 13 ILM 238 (1974)

Talmudic civil law sources

Mishnah
Bava Mezia, 3:2
M. Avot, 5:10

Talmud
Baba Kamma, 20a–21a
Baba Mezia, 35b, 42b

Commentaries
R. Solomon b. Abraham Aderet, *Hidushe Ha-Rashba to Baba Kamma*, 21a
R. Hanoch H. Agus, II *Marheshet*, 35:2b
R. Isaac Arieli, *Eynayim La-Mishpat, Baba Batra*, 4b
R. Joseph Caro, *Bet Yosef to the Tur, Hoshen Mishpat*, 363:5
R. Jacob Joshua Falk, *Pnei Yehoshua to Baba Kamma*, 20a–20b
Israel Z. Gustman, *Kuntresei Shiurim to Baba Kamma*, 12
R. Joseph Habiba, *Nimmukei Yoseph to Baba Kamma*, 9
R. Moses Isserles, *Darkei Mosheh to the Tur, Hoshen Mishpat*, 363:2
R. Eliezer b. Natan, *Sefer Ra'avan, Baba Kamma*, 21a
R. Efrayim Navon, *Mahane Efrayim, Hilkhot Gezela*, 10
Novellae of R. Shim'on Yehuda Ha-Kohen to Baba Kamma, 19–20
Novellae of R. Hayyim of Telz to Baba Batra, 109
Novellae of R. Hayyim of Telz to Baba Kamma, 39
Sefer Me'irat Eynayim to the Shulhan Arukh, 363:14
R. Meir Simhah of Dvinsk, *Ohr Sameah on Mishneh Torah, Hilkhot Nizkei Mamon*, 3:2

R. David Tevel, *Nahalat David to Baba Kamma*, 21a

Codes
Arukh Ha-Shulhan, *Hoshen Mishpat*, 363:19
Maimonides, *Hilkhot Skhirut*, 1:6
Maimonides, *Torts, Robbery and Lost Articles*, 3:9
Shulhan Arukh, Hoshen Mishpat, 307:5, 363:5–10
Tur, *Hoshen Mishpat*, 363:5

Responsa
R. Hayyim Yair Bachrach, *Responsa Havat Yair, responsum* 186
R. Meir b. Baruch, IV *Responsa Maharam of Rotenberg, responsum* 39
R. Ezekiel Landau, II *Responsa Noda Bihudah, Hoshen Mishpat, responsum* 24
R. Abraham Samuel of Raseiniai, *Responsa Amude Esh*, 67
R. Malkiel Zvi Tennenbaum, *Responsa Divrei Malkiel*, 3:157
R. Joab Joshua Weingarten, *Responsa Helkat Yoav, Hoshen Mishpat*, 9

Secondary sources

Note all books are published in the US or the UK unless otherwise indicated.

Books

Ackerman, Bruce A., *Social Justice in the Liberal State* (1980)
Akinsanya, Adeoyea A., *The Expropriation of Multinational Property in the Third World* (1980)
Aristotle, *Nicomachean Ethics* (Terence Irwin trans. 1985)
Baron, Salo W., *The Jewish Community: Its History and Structure to the American Revolution* (1942) (3 vols.)
Barry, Brian M., *Theories of Justice* (1989)
Batson, C. Daniel, *The Altruism Question: Toward a Social-Psychological Answer* (1991)
Beatson, Jack, *The Use and Abuse of Unjust Enrichment: Essays on the Law of Restitution* (1991)
Bellah, Robert N., *et al.*, *Habits of the Heart: Individualism and Commitment in American Life* (1985)
Bentham, Jeremy, *The Theory of Legislation* (Richard Hildreth trans. C. K. Ogden ed. 1931)
Berlin, Isaiah, *Four Essays on Liberty* (1969)
The Crooked Timber of Humanity: Chapters in the History of Ideas (Henry Hardy ed. 1991)
Birks, Peter, *An Introduction to the Law of Restitution* (paperback edn. with revisions 1989)
Blass, Jonathan, *Jewish Law for Israel: Unjust Enrichment Law* (1991) (Israel)
Braybrooke, David, *Meeting Needs* (1987)
Brealey, Richard A. and Myers, Stewart C., *Principles of Corporate Finance* (4th edn. 1991)

Burrows, Andrew S., *The Law of Restitution* (1993)
Calabresi, Guido, *Ideals, Beliefs, Attitudes and the Law: Private Law Perspectives on a Public Law Problem* (1985)
Chisum, Donald S., *Patents* (permanent edn. revised 1993 and Supplement 1994) (8 vols.)
Christman, John, *The Myth of Property: Toward an Egalitarian Theory of Ownership* (1994)
Cohen, Boaz, *Law and Tradition in Judaism* (1959)
Coleman, Jules L., *Markets, Morals and the Law* (1988)
Risks and Wrongs (1992)
Danielsen, Dan and Engle, Karen (eds.), *After Identity: A Reader in Law and Culture* (1995)
Dawson, John P., *Unjust Enrichment – A Comparative Analysis* (1951)
Dell, Sidney, *The United Nations and International Business* (1990)
Dicke, Detlev Chr. (ed.), *Foreign Investment in the Present and a New International Economic Order* (1987) (Switzerland)
Dittmar, Helga, *The Social Psychology of Material Possessions: To Have Is To Be* (1992)
Dobbs, Dan B., *Handbook on the Law of Remedies: Damages – Equity – Restitution* (2nd edn. 1993)
Douthwaite, Graham, *Attorney Guide to Restitution* (1977)
Dukeminier, Jesse and Krier, James E., *Property* (3rd edn. 1993).
Dworkin, Ronald, *Law's Empire* (1986)
Ellickson, Robert C., *Order without Law: How Neighbors Settle Disputes* (1991)
Elon, Menachem, *Jewish Law: History, Sources, Principles* (1994)
Etzioni, Amitai, *The Moral Dimension: Toward a New Economics* (1988)
Falk, Ze'ev W., *Legal Values and Judaism: Towards a Philosophy of Halakha* (1980) (Israel)
Finn, P. D. (ed.), *Essays on Restitution* (1990) (Australia)
Fishkin, James, *The Limits of Obligation* (1982)
Fletcher, George P., *Loyalty: An Essay on the Morality of Relationships* (1993)
Frank, Daniel (ed.), *Autonomy and Judaism: The Individual and the Community in Jewish Philosophical Thought* (1992) (Canada)
Fridman, G. H. L., *Restitution* (2nd edn. 1992)
Fridman, G. H. L. and McLeod, James G., *Restitution* (1982) (Canada)
Friedman, Lawrence, *The Republic of Choice* (1990)
Friedman, Milton, *Capitalism and Freedom* (1962)
Friedman, S., *Expropriation in International Law* (Ivor C. Jackson trans. 1953)
Friedmann, Daniel, *The Law of Unjust Enrichment* (2nd edn. 1982 and Supplement 1988) (Israel)
Frisch, Ephraim, *An Historical Survey of Jewish Philanthropy* (1924)
Galston, William A., *Liberal Purposes: Goods, Virtues, and Diversity in the Liberal State* (1991)
Garcia-Amador, F. V., *The Changing Law of International Claims* (1984) (2 vols.)

The Emerging International Law of Development: A New Dimension of International Economic Law (1990)
Gauthier, David, *Morals by Agreement* (1986)
Geertz, Clifford, *Local Knowledge: Further Essays in Interpretive Anthropology* (1983)
The Interpretation of Cultures: Selected Essays (1973)
Glendon, Mary Ann *et al.*, *Comparative Legal Traditions* (1985)
Goff, Lord of Chieveley and Jones, Gareth, *The Law of Restitution* (4th edn. 1993)
Goldstein, Paul, *Copyright* (2nd edn. 1996) (4 vols.)
Goodman, Lenn E., *On Justice: An Essay in Jewish Philosophy* (1991)
Griffin, James, *Well-Being: Its Meaning, Measurement and Moral Importance* (1986)
Hayek, F. A., *The Fatal Conceit: The Errors of Socialism* (1988)
Herzog, Isaac, *The Main Institutions of Jewish Law: The Law of Obligations* (2nd edn. 1967) (2 vols.)
Holgren, Carol J. (ed.), *Private Investors Abroad – Problems and Solutions in International Business in 1989* (1989)
Horowitz, George, *The Spirit of Jewish Law* (1973)
Horwitz, Robert H. (ed.), *The Moral Foundations of the American Republic* (3rd edn. 1986)
Hossain, Kamal and Chowdhury, Subrata Roy (eds.), *Permanent Sovereignty Over Natural Resources in International Law: Principles and Practice* (1984)
Hutchinson, Allan C. and Green, Leslie J. M. (eds.), *Law and Community: The End of Individualism* (1989) (Canada)
Ignatieff, Michael, *The Needs of Strangers* (1984)
Irani, K. D. and Silver, Morris (eds.), *Social Justice in the Ancient World* (1995)
Jackson, R. M., *The History of Quasi-Contract in English Law* (1936)
Jain, Subhash C., *Nationalization of Foreign Property: A Study in North–South Dialogue* (1983) (India)
Keeton, W. Page, *et al.*, *Prosser and Keeton on the Law of Torts* (5th edn. 1984)
Khan, Rahmatullah, *The Iran–United States Claims Tribunal: Controversies, Cases, and Contribution* (1990) (Netherlands)
Kirschenbaum, Aaron, *Equity in Jewish Law: Halakhaic Perspective in Law: Formalism and Flexibility in Jewish Civil Law* (1991)
Klippert, George B., *Unjust Enrichment* (1983) (Canada)
Krausz, Michael (ed.), *Relativism: Interpretation and Confrontation* (1989)
Lamm, Norman and Wurzburger, Walter S. (eds.), *A Treasury of Tradition* (1967)
Lauterpacht, Elihu, *Aspects of the Administration of International Justice* (1991)
Lauterpacht, Hersch O., *Collected Papers* (1975)
Oppenheim on International Law (8th edn. 1955) (2 vols.)
Laycock, Douglas, *Modern American Remedies: Cases and Materials* (2nd edn. 1994)

Levine, Aaron, *Economics and Jewish Law* (1987)
Free Enterprise and Jewish Law: Aspects of Jewish Business Ethics (1980)
Lew, Myer S., *The Humanity of Jewish Law* (1985)
Lillich, Richard B. (ed.), *International Law of State Responsibility for Injuries to Aliens* (1983)
The Valuation of Nationalized Property in International Law (1972–87) (4 vols.)
Lillich, Richard B. and Weston, Burns H., *International Claims: Their Settlement by Lump Sum Agreements* (1975) (2 vols.)
Lipson, Charles, *Standing Guard: Protecting Foreign Capital in the Nineteenth and Twentieth Centuries* (1985)
Llewellyn, Karl L., *Jurisprudence: Realism in Theory and in Practice* (1962)
Lucash, Frank S. (ed.), *Justice and Equality: Here and Now* (1986)
Lukes, Steven, *Individualism* (1973)
Macedo, Stephen, *Liberal Virtues: Citizenship, Virtues, and Community in Liberal Constitutionalism* (1990)
MacIntyre, Alasdair, *After Virtue: A Study in Moral Theory* (2nd edn. 1984)
Maddaugh, Peter D. and McCamus, John D., *The Law of Restitution* (1990) (Canada)
Makarczyk, Jerzy, *Principles of a New International Economic Order* (1988) (Netherlands)
Mansbridge, Jane J. (ed.), *Beyond Self Interest* (1990)
Mapp, Wayne, *The Iran–United States Claims Tribunal: The First Ten Years 1981–1991* (1993)
McCarthy, J. Thomas, *The Right of Publicity and Privacy* (permanent edn. revised 1994)
Trademarks and Unfair Competition (permanent edn. revised 1994) (4 vols.)
McClosky, Herbert and Zaller, John, *The American Ethos: Public Attitudes toward Capitalism and Democracy* (1984)
McMurrin, Sterling M. (ed.), *Liberty, Equality, and Law: Selected Tanner Lectures on Moral Philosophy* (1987)
Milgrim, Roger M., *Milgrim on Trade Secrets* (permanent edn. and Supplement 1995) (3 vols.)
Miller, David (ed.), *Liberty* (1991)
Miller, Richard S. and Stanger, Ronald J. (eds.), *Essays on Expropriation* (1967)
Minkowitch, Meyer, *Studies in Talmudic Law* (1956) (Israel)
Mouri, Allahyar, *The International Law of Expropriation as Reflected in the Work of the Iran–US Claims Tribunal* (1994) (Netherlands)
Munzer, Stephen R., *A Theory of Property* (1990)
Nagel, Thomas, *Equality and Partiality* (1991)
The Possibility of Altruism (1978)
Nedelsky, Jennifer, *Private Property and the Limits of American Constitutionalism: The Madisonian Framework and its Legacy* (1990)
Nimmer, Melville B. and Nimmer, David, *Nimmer on Copyright* (permanent

edn. revised 1996) (4 vols.)
Nozick, Robert, *Anarchy, State, and Utopia* (1974)
The Examined Life: Philosophical Mediations (1989)
Palmer, George E., *The Law of Restitution* (1978 and Supplement 1995) (4 vols.)
Panagiotou, Spiro (ed.), *Justice, Law and Method in Plato and Aristotle* (1987) (Canada)
Patterson, L. Ray and Lindberg, Stanley W., *The Nature of Copyright: A Law of Users' Rights* (1991)
Paul, Ellen F. *et al.* (eds.), *Property Rights* (1994)
Posner, Richard A., *Economic Analysis of Law* (4th edn. 1992)
Proshansky, Harold M. *et al.* (eds.), *Environmental Psychology: People and Their Physical Settings* (2nd edn. 1976)
Prott, Lyndel v. and O'Keefe, P. J., *Law and the Cultural Heritage*, vol. 3: *Movement* (1989)
Radin, Margaret J., *Reinterpreting Property* (1993)
Rakover, Nahum, *Unjust Enrichment in Jewish Law* (1987) (Israel)
Rawls, John, *A Theory of Justice* (1971)
Raz, Joseph, *The Morality of Freedom* (1986)
Reeve, Andrew, *Property* (1986)
Rodman, Kenneth A., *Sanctity Versus Sovereignty: The United States and the Nationalization of Natural Resource Investments* (1988)
Rorty, Richard, *Objectivity, Relativism, and Truth* (Philosophical Papers 1) (1991)
Rudmin, F. W. (ed.), *To Have Possessions: A Handbook on Ownership and Property* (1991) (Special Issue 6(6) of *Journal of Social Behavior and Personality*)
Sandel, Michael J., *Liberalism and the Limits of Justice* (1982)
Sandel, Michael J. (ed.), *Liberalism and Its Critics* (1984)
Schachter, Oscar, *International Law in Theory and Practice* (1991)
Sharing the World's Resources (1977)
Schauer, Frederick, *Playing by the Rules: A Philosophical Examination of Rule-Based Decision-Making in Law and in Life* (1991)
Shafer, Byron E. (ed.), *Is America Different?: A New Look at American Exceptionalism* (1991)
Shapiro, Alan C., *Multinational Financial Management* (3rd edn. 1989)
Shea, Donald R., *The Calvo Clause: A Problem of Inter-American and International Law and Diplomacy* (1955)
Smolla, Rodney A., *Law of Defamation* (permanent edn. revised 1991)
Sornarajah, M., *The Pursuit of Nationalized Property* (1986) (Netherlands)
Spero, Shubert, *Morality, Halakha and the Jewish Tradition* (1983)
Steiner Henry J. *et al.*, *Transnational Legal Problems: Materials and Text* (4th edn. 1994)
Stoljar, Samuel J., *The Law of Quasi Contracts* (2nd edn. 1989) (Australia)
Street, Harry, *Principles of the Law of Damages* (1962)

Tamari, Meir, *With All Your Possessions: Jewish Ethics and Economic Life* (1986)
Taylor, Charles, *Philosophy and the Human Sciences* (Philosophical Papers 2) (1985)
Sources of the Self: The Making of the Modern Identity (1989)
Thomson, Garrett, *Needs* (1987)
Waldron, Jeremy, *The Right to Private Property* (1988)
Walzer, Michael, *Spheres of Justice: A Defense of Pluralism and Equality* (1983)
Watson, Alan, *Legal Transplants: An Approach to Comparative Law* (2nd edn. 1993)
Waxman, Meyer, *Judaism: Religion and Ethics* (1958)
Weinberg, Steven, *Dreams of a Final Theory* (1992)
Westberg, John A., *International Transactions and Claims Involving Private Parties* (1991)
Winfield, Sir P. H., *The Law of Quasi-Contracts* (1952)
Woodmansee, Martha and Jaszi, Peter (eds.), *The Construction of Authorship: Textual Appropriation in Law and Literature* (1994)
Woodward, Frederic C., *The Law of Quasi Contracts* (1913)
Zipperstein, Edward, *Business Ethics in Jewish Law* (1981)
Zweigert, Konard and Kotz, Hein, *An Introduction to Comparative Law: The Institutions of Private Law* (2nd revised edn. Tony Weir trans. 1992)

Articles

Amerasinghe, C. F., "Issues of Compensation for the Taking of Alien Property in the Light of Recent Cases and Practice," 41 *International and Comparative Law Quarterly* 22 (1992)
Asante, Samuel K. B., "International Law and Foreign Investment: A Reappraisal," 37 *International and Comparative Law Quarterly* 588 (1988)
Baker, C. Edwin, "Property and Its Relation to Constitutionally Protected Liberty," 134 *University of Pennsylvania Law Review* 741 (1986)
Balkin, J. M., "Ideology as Constraint," 43 *Stanford Law Review* 1,133 (1991)
"Understanding Legal Understanding: The Legal Subject and the Problem of Legal Coherence," 103 *Yale Law Journal* 105 (1993)
Barker, Kit, "Unjust Enrichment: Containing the Beast," 15 *Oxford Journal of Legal Studies* 457 (1995)
Belk, Russell W., "Possessions and the Extended Self," 15 *Journal of Consumer Research* 139 (1988)
Berryman, Jeff, "The Case for Restitutionary Damages over Punitive Damages: Teaching the Wrongdoer that Tort Does Not Pay," 73 *Canadian Bar Review* 320 (1994)
Bezanson, Randall P., "The Libel Suit in Retrospect: What Plaintiffs Want and What Plaintiffs Get," 74 *California Law Review* 789 (1986)
Birks, Peter, "Civil Wrongs: A New World," *1990–91 Butterworths Lectures* 55
"Property in the Profits of Wrongdoing," 24 *Western Australia Law Review* 9 (1994)

Blakeslee, Merritt R., "Standard of Compensation: Prompt, Adequate and Effective Versus Appropriate Compensation," 89 *American Journal of International Law* 385 (1995)

Bohlen, Francis H., "Incomplete Privilege to Inflict Intentional Invasions of Interests of Property and Personality," 39 *Harvard Law Review* 307 (1926)

Bordan, Gregory, "The Law of Construction Privileges: Corrective Justice or Distributive Justice," 2 *Canadian Journal of Law and Jurisprudence* 57 (1989)

Bowett, Derek W., "Claims Between States and Private Entities: The Twilight Zone of International Law," 35 *Catholic University Law Review* 929 (1986)

Brady, Viola C., "The Duty to Rescue in Tort Law: Implications of Research on Altruism," 55 *Indiana Law Journal* 551 (1980)

Burrows, Andrew S., "Contract, Tort and Restitution – A Satisfactory Division or Not?" 99 *Law Quarterly Review* 217 (1983)

Calabresi, Guido, "Concerning Cause and the Law of Torts: An Essay for Harry Kalven, Jr.," 43 *University of Chicago Law Review* 69 (1975)

Calabresi, Guido and Melamed, A. Douglas, "Property Rules, Liability Rules, and Inalienability: One View of the Cathedral," 85 *Harvard Law Review* 1,089 (1972)

Caldwell, Lynton K., "Land and the Law: Problems in Legal Philosophy," 1986 *University of Illinois Law Review* 319

Charney, David, "Hypothetical Bargains: The Normative Structure of Contract Interpretation," 89 *Michigan Law Review* 1,815 (1991)

Coleman, Andrew W., "Copyright Damages and the Value of the Infringing Use: Restitutionary Recovery in Copyright Infringement Actions," 21 *AIPLA Quarterly Journal* 91 (1993)

Coleman, Jules L., "The Structure of Tort Law (Book Review)," 97 *Yale Law Journal* 1,233 (1988)

Cooke, Elizabeth, "Trespass, Mesne Profits and Restitution," 110 *Law Quarterly Review* 420 (1994)

Cover, Robert M., "Obligation: A Jewish Jurisprudence of the Social Order," 5 *Journal of Law and Religion* 65 (1987)

Dali, Justine, "Has Mexico Crossed the Border on State Responsibility for Economic Injury to Aliens? Foreign Investment and the Calvo Clause in Mexico After the NAFTA," 25 *St. Mary Law Journal* 1,147 (1994)

Dan Cohen, Meir, "In Defense of Defiance," 23 *Philosophy and Public Affairs* 24 (1994)

Dawson, Frank G. and Weston, Burns H., "'Prompt, Adequate and Effective': A Universal Standard of Compensation?" 30 *Fordham Law Review* 727 (1962)

Dawson, John P., "Restitution or Damages," 20 *Ohio State Law Journal* 175 (1959)

"Restitution Without Enrichment," 61 *Boston University Law Review* 563

(1981)
Dozler, Rudolf, "New Foundations of the Law of Expropriation of Alien Property," 75 *American Journal of International Law* 553 (1981)
Drescher, Thomas D., "The Transformation and Evolution of Trademarks – From Signals to Symbols to Myth," 82 *Trademark Reporter* 301 (1992)
Dworkin, Ronald, "Comment on Narveson: In Defense of Equality," 1(1) *Social Philosophy and Policy* 24 (1983)
"What is Equality? Part 2: Equality of Resources," 10 *Philosophy and Public Affairs* 283 (1981)
Elon, Menachem, "More About Research into Jewish Law," 8 *Mishpatim* 99 (1977) (Israel)
Englard, Izhak, "Research on Jewish Law: Its Nature and Function," 7 *Mishpatim* 34 (1976) (Israel)
"The Interaction of Morality and Jewish Law," 7 *Jewish Law Annual* 114 (1988)
Epstein, Richard A., "The Ubiquity of the Benefit Principle," 67 *Southern California Law Review* 1,369 (1994)
Eskridge, William N. Jr., "The New Textualism," 37 *UCLA Law Review* 621 (1990)
Ewald, William, "Comparative Jurisprudence (I): What Was it Like to Try a Rat?" 143 *University of Pennsylvania Law Review* 1,889 (1995)
Farnsworth, E. Allan, "Your Loss or My Gain? The Dilemma of the Disgorgement Principle in Breach of Contract," 94 *Yale Law Journal* 1,339 (1985)
Fiss, Owen M., "The Supreme Court, 1978 Term – Foreword: The Forms of Justice," 93 *Harvard Law Review* 1 (1979)
Flakser, Izhak, "Yishuv Piskei Ha-Rema," 13 *No'am* 51 (1970) (Israel)
Frankenberg, Gunter, "Critical Comparisons: Re-Thinking Comparative Law," 26 *Harvard International Law Journal* 411 (1985)
Friedmann, Daniel, "Restitution of Benefits Obtained Through the Appropriation of Property or the Commission of a Wrong," 80 *Columbia Law Review* 504 (1980)
"The Efficient Breach Fallacy," 18 *Journal of Legal Studies* 1 (1989)
Friedmann, Wolfgang, "Social Conflict and the Protection of Foreign Investment," 57 *Proceedings of the American Society of International Law* 126 (1963)
Gainer, Greta, "Nationalization: The Dichotomy Between Western and Third World Perspectives in International Law," 26 *Howard Law Journal* 1,547 (1983)
Gallie, W. B., "Essentially Contested Concepts," 56 *Proceedings of the Aristotelian Society* 167 (New Ser. 1956)
Gann, Pamela B., "Compensation Standard for Expropriation," 23 *Columbia Journal of Transnational Law* 615 (1985)
Ginsburg, Jane C., "Creation and Commercial Value: Copyright Protection of Works of Information," 90 *Columbia Law Review* 1,865 (1990)

Glendon, Mary Ann, "Individualism and Communitarianism in Contemporary Legal Systems: Tensions and Accommodations," (1993) *Brigham Young University Law Review* 385

Gutman, Amy, "Communitarian Critics of Liberalism," 14 *Philosophy and Public Affairs* 308 (1985)

Haddock, David D. *et al.*, "An Ordinary Economic Rationale for Extraordinary Legal Sanctions," 78 *California Law Review* 1 (1990)

Halpern, Sheldon W., "The Right of Publicity: Commercial Exploitation of the Associative Value of Personality," 39 *Vanderbilt Law Review* 1,199 (1986)

Haut, Irwin H., "Abuse of Rights and Unjust Enrichment: A Proposed Restatement of Jewish Law," 2 *National Jewish Law Review* 31 (1987)

Hedley, Stephen, "The Myth of "'Waiver of Tort,'" 100 *Law Quarterly Review* 653 (1984)

"Unjust Enrichment," 54 *Cambridge Law Journal* 578 (1995)

Hill, Jonathan, "Comparative Law, Law Reform and Legal Theory," 9 *Oxford Journal of Legal Studies* 101 (1989)

Hodder, James G., "Profiting from Tortious Use of Property: A Reply to the Lost Bargain Theory," 42 *University of Toronto Faculty Law Review* 105 (1984)

Huber, Peter K., "Mistaken Transfers and Profitable Infringements of Property Rights: An Economic Analysis," 49 *Louisiana Law Review* 71 (1988)

Hughes, Justin, "The Philosophy of Intellectual Property," 77 *Georgetown Law Journal* 287 (1988)

Hunter, H. O., "Measuring the Unjust Enrichment in a Restitution Case," 12 *Sydney Law Review* 76 (1989) (Australia)

Jackman, I. M., "'Restitution for Wrongs," 48 *Cambridge Law Journal* 302 (1989)

Jackson, Bernard S., "Introduction to Symposium: Unjust Enrichment," 3 *Jewish Law Annual* 3 (1980)

Jaffey, Peter, "Restitutionary Damages and Disgorgement," 3 *Restitution Law Review* 30 (1995)

Keeton, Wade R., "Monetary Recovery Under the Copyright Act," 65 *Oregon Law Review* 809 (1986)

Kennedy, Duncan, "Distributive and Paternalist Motives in Contract and Tort Law, With Special Reference to Compulsory Terms and Unequal Bargaining Power," 41 *Maryland Law Review* 563 (1982)

"Form and Substance in Private Law Adjudication," 89 *Harvard Law Review* 1,685 (1976)

Knowles, Dudley, "Hegel on Property and Personality," 33 *Philosophical Quarterly* 45 (1983)

Koelemay, James M. Jr., "A Practical Guide to Monetary Relief in Trademark Infringement Cases," 75 *Trademark Reporter* 263 (1995)

"Monetary Relief for Trademark Infringement under the Lenham Act,"

72 *Trademark Reporter* 458 (1982)

Kohler, Kaufman, "The Historical Development of Jewish Charity," in *Hebrew Union College and other Addresses* 229 (1933)

Kronman, Anthony T., "Contract Law and Distributive Justice," 89 *Yale Law Journal* 472 (1980)

Kull, Andrew, "Rationalizing Restitution," 83 *California Law Review* 1,196 (1995)

Large, Donald W., "This Land is Whose Land? Changing Concepts of Land as Property," 1973 *Wisconsin Law Review* 1,039

Laycock, Douglas, "The Scope and Significance of Restitution," 67 *Texas Law Review* 1,277 (1989)

Leebron, David W., "A Game Theoretic Approach to the Regulation of Foreign Direct Investment and the Multinational Corporation," 60 *University of Cincinnati Law Review* 305 (1991)

Leigh, Monroe, "Decision," 76 *American Journal of International Law* 847 (1982)

Levi, Tali, "NAFTA's Provision for Compensation in the Event of Expropriation: A Reassessment of the 'Prompt, Adequate and Effective' Standard," 31 *Stanford Journal of International Law* 423 (1995)

Lichtenstein, Aharon, "Towards an Understanding of 'Coercion over Sodom Qualities,'" in I *Hagut Ivrit Be'Amerika* 362 (M. Zohori *et al.* eds. 1972) (Israel)

Lieblich, William C., "Determinations by International Tribunals of the Economic Value of Expropriated Enterprises," 7 *Journal of International Arbitration* 37 (1990) (Switzerland)

Lifshitz, Berahyahu, "'One Derives a Benefit and the Other Sustains no Loss' – 'The Receipt of the Benefit did not Involve a Loss to the Benefactor'?" 37 *Hapraklit* 203 (1986) (Israel)

Lillich, Richard B. and Weston, Burns H., "Lump Sum Agreements: Their Continuing Contribution to the Law of International Claims," 82 *American Journal of International Law* 69 (1988)

Macaulay, Stewart, "Restitution in Context," 107 *University of Pennsylvania Law Review* 1,133 (1959)

Macedo, Stephen, "Capitalism, Citizenship and Community," 6(1) *Social Philosophy and Policy* 113 (1988)

Mann, F. A., "Foreign Investment and the International Court of Justice: The ELSI Case," 86 *American Journal of International Law* 92 (1992)

Mather, Henry, "Restitution as a Remedy for Breach of Contract: The Case of the Partially Performing Seller," 92 *Yale Law Journal* 14 (1982)

McBride, Nicholas J. and McGrath Paul, "The Nature of Restitution," 15 *Oxford Journal of Legal Studies* 33 (1995)

McCarthy, E. Doyle, "Toward a Sociology of the Physical World: George Herbert Mead on Physical Objects," 5 *Studies in Symbolic Interaction* 105 (1984)

McCarthy, J. Thomas, "Melville B. Nimmer and the Right of Publicity: A

Tribute," 34 *UCLA Law Review* 1,703 (1987)
Mendelson, M. H., "Agora: What Price Expropriation?: Compensation for Expropriation: The Case Law," 79 *American Journal of International Law* 414 (1985)
Mensch, Elizabeth V., "The Colonial Origins of Liberal Property Rights," 31 *Buffalo Law Review* 635 (1982)
Merrill, Thomas W., "American Legal History: Zero-Sum Madison," 90 *Michigan Law Review* 1,392 (1992) (book review)
Miller, David, "Distributive Justice: What the People Think," 102 *Ethics* 555 (1992)
"In What Sense Must Socialism Be Communitarian," 6(2) *Social Philosophy and Policy* 51 (1989)
Muller, Maarten H., "Compensation for Nationalization: A North–South Dialogue," 19 *Columbia Journal of Transnational Law* 35 (1981)
Narveson, Jan, "Reply to Dworkin," 1(1) *Social Philosophy and Policy* 41 (1983)
Norton, Patrick M., "A Law of the Future or a Law of the Past? Modern Tribunals and the International Law of Expropriation," 85 *American Journal of International Law* 474 (1991)
"Note, Distributive Liberty: A Relational Model of Freedom, Coercion, and Property Law," 107 *Harvard Law Review* 859 (1994)
"Note, General Principles of Law in International Commercial Arbitration," 101 *Harvard Law Review* 1,816 (1988)
Oesterle, Dale A., "Deficiencies of the Restitutionary Right to Trace Misappropriated Property in Equity and in UCC § 9-306," 68 *Cornell Law Review* 172 (1983)
Olivecrona, Karl, "Locke's Theory on Appropriation," 24 *Philosophical Quarterly* 220 (1974)
Palmer, Tom G., "Are Patents and Copyrights Morally Justified? The Philosophy of Property Rights and Ideal Objects," 13 *Harvard Journal of Law and Public Policy* 817 (1990)
Pellonpaa, M. and Fitzmaurice, M., "Taking of Property in the Practice of the Iran–United States Claims Tribunal," 19 *Netherlands Yearbook of International Law* 53 (1988)
Pincus, Laura B., "The Computation of Damages in Patent Infringement Cases," 5 *Harvard Journal of Law and Technology* 95 (1991)
Post, Robert C., "The Social Foundations of Defamation Law: Reputation and the Constitution," 74 *California Law Review* 691 (1986)
Prelinger, Ernst, "Extension and Structure of the Self," 47 *Journal of Psychology* 13 (1959)
Radin, Margaret J., "Market-Inalienability," 100 *Harvard Law Review* 1,849 (1987)
"Property and Personhood," 34 *Stanford Law Review* 957 (1982)
"Residential Rent Control," 15 *Philosophy and Public Affairs* 350 (1986)
Reich, Charles, "The New Property," 73 *Yale Law Journal* 733 (1964)
Robinson, Davis R., "Expropriation in the Restatement (Revised)," 78

American Journal of International Law 176 (1984)
Schachter, Oscar, "Agora: What Price Expropriation?: Compensation Cases – Leading and Misleading," 79 *American Journal of International Law* 420 (1985)
"Compensation for Expropriation," 78 *American Journal of International Law* 121 (1984)
Schnably, Stephen J., "Property and Pragmatism: A Critique of Radin's Theory of Property and Personhood," 45 *Stanford Law Review* 347 (1993)
Schwebel, Stephen M., "The Legal Effect of Resolutions and Cases of Conduct of the United Nations," 7 *Forum Internationale* 1 (1985) (Netherlands)
"The Story of the UN's Declaration on Permanent Sovereignty Over Natural Resources," 49 *American Bar Association Journal* 463 (1963)
Sharp, Robert J. and Waddams, S. W., "Damages for Lost Opportunities to Bargain," 2 *Oxford Journal of Legal Studies* 290 (1982)
Shilo, Shmuel, "'Kofin Al Midat Sdom': Jewish Law's Concept of Abuse of Rights," 15 *Israel Law Review* 49 (1980) (Israel)
Singer, Joseph W., "The Reliance Interest in Property," 40 *Stanford Law Review* 611 (1988)
Singer, Joseph William and Beermann, Jack M., "The Social Origins of Property," 6 *Canadian Journal of Law and Jurisprudence* 217 (1993)
Smith, Richard J., "The United States Government Perspective on Expropriation and Investment in Developing Countries," 9 *Vanderbilt Journal of Transnational Law* 517 (1976)
Solomon, Norman, "Concepts of Zeh Neheneh . . . in the Analytic School," 3 *Jewish Law Annual* 49 (1980)
Stevens, David, "Restitution, Property, and the Cause of Action in Unjust Enrichment: Getting by with Fewer Things," 39 *University of Toronto Law Journal* 258 (1989) (Canada)
Stillman, Peter G., "Property, Freedom, and Individuality in Hegel's and Marx's Political Thought," in *Property: Nomos XXII* 130 (J. Roland Pennock and John W. Chapman eds. 1980)
Stone, Suzanne L. "In Pursuit of the Counter-Text: The Turn to the Jewish Legal Model in Contemporary American Legal Theory," 106 *Harvard Law Review* 813 (1993)
Sunstein, Cass R., "Preferences and Politics," 20 *Philosophy and Public Affairs* 3 (1991)
Swann, Peter B., "Maryland Uniform Trade Secrets Act," 49 *Maryland Law Review* 1,056 (1990)
Underkuffler, Laura S., "On Property: An Essay," 100 *Yale Law Journal* 127 (1990)
Verwey, Wil D. and Schrijver, Nico J., "The Taking of Foreign Property Under International Law: A New Legal Perspective?" 15 *Netherlands Yearbook of International Law* 3 (1984)
von Mehren, Robert B. and Kourides, P. Nicholas, "International

Arbitration Between States and Foreign Private Parties: The Libyan Nationalization Cases," 75 *American Journal of International Law* 476 (1981)

Waldron, Jeremy, "Criticizing the Economic Analysis of Law," 99 *Yale Law Journal* 1,441 (1990)

Walzer, Michael, "The Communitarian Critique of Liberalism," 18 *Political Theory* 6 (1990)

Warren, Samuel D. and Brandeis, Louis D., "The Right to Privacy," 4 *Harvard Law Review* 193 (1890)

Weinrib, Ernest J., "Legal Formalism: On the Immanent Rationality of Law," 97 *Yale Law Journal* 949 (1988)

"Liberty, Community, and Corrective Justice," 1 *Canadian Journal of Law and Jurisprudence* 3 (1988)

"Right and Advantage in Private Law," 10 *Cardozo Law Review* 1,283 (1989)

Weller, James W., "International Parties, Breach of Contract, and the Recovery of Future Profits," 15 *Hofstra Law Review* 323 (1987)

Wiesner, Don and Cava, Anita, "Stealing Trade Secrets Ethically," 47 *Maryland Law Review* 1,076 (1988)

Wonnell, Christopher T., "Replacing the Unitary Principle of Unjust Enrichment," 45 *Emory Law Journal* 153 (1996)

York, Kenneth H., "Extension of Restitutional Remedies in the Tort Field," 4 *UCLA Law Review* 499 (1957)

Ziemmerman, Diane L., "Requiem for a Heavyweight: A Farewell to Warren and Brandeis's Privacy Tort," 68 *Cornell Law Review* 291 (1983)

Zimmermann, Reinhard, "Unjustified Enrichment: the Modern Civilian Approach," 15 *Oxford Journal of Legal Studies* 403 (1995)

Others

Restatements

Restatement (Third) of the Foreign Relations Law (1987)

Restatement of Restitution (1937)

Restatement (Second) of Restitution (Tentative Draft, 1983–84)

Restatement (First) of Torts (1939)

Restatement (Second) of Torts (1965)

Restatement (Third) of Unfair Competition (1995)

Annotations

"Annotation, Measure of Damages for Destruction of or Injury to Trees and Shrubbery," 69 ALR 2d 1,335 (1960)

"Annotation, Right of Trespasser to Credit for Expenditures in Producing, as Against His Liability for Value of, Oil or Minerals," 21 ALR 2d 380 (1952)

Donaldson, Russell G., "Annotation, False Light Invasion of Privacy –

Defenses and Remedies," 57 ALR 4th 244 (1987)
Gross, Alois V., "Annotation, Measure of Damages and Profits to which Copyright Owner is Entitled under 17 USCS § 504(b)," 100 ALR Fed. 258 (1990)
Kobylak, Wesley, "Annotation, Factors to be Considered in Determining a 'Reasonable Royalty' for Purposes of Calculating Damages for Patent Infringement Under 35 USCS § 284," 66 ALR Fed. 186 (1984)
Rosenhouse, Michael A., "Annotation, Proper Measure and Elements of Damages for Misappropriation of Trade Secret," 11 ALR 4th 12 (1982)
Vinluan, R. A., "Annotation, Measure of Damages for Wrongful Removal of Earth, Sand, or Gravel from Land," 1 ALR 3d 801 (1965)
Zupanec, Donald M., "Annotation, Disclosure of Trade Secrets as Abandonment of Secrecy," 92 ALR 3d 138 (1982)

Miscellaneous

Black's Law Dictionary (6th edn. 1990)
Law Commission Paper No. 132 on Aggravated, Exemplary and Restitutionary Damages (1993)
World Bank Group, *Guidelines on the Treatment of Foreign Direct Investment*, 31 ILM 1,366, 1,383 (1992)
"Zeh Neheneh Ve-zeh Lo Haser," in 12 *Encyclopedia Talmudit* 1 (1967) (Israel)

Index

CAMBRIDGE STUDIES IN INTERNATIONAL AND COMPARATIVE LAW

Books in the series

1 *Principles of the institutional law of international organizations*
C. F. Amerasinghe

2 *Fragmentation and the international law relations of micro-states*
Jorri Duursma

3 *The polar regions and the development of international law*
Donald R. Rothwell

4 *Sovereignty over natural resources*
Nico Schrijver

5 *Ethics and authority in international law*
Alfred P. Rubin

6 *Religious liberty and international law in Europe*
Malcolm D. Evans

7 *Unjust enrichment: A study of private law and public values*
Hanoch Dagan

8 *Trade and the environment: EC and US law in comparison*
Damien Geradin